THE STRONG NAME

THE STRONG NAME

BY

JAMES S. STEWART, B.D.

NORTH MORNINGSIDE CHURCH, EDINBURGH

AUTHOR OF

"THE GATES OF NEW LIFE" "A MAN IN CHRIST" ETC.

"I bind unto myself to-day
The strong Name of the Trinity."
ST. PATRICK.

NEW YORK

CHARLES SCRIBNER'S SONS

1941

TO

THE MEMORY OF

MY FATHER

WHO DID JUSTLY
AND LOVED MERCY
AND WALKED HUMBLY WITH HIS GOD

CONTENTS

THE GRACE OF THE LORD JESUS CHRIST

THE LOVE OF GOD

CONTENTS

THE COMMUNION OF THE HOLY GHOST

(Of these studies, three have already appeared—number IX. in *The Speaker's Bible*, and numbers X. and XVI. in *The Expository Times*. I am grateful to the editors and publishers for permission to include them here.)

THE
GRACE OF THE LORD JESUS CHRIST

" And why not grace ? Why not God's grace ? . . . We walk
upon it, we breathe it ; we live and die by it ; it makes the nails and
axles of the universe."—R. L. STEVENSON.

" I fancy that as we grow older, as we think longer and work
harder and learn to sympathize more intelligently, the one thing we
long to be able to pass on to men is a vast commanding sense of the
grace of the Eternal. Compared with that, all else is but the small
dust of the balance."—H. R. MACKINTOSH.

I

SURSUM CORDA !

"When these things begin to come to pass, then look up, and lift up your heads ; for your redemption draweth nigh."—LUKE xxi. 28

WHEN Jesus spoke these words, He turned history upside down. Once this has been said, everything that makes up the usual stock-in-trade of a whole tribe of worldly-wise commentators on the human scene is rendered obsolete for ever. All our habitual judgments and valuations are challenged and overruled by this piercing, dramatic insight of the Son of God.

"When these things begin to come to pass." Glance back across the chapter and see what things are meant. It is no description of calm weather and peaceful prospects that meets you here. It is the most devastating catalogue of crisis and convulsion, of formidable, ruthless forces playing havoc with good men's dreams. These words of Jesus are full of the crash and thunder of the storm—nation rising against nation, and kingdom against kingdom ; earthquakes, famines, pestilences, fearful sights and signs from heaven ; persecutions, inquisitions, racial hatreds, martyrdoms ; the whole world gone mad, and "men's hearts failing them for fear, and for looking after those things which are coming on the earth." When these things come to pass, said Jesus, these intolerably grim and harrowing things, these things of which the tender conscience would say that they just do not bear thinking about ; when all you can do is helplessly to watch the human situation deteriorating, and the frenzied altercations growing still more turbulent and furious, and the tide of violence mounting till it is rushing like a great river in spate ; when your own mind is confused, and your nerves

3

reeling, and your spirit near despair—then, said Jesus, look
up ! Lift up your heads !

Do you not feel that this chapter might have sprung
straight out of the background of the present day ? We
shall be far wrong if we suppose that this was simply Jesus'
forecast of the fearful fate that Rome was keeping in store
for Jerusalem the city of God. It was that, no doubt, but
certainly it was also far more. " When these things begin
to come to pass " : who can ponder the picture here, and
not feel that it is supremely relevant now ?

Moreover, there is this to be said. You have not faced
the real seriousness of any Dark Age in the world's history,
or of any dark night in your own personal experience, when
you have simply recounted the external facts of the situation.
For far more ominous than the physical facts are the
potential spiritual consequences of the facts. I mean that
there is always a possibility that an individual, or a whole
age, under the pressure of terrible events, may suffer total
eclipse in the region of faith. Things may go so radically
and bitterly wrong that the basic convictions on which life is
built are shaken, and the very foundations begin to rock and
quiver, and the whole edifice threatens to collapse before
the assault of the ultimate doubt. That, nothing less, is the
really sinister menace—that hour of awful darkness in which
the human heart begins to suspect that there is no rationality
anywhere, that right and wrong and good and evil are mere
figures of speech, not solid and substantial facts ; that divine
Fatherhood is a myth, and providence an illusion, and any
spiritual interpretation of life a fantastic self-deception, and
all man's striving purposeless and futile. " When these
things begin to come to pass," said Jesus, " when that fierce
threat is getting you by the throat, that stifling doubt
endeavouring to suffocate your soul, then——" What then ?

Finish the sentence ! Shall we say, " When these things
come, all hope abandon " ? That is what our natural instinct
says. " The lights that you have seen extinguished can

never be rekindled. The blessed hours of peace and confidence and joy in the Lord are coming back no more. You may as well hang up your harps upon the willows once for all, and forget you ever learnt the happy songs of Zion, and resign yourselves to the miseries of Babylon, and to the slow doom, pitiless, unending. When these things come to pass, then—farewell hope ! Enter—despair ! And weep for the days that are dead." So speaks the wisdom of the world. So speaks perhaps, in such a day as this, the voice of our own hearts. But not so speaks Christ ! Not so speaks the One who above all others has a right to speak. " When these things come, then *look up, and lift up your heads* ; for your redemption draweth nigh."

With that flashing thrust of divine insight, He challenges and reverses and contradicts our all too human interpretation of the world and of our own tangled experience. I do want you to grasp the thrilling and really revolutionary truth to which these words of Jesus point. It is this, that the same crises, calamities, hours of desolation and heartbreak, which to the natural man constitute a flat denial of God—these very things are actually, to the spiritual man, a new tremendous revelation of God. They shake the faith of the one, they confirm the faith of the other. " This is the end of everything," says the one. " No," says the other, " this is my God marching on in judgment and in mercy." And all the prophetic spirits who have ever lived have verified Christ's interpretation and discovery, and cry to us to-day to believe it, for it is true.

> " For we are afar with the dawning
>   And the suns that are not yet high,
>   And out of the infinite morning
>   Intrepid you hear us cry—
>   How, spite of your human scorning,
>   Once more God's future draws nigh."

When these things come to pass, says Jesus, when all the ways of life are darkened, and you can scarce see the road beneath your feet, when the terror by night is a grim reality, and your soul is bowed to the ground beneath the weary load of bitter disillusionment and cares that sap your strength away—then look up! Lift up your head! Think not that the immediate aspect of things is the final truth. If the valley is black and murky, remember the stars! If the shadow of Herod is darkening the world, hark to the angels singing over Bethlehem! If your soul is stumbling in the gloom, reach out for the hand of the Lord!

Would it not be true to say that it is precisely this faculty of looking up, that is to say, of adding on to life a new dimension, which differentiates man from all the rest of creation? And (to digress from our main theme for a moment) think of all the blessed ministries God has devised, for the specific purpose—it would seem—of helping and enabling us, even in the darkest days, to stand with lifted head! The gracious ministry of home; the light in the dear eyes of a woman who has given you her heart, and has been amazingly loyal to you through everything, and patient and understanding; the memory of an hour when, awed and strangely thrilled, you stood beside a cradle, and vowed that for the sake of that new, tender, helpless life committed to your care you would sanctify yourself, and walk for ever in the light; and all the rich manifold variety of God's other avenues of approach, in Nature, and music, and the sacrament of friendship where heart speaks to heart; and unexpected acts of kindness that touch grey days with loveliness and colour; and deeds of sudden chivalry that make an old world young again; and moments when the House of God has been to you no ordinary meeting-place, but a veritable shrine, a gate of heaven, because of the authentic presence of the Lord— are these not all means that God has lovingly devised to enable us, however dark and rough the way, however crushing and oppressive the tyranny of circumstance, to look up, and lift our heads, and stabilize our staggering souls by a rediscovery of the unseen and the eternal?

But to return. I ask you to observe that Christ's appeal to His followers to lift up their heads in desperate days was no piece of sentimental bravado, encouraging baseless hopes. There was a reason for the upward look ; and very definitely and unequivocally He told them of it. " *For your redemption draweth nigh.*" In other words, when things are at their worst, you had better be alert and wakeful, more vigilant then than ever, for that is the likeliest hour for a new decisive emergence of the Spirit of God upon the scene.

Has not that insight of Jesus been verified repeatedly by the facts of history and experience ? Think, for instance, of the witness of the Old Testament. What were the times in the annals of Israel when the Hebrew religious genius recorded its greatest achievements, and faith made another forward leap ? Not the peaceful, prosperous days of a Solomon in all his glory. No, but the days of deluge and disaster, when the proud waters of the Babylonian wrath were going over Israel's soul—then the faith leapt to life, then the very pressure of catastrophe threw up another prophet, and another, to cry aloud and reassert the unshaken, everlasting spiritual realities. And what was that but redemption drawing near ?

Or think of the history of the Christian Church. What have been the eras of the Church's greatest influence ? What have been the moments of its most powerful impact on the world ? Not the epochs of its visible might and splendour ; not the age succeeding Constantine, when Christianity became imperialistic, and all the kingdoms of the world and the glory of them seemed ready to bow beneath the sceptre of the Christ ; not the days of the great medieval pontiffs, when Christ's vicar in Rome wielded a sovereignty more absolute than that of any secular monarch on the earth ; not the later nineteenth century, when the Church became infected with the prevailing humanistic optimism, which was quite sure that man was the architect of his own destinies, that a wonderful utopian kingdom of God was waiting him just round the corner, and that the very momentum of his progress was bound to carry him thither. Not in such times as these has the Church exercised its strongest leverage upon the soul and conscience of the world : but in days when it has been crucified with Christ, and has counted all things but loss for His sake ; days when, smitten with a great contrition and repentance, it has cried out to God from the depths. Then indeed—in a Francis, a Luther, a Wesley—the time of the singing of birds has come, and the air has been full of the Hallelujahs of revival. And what is that but redemption drawing nigh ?

Or you can see it in the realm of personal experience. The man who has had all fortune's favours showered upon him is not generally the man whom God finds it easiest to reach ; and a soul that is completely at ease in Zion, and comfortably conscious of its own rectitude and resources, can be a desperately difficult target even for the winged arrows of Christ. But show me a man who has reached the point of saying, " I'm beaten ! I'm just about done for. I thought once that I could manage life successfully, that I had qualifications and reserves of power adequate to any demands it would make upon me, that the arm of flesh could drive a path for me through any obstacles I might ever have to meet ; but now, I am at the end of my tether, now the radical lie in all that humanist philosophy is being found out, now I know exactly what I am, a poor, lame, helpless creature; and O wretched man that I am ! who shall deliver me ? " —show me a man like that, and I will tell you, There is a man to whom God is on the way, and his redemption is drawing nigh !

There, then, is the fact—that again and again in the history of the world, in the life of the Church, in the experience of the individual, the darkest and most hopeless hours have preluded a new advent and invasion of the Spirit of God. Of that fact there is no manner of doubt.

But I wonder can we, ere we close, go one step further, and point to a possible explanation of the fact ? I think we can. Why is it that God acts in such a paradoxical way, using the blackest and most desperately unlikely hour for His entrance upon the scene ? I believe the explanation is this—that *it is precisely in such hours that the one thing which most impedes the divine activity is apt to get broken down* : and that is *man's self-trust.* Sooner or later we have to face the uncomfortable truth that the greatest barrier to the fashioning of a new world, to the vitalizing of a dynamic Church, to the growing of a Christlike character, is just man's stubborn trust in himself. It is the last thing that even the religious man is prepared to give up. But give it up he must, or else be finally frustrated in his quest for the pearl of great price, which is the kingdom of God in the heart.

I am not thinking now, mark you, of conscious and Pharisaic self-righteousness : that, if you believe the New Testament, is the most damning sin of all, far more dangerous, more utterly certain (as Jesus said) to disqualify a soul for life eternal than even the gross sins of the flesh. But I am not thinking of that. I am thinking of human nature's tenacious and ineradicable instinct to trust its own achievements. " Most men," said Thomas Erskine of Linlathen, " are so possessed by themselves that they have no vacuum into which God's deep water may rise." The whole of life is evidence of that. Man is intellectual, and trusts his science to redeem the world and build the New Jerusalem. He is patriotic, and trusts his race or nation to secure the future of civilization. He is philanthropic, and trusts his humanistic ideals to permeate the lump of social life till the whole is leavened. He is religious, and trusts his Church to organize the kingdom of heaven into existence. He is moral, and trusts his personal virtues to justify him in the sight of God.

" Have I not worked hard ? " he asks himself, assessing his own spiritual worth. " Have I not been a man of my

2

word ? Have I not lived a disciplined life, and fought down temptation, and cultivated virtues, and been assiduous in the ordinances of religion, and paid my debts, and given to charity, and honoured all men, and loved the brotherhood, and feared God, and honoured the king ? " These are the things we carry in our hands right up to the throne of grace, as if they gave us a claim upon God, and earned us His favourable consideration, and merited salvation. " See, Lord," we exclaim, " all this in my hands I bring ! I would not dream of coming empty-handed. All this can go down to the credit side of the account ! "

What we so tragically fail to realize is that by that instinctive attitude, that native trust in our own virtues and achievements, we are automatically excluding ourselves from the very blessings which we hoped to reach. Our very spirituality, if you will understand me, is robbing us of God's Spirit. Not so does the true redemption ever draw nigh ! The sacrifices of God are not an imposing array of creditable achievements. The sacrifices of God are a broken spirit and a contrite heart. If something really breaks you down, so that virtues and good works count no longer, and you cry with Job " I abhor myself, and repent in dust and ashes " ; if some day of storm and darkness leaves you stripped of every shred of satisfied self-trust, and of every vestige of conscious claim upon God—*then* look up, for your redemption will be coming over the horizon. But not before !

You have to experience the darkness that descends when all the flickering candles of personal merit have gone out, before you can discern, rising out of the gloom to meet you, the light that never was on sea or land. You have to feel the foundations shake beneath your feet, before you can sing " Rock of Ages " as it should be sung. You have to " faint for the flaming of Christ's advent feet," and cry " Watchman, what of the night ? " before you can know the thrill of Christmas morning, and the glory of the Word made flesh, and the sheer irrepressible excitement of that ringing, tumultuous shout—" Blessed is He that cometh in the name of the Lord ! " You have to have looked into the horrible abyss of doubt and despair before you can really believe. You have to see everything falling from your grasp, and to cry " Nothing in my hands I bring," before Christ's strong pierced hands can grip and hold you. You have to suffer crucifixion in the region of self, before you can rise from the dead the third day with the new life of God throbbing in your heart.

So when these things come to pass, these desolating things that leave all self-trust shattered and in ruin, look up, and lift up your head, knowing that your light is come, that the glory of the Lord is risen upon you, and your redemption draweth nigh !

Even so, come, Lord Jesus.

II

THE MIRACLE OF RECONCILIATION

"God was in Christ, reconciling the world unto himself. . . . We pray you in Christ's stead, be ye reconciled to God."—2 Cor. iv. 19, 20.

IT is at once the glory and the doom of man to have been made for fellowship with God. Of all the faculties and capacities which he possesses, incomparably the greatest is his capacity for God. It is his glory, for it opens up before him endless vistas of spiritual achievement. It is his doom, because he can never wholly escape the compulsion of his destiny, nor be satisfied while the soul within him starves. " Restless is our heart," said St. Augustine, " until it find rest in Thee."

Reconciliation with God is therefore the cardinal issue, far and away the most crucial problem confronting the soul of man to-day.

That this is the main problem is, however, by no means universally admitted or recognized. The man who, diagnosing his personal situation, has reached the point of saying " My heart is restless until it rests in God," is clearly already well on the way towards the peace that passes understanding. But the trouble is that there are so many who would assent to St. Augustine's first clause, to whom it would simply never occur to go on and say the second. They put the full-stop in the middle. " Restless is our heart "—that they admit. That they realize. That, they feel, it would serve no purpose to deny. Their heart is ill at ease, dissatisfied, heavy-laden. But—" until it rest in Thee " ? Ah, they say, that is different ! That we do not admit. That is not our psychology of the matter. In other words, they are prepared to recognize that somewhere there is a deep disharmony in their nature, something setting up a friction : what they are not prepared to recognize is that it is a disharmony with God.

Or turn from the individual, and contemplate the world —this restless, heaving, fevered world. No one can look at the world to-day, and observe the tragic disillusionments and rampant degradations, without being driven to the conclusion that something in the organism of the human race has gone mysteriously and terribly wrong. " Restless is the world's heart." But amongst those who agree on that, would there be anything like a consensus of opinion that what is wrong is a disturbed, defective God-relationship, and that no cheerful slogans about brotherhood or democracy or progress can ultimately avail anything apart from a return to the living God ? The world is convulsively restless, and it knows it. What it has not yet brought itself to say is —" until we find rest *in Thee.*"

There, then, is the problem. Man's inability to diagnose correctly his own malady—that is what makes his plight so critical. The words do not leap to our lips, as they did with the psalmist : " Against Thee, Thee only, have I sinned." That piercing insight is not ours. God pity us, it is sometimes the last thing we think of saying.

Now here we are laying our finger on what is undoubtedly the most ominous feature of the mystery of evil, and the most crucial difficulty in the way of reconciliation. The trouble is precisely that the sinful soul does not recognize, and by the very nature of the case is precluded from recognizing, what has been going on within itself. It might seem natural to suppose that every time a man sins, he would know a little more about sin, its nature and its methods. Actually the exact reverse is true. Every time he sins, he is making himself less capable of realizing what sin is, less likely to recognize that he is a sinner ; for the ugly thing (and this, I feel sure, has never been sufficiently grasped), the really diabolical thing about sin is that it perverts a man's judg-

ment. It stops him from seeing straight. In the words of
Robert Burns—

> " it hardens a' within,
> And petrifies the feeling."

Hence every time any of us sins, we are making it not more,
but less possible, for ourselves to appreciate what sin is ; and
therefore not more but less likely that we shall feel there
is anything to be forgiven. Every time I indulge in pride,
selfishness, or censoriousness, I am reducing my power to
realize how essentially hateful and unchristlike pride, selfishness, and censoriousness are. Every time I reject some voice
in conscience, I am making it certain that next time that
voice is going to speak not more, but less, imperiously and
convincingly. Until we have grasped this, we have not
begun to glimpse the terrible nature of the problem God
had upon His hands when He faced the task of man's redemption. In the grave language of Whittier—

> " A tenderer light than moon or sun,
>   Than song of earth a sweeter hymn,
> May shine and sound forever on,
>   And thou be deaf and dim.
>
> Forever round the Mercy-seat
>   The guiding lights of Love shall burn:
> But what if, habit-bound, thy feet
>   Shall lack the will to turn ?
>
> What if thine eye refuse to see,
>   Thine ear of Heaven's free welcome fail,
> And thou a willing captive be,
>   Thyself thy own dark jail ? "

It is worth remarking that here we find a clue to the
understanding of what Jesus had in mind when He spoke
about the unforgivable sin. What our Lord, in His dark,
mysterious reference to the " blasphemy against the Holy
Spirit " intended to convey was not that some specific acts
of sin might be so base and heinous as to be beyond remission :

rather, He was thinking of what might conceivably be the final outcome of the vicious circle set up by sin's insensitizing process—a condition in which the last vestiges of the power to recognize and respond to truth and love would have been burnt out of the soul. Even divine forgiveness, it is clear, could not operate in the presence of such a total destruction of personality. Jesus, in this passage, was pushing the truth of sin's blinding action to its logical limit.

Whether any soul has ever reached that stage, He did not say ; nor is it for us to inquire. We can thank God that every twinge of conscience we feel, and every spasm of remorse that ever troubles this tragic world, is a token of life and a herald of hope. We can thank Him that, subject as these souls of ours are to the crippling defects and the bitter thraldom which a sinful nature imposes, they are not without their times of insight, when the eternal values come into their own. It is this truth which Robert Browning has expressed so memorably :

> " Oh, we're sunk enough here, God knows !
> But not quite so sunk that moments,
> Sure tho' seldom, are denied us,
> When the spirit's true endowments
> Stand out plainly from its false ones . . .
> There are flashes struck from midnights,
> There are fire-flames noondays kindle."

But the question is, Will that suffice ? Is it enough to save a man from the predicament in which sin lands him ? Is it adequate to heal and to remake the world ? And the answer comes, Not that ! Something more radical is needed if the vicious circle of which we have spoken is to be broken into decisively. The moment of vision is not dynamic enough to effect the casting off of the chain, nor is the " flash struck from midnight " permanent enough to dispel the darkness. It may, indeed, only serve to make the darkness deeper. It will almost certainly have that effect, if it throws into sudden relief the real nature of the situation sin creates, or

gives the sinner some inkling of the hopelessly disqualifying
influence of his sin.

> " Intense the agony
> When the ear begins to hear, and the eye begins to see ;
> When the pulse begins to throb, and the brain to think again ;
> The soul to feel the flesh, and the flesh to feel the chain."

It is then that there is heard the cry, " O wretched man that
I am ! Who shall deliver me ? "

Certainly not myself ! That, at any rate, is clear. Certainly not anything in human nature. Certainly not any
power of will or intellect or emotion operating from within
the sinful process. To talk of man reconciling God is simply
irrelevant ; and all the theologies and ritual systems which
have followed that line have missed the point completely.
It is sheer trifling with a tragedy to talk airily of the soul's
freedom to refashion its own destiny and rehabilitate its
own reputation. The fact is, we are doubly disqualified from
initiating any sort of action to right the wrong relationship.
For on the one hand, as we have seen, the very sin from
which all our trouble springs has the effect of blinding us
progressively to what the real malady is ; and on the other
hand, even if we could fully recognize our need, we should
be powerless to match ourselves against it, and the only result
of such a recognition would be a devastating, intolerable
despair. No, unless the accumulated, ever-tightening bondage
in which the soul is rigidly encased can be shattered from
outside, by the intervention of some personal power never
implicated in that bondage ; unless the deepening shades of
the prison-house can be penetrated by some sudden, supernatural light ; unless the kingdom of evil can at some point
be intersected, broken into vertically from above, by a kingdom of grace—there is no hope at all. Change the angle of
the psalmist's words, " Against Thee, Thee only, have I
sinned," and they become, " Thou must save, and Thou
alone." God must act first, and act decisively.

Martin Luther was indeed right when he said that your

plight and mine was *nodus deo vindice dignus*—a knot which
it needs a God's help to unravel.

The question, then, is this : How does God act to break
through the bondage of blindness and corruption which
shuts the sinner in ? It is manifest that no one who is
himself involved in sin, no one whose insight has been im-
paired in any degree by evil, can enter redeemingly into the
experience of sinful men. But suppose one day a perfect
life should appear upon the earth, suppose at a single point—
in one soul out of all the myriads of souls—the fatal drift
of evil should be arrested, suppose that in one personality
the absolute union with God which is the meaning of sinlessness should be realized, then obviously you would have a
new, incalculable factor appearing upon the scene. You
would have arriving in this world of darkness a light which
literally had never been on sea or land before. Now do you
see what might happen ? That incalculable factor, arriving
in history, might liberate incalculable energies. It might set
in motion a force strong enough even to do the one crucial
thing which is humanly impossible, namely, to break into
the vicious circle which has closed around man remorselessly
by the very logic of his sin. It might be that that flash of
light, being unlike any other ever known or seen upon the
earth, would shatter the blindness sin creates, and carry
right into the sinner's soul the truth about himself and about
his God.

It is the claim of Christianity that this has happened.
In Jesus the supposition has become an actuality. The
unprecedented factor has appeared. In His perfect life and
sinless personality, there has entered history a light capable
of piercing the darkness of our dulled and blunted faculties,
capable of bursting the bondage of sin's blindness—because
it is the lightning-flash of God. " In Him was life, and the
life was the light of men."

I wish at this point to suggest that, to understand Christ's mastery over sin, we ought to view it in the light of His mastery over Nature and disease. Think of what we call the miraculous element in the Gospels—the mighty works of healing, the controlling of wind and wave, the casting out of demons. Do you not feel that the explanation of these things lies at the point where Jesus differs from us for ever, namely, His sinlessness ? These mighty deeds were the impact of a sinless personality upon its environment. The poet sang—

> " My strength is as the strength of ten,
> Because my heart is pure."

Does that not suggest that, given absolute purity and an entirely untainted soul, given a perfectly undimmed vision of the face of God, there might suddenly be loosed upon the world a strength greater even than the strength of any ten, or any hundred, or any thousand souls like ours which are involved in the limitations sin imposes ? This is the incalculable factor ; and the " signs and wonders " of the New Testament are best understood, not as an interference with natural law, but as the coming into action of a higher law inherent in this unprecedented fact. Indeed, granted a sinless personality, even resurrection from the dead on the third day might become more inevitable than astonishing.

Now you see the point. The Gospel miracles can light up the whole question of man's deliverance from sin, precisely because this deliverance is itself the supreme miracle. The mastery over Nature and the mastery over sin are two aspects of one and the selfsame power. Did not Jesus say so Himself ? " Whether is it easier," He demanded of the scribes, " to say to the sick of the palsy, Thy sins be forgiven thee ; or to say, Arise, and take up thy bed, and walk ? " Neither the one nor the other—neither the instantaneous curing of disease nor the reconciling of a soul to God—lay within human reach. " But," went on Jesus, " that ye may know the Son of man hath power on earth to forgive sins, (He saith to the sick of the palsy), I say unto thee, Arise, and take up thy bed, and go thy way. And immediately he arose." God could do both things—master the disease, and master sin —through the personality of Jesus, which was uniquely creative because uniquely without sin. And just as on another day the light which was in Christ was able to pierce the gloom of poor Bartimaeus' physical blindness, and to make the man see, so it was able also to penetrate that deeper because unconscious darkness of souls dulled and fogged and blinded by their sin, and to make *them* see—see themselves, and see the face of God.

That this is actually what occurred when Jesus and sinners met is written clear on page after page of the Gospels. If you were to make a study of the personal interviews Jesus had with individuals, you would discover that in almost every case two things happened to the man or the woman who encountered Jesus, two dramatically opposite things —the one an absolutely devastating sense of shame, the other an absolutely glorious feeling of liberation.

Take just one instance. You will remember there was a day, near the beginning of the story, when Simon Peter, finding himself in the presence of Jesus, suddenly fell upon his face in the bottom of his boat, crying " Depart from me, for I am a sinful man, O Lord ! " I fancy that the apostle, in some of the sermons he preached after Pentecost, must have told and re-told the story of that day. " I looked at Him, and He looked at me," said Peter, " and in that moment I knew that every wound and weakness of my nature was open to His glance. I knew that those clear, steady eyes saw everything—the insincerities, the selfishnesses, the shabby, pitiful subterfuges. I suddenly knew that that was the kind of person I was. It was not that He spoke words of judgment to me—He did not need to probe or cross-examine or condemn : in His presence, I knew. It was just as if a veil had been torn away from my eyes, and for the first time

in my life I really saw myself ; and God pity me, it was a
tragic sight ! I could not bear it ; and I cried—' Let me
alone ! Depart from me, for I am a sinful man, O Lord.' "
Always that was the first reaction when the light of Christ
pierced the sinner's blindness—a scorching sense of shame.

Is it not so still ? Look into your own heart. Do you
remember an hour when the face of Jesus rose before you,
when the fact of Christ flashed upon your inward vision ?
Was that a comfortable experience ? Did it immediately
suffuse you with a delectable glow of calm content ? You
know it did not. It disturbed, and stung, and pierced, and
hurt. It brought not peace but a sword. It smashed down
all defences, and crumbled them to dust. Comfortable ?
I think not. " O Christ, leave me ! Take your eyes off me !
They are burning out my soul. I am a sinful man, O Lord !"

But come back for a moment to the evidence of the
Gospels. The extraordinary thing is this—that the flash of
light from the personality of Jesus which induced in those
men and women the most abysmal shame also kindled the
most marvellous confidence and hope. I think I can hear
Peter continuing his sermon. " O it was wonderful," he
exclaimed, " the thing that happened next ! I had begged
Jesus to depart, but there He stayed beside me : and suddenly
I grew conscious that I was in the presence of a love such as
I had never in this life imagined possible, a kindness and an
understanding and a compassion such as I had found nowhere
else on earth. In that moment, I knew I could start afresh.
I knew I could stand up and live, and face the world like a
conqueror. I knew that heaven itself was at peace with me.
I knew the joy of the reconciled, the new song of the forgiven
and the free. No longer did I cry, ' Depart, O Lord ' ; but
this was all my prayer—' Nearer, my God, to Thee, nearer
to Thee ! ' "

And if that was the experience of Peter, it is also the
experience of countless thousands who have met Jesus on
the road. For the lightning-flash of God which pierces the

defences of our blindness and sin is the light of redeeming love.

All this is focused at the cross. All the powers of God, on the one hand to desolate the soul with shame, on the other to kindle it with joy unspeakable and full of glory, are concentrated there. When I turn my eyes to the cross and gaze on Calvary, what happens ? This, first—the defences of self-excusing and rationalization behind which my sin so subtly hides from me its true colours are penetrated and shattered once for all. That death-ray of the cross breaks every illusion down ; and the truth about sin, the world's sin and my sin—its despicable meanness, its hateful ugliness—stands openly revealed. For suddenly, as I look upon that deadly tree and its pure Victim, a voice within me cries—" There is what your sin means : behold your handiwork ! " Is there any awakening in life half so terrible as that ?

But I am sure Christ meant it to happen. I am sure He chose the road of the cross deliberately, with that end in view. His death, He knew, would flash into the sinner's self-created darkness a light that would never be put out ; and men would understand at last what sin is in its essential nature, and what it means to God. If the modern man is not worrying about his sins, that simply shows that the modern man has never been to Calvary. I cannot possibly stand there, and still delude myself into imagining that sin does not matter : it matters decisively for me, and it matters terribly to God. It means—from God's side of things—an eternal crucifixion, an age-long passion, " the Lamb slain from the foundation of the world," the unseen terrible background to that shattering moment in history when absolute sinless purity saw suddenly down into the uncovered hell of a whole world's iniquity, and God was forsaken by God. No wonder that in the Book of Revelation the souls of sinful men, being confronted with the wounds of the Lamb whom they have pierced, are heard crying to the mountains " Fall on us," and to the rocks " Hide us from His face ! " And when I see in that Christ of incarnate love the wounds my cruel hands have made, then there breaks from my lips the despairing cry that for one so wretched and abandoned there can be no forgiveness in this world or the next.

But stay ! The double effect which Jesus produced in those whom He encountered is supremely manifested here. The paradox of the cross is this—that it is at once the generator of the most frightful shame that ever prostrated the human spirit to the depths, and the source of the most glorious hope that ever sent man's courage soaring to the heights. Why is it that the cross, the Roman gallows-tree, fearful symbol of deepest tragedy and iniquity, has become the magnet of mankind,

> " The sinner's refuge here below,
> The angel's theme in heaven above " ?

How is it that this thing has impregnated humanity with such a dynamic, deathless hope ? Why have all the greatest revivals of religion down the ages thrust the cross before the outcasts' eyes ? Why do all the noblest hymns of the cross tremble with a kind of inexpressible excitement and breathless wonder ? Why has that green hill far away become for millions the centre of the world ? Why can the thought and the memory of it move me to-day to the very depths of my being ? Surely the reason is this—this glorious paradox —that in the very place where I become aware of a guilt that breaks my heart, there comes to meet me a love that passes knowledge. For Calvary was not just Pilate's deed, nor the deed of Judas, or Caiaphas, or the crowd ; nor was it only my deed, and yours, and the deed of all the stubborn, sinning sons of men. It was God's deed, God in action to take the tragic wrongness of this wayward, warring world upon His own heart, God defeating the principalities and powers of darkness at the very point of their proudest triumph, and shattering the shackles of their tyranny, to set the prisoners free. And so the beam that shines from the cross, the very light which pierces and condemns, and wrecks my self-defences, heals also and blesses and gives life ; and the shame of the despairing becomes the joy of the reconciled.

It is all contained in the three great keywords of the Gospel of St. John—Light, Love, Life. In Jesus, in His sinless personality and supremely in His cross, there has broken through upon the world a revealing Light stronger than sin's blindness, " piercing," as the writer to the Hebrews puts it, " to the dividing asunder of soul and spirit, a discerner of the thoughts and intents of the heart." In Him again, in His person and His death, there has appeared upon the battlefield of man's defeat a Love that travels in the greatness of its strength, mighty to save, that looks forth as the morning of a diviner day, fair as the moon, clear as the sun, and—towards man's ancient enemies—terrible as an army with banners. The Light without the Love would terrify me and breed despair ; the Love without the Light would be powerless to reach my soul ; but the Light and the Love together generate Life—a Life which, as I enter into union with Christ by faith, becomes a present possession, eternal and death-defying, because it is the very life of God. And in this, the reconciling ministry of Jesus finds its consummation and its crown.

> " Long my imprisoned spirit lay
>   Fast bound in sin and nature's night ;
> Thine eye diffused a quickening ray,—
>   I woke, the dungeon flamed with light ;
> My chains fell off, my heart was free,
> I rose, went forth, and followed Thee."

III

SPIRITS IN PRISON

"He went and preached unto the spirits in prison."—1 Pet. iii. 19.

THERE was one strange question which haunted the imagination of the early Church : Where was Jesus between the crucifixion and the resurrection ? What was the spirit of Jesus doing, while His body lay in the rock tomb in Joseph of Arimathea's garden ? That gap in the narrative gave scope for much curious speculation. Here, it was felt, was a fascinating and dramatic theme for reverent inquiry. In those silent hours between Good Friday and Easter, when heaven and earth seemed hushed and in suspense, where was Jesus ? What was He doing then ?

The answer given to that question by the early Church was determined in part by the Jewish cosmogony it had inherited. To the Jew, death meant a transition from the land of light and activity to the shadowy abode of the under-world. There in that dim subterranean realm of Sheol, the souls of the departed, both good and evil, were assembled, awaiting the final hour of destiny.

Must not Jesus Christ, argued the fathers of the Church, Himself have travelled thither ? " He was crucified, dead, and buried." What could that mean but that the Lord of light had passed, as all the sons of men must pass, into the land of ghosts and shades ? Hence the abrupt statement of the Creed, " He descended into Hell "—the word in that usage signifying, not the realm of the doomed and lost, but an intermediate state, the Greek " Hades," lying just beyond death's dark, mysterious portal.

But Jesus, they always said, had gone there with a mission and a purpose. His journey had a double meaning. For in

that underworld of the departed, there dwelt the spirits of
Old Testament saints who had died before the Gospel came ;
and Christ went to tell them of the new and final revelation,
and to make their hope secure. There, too, in the land of
Sheol were gathered those who in ages past had rebelled
against God and arrogantly sinned against His grace : to
them Christ carried now the message He had proclaimed on
earth, and the offer of salvation. Such was the vivid imagery
in which the early Christians sought to picture to themselves
the interim activity of their Lord between the moment
when He bowed His head in death on Calvary and the moment
when the bonds of death were broken and He rose triumphant.
He was not resting from His labours then, they said. He was
still about His Father's business. " He went and preached
unto the spirits in prison."

You will understand how this daring conception, the
product of a swift and penetrating spiritual insight, lent
itself readily to dramatic treatment. Thus, for example,
the so-called *Gospel of Nicodemus* describes how on the day
of Calvary the underworld was suddenly suffused with a
strange, unearthly light, and the voice of John the Baptist
was heard proclaiming that Christ was on the way ; whereupon Satan and the king of the dead held a hurried, anxious
consultation, only to be interrupted by a sound like thunder,
and a voice crying through the dark—" Lift up your heads,
O ye gates ; and be ye lift up, ye everlasting doors ; and the
King of glory shall come in." The keepers of Sheol trembled
at the cry, and the bolts and bars with which they had made
fast the doors were beginning to give way. " Who is this
King of glory ? " they inquired ; and the whole domain of
darkness shook when the gates went crashing, and there rose
and echoed and re-echoed the cry, " The Lord of hosts, He
is the King of glory ! " So into that realm of ancient night
came Christ the Victor from the cross. Satan was bound,
the king of the dead dethroned, and all the spirits in prison
set free. What shall we call them, those early Christian

3

delineations ? Imagery, romanticism, rhapsodizing ? Yes,
perhaps—yet surely symbolical of a great and glorious
truth. Here is nothing less than the very heart and essence
of the Gospel dramatized, the eternal reality of the divine
redemptive passion made graphic, almost startling, in a
parable. " He descended into hell." " He preached unto
the spirits in prison."

Enough, however, of the scaffolding of the idea, its framework of Jewish cosmogony and early Christian dogma. Let
us push beyond that now to the essential message which
lies here, so challenging to mind and conscience. " Spirits
in prison "—does that not exactly describe a multitude of
souls to-day ? Often you can see it on their faces. You can
hear it in their talk. You can sense it in their whole attitude
to life. You and I have perhaps encountered more than a
hint of it in our own experience. We have had hours when
there came rushing in upon us the uneasy suspicion that in
some degree we were spirits in prison ourselves. And here it
stands written : " Christ preached to the spirits in prison."
He is the only liberator ; and only through the possession
of a vital Christian faith can the wretchedness of perpetual
frustration and thraldom and repression become the joyous
confidence of fulfilment and mastery and release.

I ask you to consider some of the great imprisoning forces
of human life ; and we shall find that in every case Christ
holds the key.

First, there is the fact of *drudgery*. How many spirits
are in bondage to that ! How many lives once buoyant and
resilient are going about their daily tasks with a kind of dull
resentment smouldering within ! Why should fate deny so
many dear desires of the heart and make havoc of so many
dreams ? Why should skies which in the morning were
fraught with sunlit promise become so grey and leaden as the
day advances ? Why should the human spirit so often be
condemned to beat its wings, like a caged bird, against the

bars, the dreary, hampering limitations of the commonplace, the deadly monotony of things, the thwarting, iron rigidity of a universe that does not seem to care or understand? Sometimes the strain grows almost unbearable. Then the hidden restlessness is apt to break forth. " I was not meant for this ! " the prisoned spirit wants to cry. " I can't go on like this indefinitely. My nerves won't stand it. I must get out ! I must get out ! "

But Christ preached to the spirits in prison. " You *can* get out," He says. " See, I have the key ! " And He stands at the door of that prison-house of drudgery, this Christ who has all the keys of life and destiny hanging at His girdle : and He takes one key, and puts it in the lock, and the door swings open on its hinges. That is not fancy. It is something Jesus Christ has done in the concrete stuff of human experience. There are men and women in every congregation who could tell you how He has done it for them. He has not miraculously lifted them out of the difficult situation in which a strange, inscrutable providence has set them. He has done something far better. He has lifted them out of their resentment at that situation, out of their restlessness and nerve-strain, into quietude of soul and liberty. They do not need to tell you that this has happened. You can see it. There is a light on their faces now, which is recognizably the peace of God that passeth understanding.

But the key ? The key with which Christ unlocks the door of drudgery, and sends the prisoner forth to freedom— do you know its name ? Its name is Consecration. For to take " the trivial round, the common task," the wear and tear of life, the very points at which perhaps our dearest hopes have gone down defeated and our dreams been brought to nought : to take all that crushing aspect of things, and by the strength of the grace of Jesus to lay it down upon the altar as our personal oblation and burnt-offering—that is the surest way to a poise and freedom and contentment which nothing can destroy. Even the most hurting experiences become then charged with meaning : "a road to lead us daily nearer God." The key is consecration ; and through the darkest night the consecrated spirit walks at liberty.

Let us pass on to something else. The second great imprisoning force in life is *the pressure of the world.* It is the obsession of the seen and temporal, the domination of the natural and the material. How many immortal spirits are in that prison-house to-day ! The tragic irony of it is that so many of them keep babbling about their emancipation. It is a strange thing surely that any soul should be in prison without knowing it. But that is what happens. There are people who imagine themselves free, because they have stopped worrying about the sanctions of ethics or the dictates of religion—not realizing that there are few things so danger-ous or damaging as the corroding acids of a materialist philosophy. Religion they dismiss as mere wish-thinking, ethics as a social contract with no inherent claim or sanctity. "This actual, tangible world is everything," they say. "The only wisdom is untrammelled self-expression. Let us eat, drink, and be merry, for to-morrow we die. And as for all dogmas and creeds, let us break their bands asunder, and cast away their cords from us ! "

It sounds confident and convinced, that spirit : but sometimes, listening closely, you will detect an undertone of hesitancy and misgiving. And indeed, if we could always pierce beneath the surface, it might surprise us to discover how much of the clever talk, the self-conscious modernity, the hectic flitting from one sensation to another, is but a shield for a spirit disillusioned with the results of its own enfranchisement, and how often the moral revolt, the boisterous agnosticism, hide an aching, starving heart—

> "The desire of the moth for the star,
> Of the night for the morrow,
> The devotion to something afar
> From the sphere of our sorrow."

But Christ preached to the spirits in prison. Christ knows those secret aches and longings behind the façade of scepticism and indifference. His kind but searching glance can scan the restlessness, the hunger, that hide behind the mask of apathy and irreligion. And there is only one key which can unlock this prison, and open the path to freedom —and its name is the Supernatural. The real need of multitudes to-day is not a new intellectual gymnastic to exercise their minds : it is a new sense of the supernatural to liberate their souls. There are people busy looking for a dialectic and a philosophy that will stabilize their position and set them firmly on their feet : what they are really requiring is a sense of God that will drive them to their knees. The soul is not going to be satisfied indefinitely with the husks of the material and the natural and the temporal. It needs something better than this earthly stuff. It needs a fourth dimension. It needs the sacraments. It needs the living God. Until it finds that, it may range the world from one end to the other, but it is a spirit in prison. And who holds the key if not Jesus of Nazareth, in whom the unseen reality without which we cannot live became actual and visible, and the eternal became near and present, and God Himself stood at our door and knocked ?

Let us pass on again. A third imprisoning force, one all too tragically familiar, is *the tyranny of sin*. There are no easy words, no palliating and sophisticating excuses, that can ever gloss over the stark fact of a guilty conscience. We may call sin, if we choose, by other names ; we may ingeniously discover that the blame, if blame there be, attaches to our heredity, our environment, our social organism, our economic system, our evolution, anything in fact except ourselves ; we may sentimentalize our sins, till they seem almost romantic, or we may rationalize them, till they appear clothed in the virtue of a pre-destined necessity. But in our inmost hearts we know that all such self-excusings are but casuistry. The plain fact is, we have done things we ought not to have done, and need not have done, and these things have left a mark. Every time we yield to evil, we add another fetter to the chain that binds us, and we know it. We know, moreover, that all our stern resolving, our vows and oaths of amendment, our fervent, fevered efforts to rectify the situation, and by a sheer act of will to neutralize the downward drag and defeat the fatal bias, are ultimately impotent and unavailing. "The strongest oaths," says Shakespeare's Prospero, "are straw to the fire i' the blood." We cannot eradicate the evil, or redeem ourselves.

> "There was a Door to which I found no Key :
> There was a Veil past which I could not see."

But Christ preached to the spirits in prison. And to-day we do not need to stand baffled before any obstructing, impenetrable veil : the veil has been "rent in twain from the top to the bottom." We are not left pathetically battering at a closed door, or crying in frantic desperation, "Let me out! Let me out!" The door stands open wide, for Christ has brought the key. Its name is the Forgiveness of God. And as He once stood at the grave of Lazarus, and cried in a voice that rang right down into the depths, "Come forth and live," so now He stands at the deep dungeon of sin's fast-bound tyranny, and cries, "Come, soul, come forth and be free! For God is at peace with you. There is nothing that need separate you from God one moment longer. Enter into the joy of your Lord!"

It is the flaming heart of the message of Calvary that this incredible thing has happened. Incredible—yes, that is our difficulty. We cannot believe it. When the burden of a troubled conscience falls from us at the foot of the cross, we are not like Christian, who let it lie, and "gave three leaps for joy, and went on singing" : we cannot believe such freedom was ever intended for guilty souls, and

with a strange, perverted sense of duty we look around for
the burden that has been struck from off our shoulders, and
tie it on again. That is not "the glorious liberty of the
children of God"! Why should we still linger amid the
shadows of the prison-house, when Christ's pierced hand has
set wide the door? We may believe in the forgiveness of
sins : but we have to do more than believe in it as a theological
statement in a creed, we have to accept it as a gift. We
have to realize that when Scripture tells us there are certain
things which God is going to remember against us no more
for ever, it means what it says. It is one of the great transfiguring moments in life when a man can say, not only " I
believe in the forgiveness of sins," but "I know He has
forgiven me!" If only, for some spirit in prison, that
moment might be now!

There, then, are three of the great imprisoning forces of
life—the fact of drudgery, the pressure of the world, the
tyranny of sin. And there are the keys by which Christ
brings release—the consecration of life, the vision of the
supernatural, the forgiveness of God. One final prison-
house remains, *the fear of death*. No Gospel for man's desperate
need, as the writer to the Hebrews saw and declared quite
bluntly, could ever be adequate or decisive which did not
include this within its scope—to " deliver them who through
fear of death were all their lifetime subject to bondage." I
do not think he meant that men fear death as a physical
fact, or shrink trembling when it comes to them. It is very
rarely that, when the darkness deepens and the last hour
draws near, a man is found afraid to die. No, the real fear
of death is something different. It is the fear that this thing
may mean the destruction of love, the ruthless separation
for ever and for ever of those who have been all in all to
each other on this earth, and have loved with every atom
of their being. It means more even than that. It means
the awful, hideous suspicion that a universe in which death

plays a part so pitiless and inexorable, must be, in the last resort, not a cosmos, but a chaos ; and that the dearest hopes and dreams we have cherished, the convictions we have laboured for and fought for and agonized for—such instincts deep within us as the difference between right and wrong, the final victory of good over evil, the emergence of a day of perfect righteousness beyond the dark night of the toil and tears and sacrifice of a thousand generations—are all inevitably doomed to bitterest disillusionment and derision, are indeed nothing but a mocking mirage across the desert of our wanderings, a chimera of the mind, " a tale full of sound and fury, signifying nothing." That is the fear of death which subjects to bondage. That is the last grim prison of the soul.

But Christ preached to the spirits in prison. And we, the imprisoned spirits who have listened to Christ, and have become aware that in Christ we are being confronted with the authentic truth of God Himself, have heard—even as John of the Revelation heard it in his prison isle of Patmos —a great voice crying across the mists and shadows of our misgiving, " Fear not ! I am He that liveth, and was dead ; and behold, I am alive for evermore—and have the keys of hell and of death." Christ has the key. Its name is Immortality.

What a glorious world of far horizons it is that meets your gaze, when that key has unlocked the door ! How wide the universe in which your spirit now walks at liberty ! Listen to this other liberating word of Jesus : " Be not afraid of them that kill the body, and after that have no more that they can do "— a magnificent, almost taunting, declaration of death's utter impotence to crush or injure the things that most vitally matter. It may kill the body ; but having done that, said Christ, it is finished, it has spent the last atom of its force. And if that is the sum-total of death's achievement, why call it king of terrors ? Why, when it has done its worst, it has not begun to touch the real heart

of life's essential glory! "Safe shall be my going," sang
Rupert Brooke,

> "Secretly armed against all death's endeavour;
> Safe though all safety's lost; safe where men fall;
> And if these poor limbs die, safest of all."

The people who have reached real peace of mind in this
present distracting life are those who are utterly at peace
about death, who have gazed full into the face of man's last
enemy, and have recognized with the thrill of excited discovery how meagre is its narrow realm, how pitiful its weakness behind the braggart show of power. And to all who
will accept it, that release from the prison of the fear of
death is freely offered in the Gospel. Christ holds the key
of immortality.

Your love is immortal. Death cannot lay a finger on
that; for love is of God, and those you have loved upon this
earth, and have been loved by, are yours for ever.

Your work is immortal. The greatest passage on immortality in the New Testament ends with the words—
"Therefore be ye stedfast, unmoveable, always abounding
in the work of the Lord, forasmuch as ye know that your
labour is not in vain in the Lord": it is not going to be
made a mockery by death, nor cast as rubbish to the void;
it is to be taken up, and conserved, and wrought into the fabric
of the final consummation towards which the whole creation
moves, a city which hath foundations, whose builder and
maker is God.

Finally, your own being is immortal. The earth and
clay of our common nature are mingled with the fire of
God; beneath the dull surface of our sinning, suffering
humanity lurks divinity; and this corruptible must put on
incorruption, and this mortal immortality. Nay, the fact is
that in union with Jesus Christ, this mortal has already put
on immortality! For in Christ, the eternal has arrived upon
the scene of time; and in fellowship with Him, our eternal
life begins here and now, is a present, actual possession.

To those who know that, what is death ? A mere
irrelevance. Let John Donne's noble words declare it :

> " Death be not proud, though some have called thee
> Mighty, and dreadfull, for, thou art not so :
> For those whom thou think'st thou dost overthrow
> Die not, poor Death ; nor yet canst thou kill me. . . .
> Thou'rt slave to fate, chance, kings, and desperate men,
> And dost with poison, war, and sickness dwell ;
> And poppy or charms can make us sleep as well
> And better than thy stroke. Why swell'st thou then ?
> One short sleep past, we wake eternally,
> And Death shall be no more : Death, thou shalt die ! "

Thanks be to God, who giveth us the victory—that victory
—through our Lord Jesus Christ.

IV

THE TRANSFORMATION OF TRAGEDY

"Thou hast turned for me my mourning into dancing: thou hast put off my sackcloth, and girded me with gladness."—Ps. xxx. 11.
"Then were the disciples glad, when they saw the Lord."—JOHN xx. 20.

THIS broken, warring world is living on the wrong side of Easter Day. That is the basic fact, and the source of all our troubles. We are back where the disciples were, between Good Friday and the Resurrection. Like them, we are groping in the dark. We are on the wrong side of Easter. We are standing helpless before the towering mystery of evil's tragic dominion, feeling our hopeless inadequacy in the face of the grim facts of sin and chaos and man's ruthless inhumanity to man. We are still fighting the spectres of the night, still searching pathetically for some man-made, humanistic solution to our problems, struggling in the morass of fear and impotence and confusion. And the supreme need of the world at this moment is to start living on the other side—the right side—of Easter. It is to know that in the Resurrection of Jesus God Himself has spoken, and God's empire of righteousness and peace and joy and liberty has been brought decisively to light.

That was the discovery which brought the Church into being, and on which Christianity has lived and gone crusading ever since.

Never was there a transformation so swift and radical and complete as that which turned eleven broken, utterly defeated men into the resolute nucleus of the greatest society this earth has ever seen—the Body of Christ, the Church of the living God. Never was there a transition more impossible to explain on purely naturalistic and psychological grounds than that which, almost in a moment, in the twinkling of an eye, carried Christ's abject, trembling followers from the lowest abyss of cowed, irrevocable despair to the sunlit heights of courage and conviction and confidence in the living God, giving them a message which flamed with assurance and a spirit rocklike and irresistible. The historian who thinks he can explain *that* in terms of auto-suggestion, or measure it by the paltry foot-rule of a humanistic, non-supernatural theology or a mechanistic psychology, is simply not being scientific. "This is the Lord's doing, and it is marvellous in our eyes." And it is that revolution, that Easter awakening, that vision of the victory of God, which this darkened earth is needing desperately to-day.

It is important for our purpose that we should reconstruct the scene in the upper room on the night that followed Calvary. Let us try to sense the atmosphere. Look at the faces of the little group of men. Listen to their conversation. Can we analyse their thoughts and their emotions? Can we read the secrets of their souls?

The first fact that arrests you is *the depth of their despair*. It is an awful thing to live for years in the light of a lovely dream, and then in one moment to see it crumpled up and smashed to atoms and destroyed. That is what life had done to them. "It is all over now," I can hear Peter saying, "all the hopes we cherished when we left our fishing-nets to follow Him, all those vivid happy days when we thought we had found the one thing supremely worth doing and it was bliss to be alive, all the high thoughts He kindled in us of a kingdom of God coming gloriously upon the earth—all finished now!" "Yes," breaks in Matthew, "I remember the day He called me. Three years ago? It seems but yesterday. He came and took me from the work I had grown to hate, for it was smirching my soul and making me feel unclean; and His coming was like the songs of morning, a new beginning, a wonderful life that was never going to end. And now— that it should have ended like this! How can I bear it?" And another voice chimes in, the voice of Simon Zelotes, who had come to Jesus from the dangerous game of nationalist politics. " I wonder if we have been living in a fool's paradise from the first, if my dreams of a kingdom in Israel were all the time pure delusion ; I wonder—was the man Judas right when he once hinted to me that our Leader had betrayed us, and led us on deliberately to disillusionment ? " " For God's sake, hold your peace," cries out John. " You shan't say a thing like that ! It is bitter enough without that added bitterness "—and then, almost with a sob, " O Jesus, Master, how can I live without you ? The world is wrecked for me, weary and empty for ever."

There, then, is the first fact you encounter in that upper room—dejection and despair. But you look again—and now you realize there is something on the men's faces besides despair : there is *shame*. The end of the story had been so discreditable to themselves. There had been such a dastardly loss of nerve. They had all, at the crucial moment, forsaken their Leader and fled. Only a few women had been there, faithful to the last. They were deserters—every man of them —and they knew it. And looking at their faces, you can see that they are worse than despondent : they are ashamed. Two nights before, says the evangelist, one of those men, looking into the face of Christ, had cried—" Though I should die with Thee, yet will I not deny Thee." " Likewise also said all the disciples." Count on us, Jesus ! Count on our loyalty absolutely ! Whatever happens to You, we will be there to share it, gladly and vehemently and with all our heart ! Then your eye travels down the Gospel page to this : " They all forsook Him and fled." Those men in the upper room on Easter Eve were bitterly, horribly ashamed. " If even one of us had played the man ! " they were thinking. " If only one of us had broken the spell of that pitiful cowardice and stood beside Him in His loneliness ! If one of us had had grit and grace enough to lose his life for Jesus ! But what an ignominious show we made, what a miserable crew we are ! After this, we'll never be able to lift up our heads again." And if there was one of them who felt that more acutely than all the rest, it was the man who had always been the acknowledged spokesman of the little group. " What was it He said to me at Caesarea ? ' Thou art no longer Simon. Thou art Peter—a rock ! And on this rock I build My Church.' That was it. This rock ! And I was so proud, so gratified about it, so full of confidence and resolution. Yet when the crisis came, I ran like the rest ; and when men challenged me about Him, I said I did not know Him, and that He meant nothing to me. This rock ! O God, forgive me—wretched, miserable me ! " Those men were not only despairing : they were ashamed.

Nor was that all. Look again, and on their faces you will see *fear*. Their Master was gone, brutally done to death : who knew but that it might be their turn next ? They had been seen with Him, they were marked men : and who could tell but that Annas and Caiaphas, having struck once, might strike again ? " The doors were shut, for fear of the Jews," says the evangelist. And when two of them made as though to slip out into the streets, " Keep that door locked ! " cried the others—for the nervous tension in the room had grown feverish and acute, and feelings were strained and overwrought—" For God's sake, shut that door, and bolt it ! " Yes, on those faces you read fear.

But look just once again and you will detect something more tragic still—deeper than despair or shame or fear— the sense of *Christ-forsakenness*. That is what had finally wrecked their universe : they had lost Him, the best and dearest Friend of all. There come to mind the haunting lines of *The Passing of Arthur*, where Tennyson tells of good Sir Bedivere standing on the shore, watching the dark barge that carried his dying King away from him for ever.

> " Long stood Sir Bedivere
> Revolving many memories, till the hull
> Look'd one black dot against the verge of dawn,
> And on the mere the wailing died away.

> But when that moan had past for evermore,
> The stillness of the dead world's winter dawn
> Amazed him, and he groan'd, ' The King is gone.' "

So the orphaned disciples revolved their many memories of Jesus. Slowly into their dazed, stunned minds the truth was sinking, that never on this earth would they set eyes on Him again ; never see Him, as they had loved to watch Him, with the little children clambering to His arms ; never listen awed and thrilled to that quiet voice speaking of the mysteries of God ; never hear the ringing royalty of its tones as it cried to the demons and the evil spirits, " Hold your peace and come forth " ; never see again the infinite compassion and gentleness in those eyes, as they gazed upon the outcast and the lonely and the leper and the broken-hearted. They were struggling to realize it : Jesus is dead. " Do you remember, Peter," John burst out, " the day you stood and cried ' Thou are the Christ, the Son of the living God ' ? How thrilled we were, how sure He was the Lord's Anointed, with all heaven's legions at His back ! And now He is dead. Do you remember how the feeling grew upon us that He was a Being of a different order from ourselves, how awed we were to hear Him at His prayers—He seemed so close to God, so deep in the mysteries we could never understand, the only begotten of the Father, full of grace and truth ? And now He is dead. He made God so marvellously real to us, so personal and present : and now He is dead. I feel," cried the brokenhearted disciple, " as if God Himself were dead—no God for us to pray to any longer, now that Christ is gone." That was the final anguish of Easter Eve, the desolation of Christ-forsakenness.

Now do you see the urgent significance of all this for ourselves ? That upper room is a kind of microcosm of our world to-day. We are still living on *that* side—the wrong side—of Easter. Keep in mind the four things we have seen there, the four attitudes to life carved deep upon the features of those men : then turn and contemplate the human scene around you now, and man's terrible twentieth-century dilemma and entanglement, the chaos of his wars, the confusion of his ethics, his powerlessness to redeem himself. Is it not apparent that all the darkness of the upper room that night—all the raw material of tragedy—is here in this world to-day ?

On the disciples' faces we saw *despair*. Is that not here to-day ? The comfortable optimism of the Victorian Age, with its gospel of inevitable progress and its jaunty evolutionism, is quite exploded now. Nor can any idealist philosophy, any social ethic, equip man to withstand the onslaught of the wild forces that are loose in the world, or to survive the damage and disaster that life's harsh actualities inflict upon his dearest hopes and dreams. John Bunyan knew what he was about when, on the first page of his book, he pictured humanity by the symbol of a man with a great burden on his back, and on his lips a lamentable cry— " What shall I do ? " We are rediscovering the seventh chapter of *Romans* to-day. We are recognizing that all our own expedients and devices are futile, a mere tinkering with the surface of a world that is wrong at the roots. Human wisdom is bankrupt, and all man's efforts haunted with despair.

But in the upper room we sensed not only despair, but *shame*. Is that not here to-day ? Why is the world so wrong ? Is it not that man himself has basely mismanaged and misused the mighty gift of freedom ? And in his heart of hearts he knows it ; and he is ashamed. He has taken his noblest faculties, and prostituted them to beastly ends. He has taken a lovely thing like science, and devised the devilry of poison gas. He has taken a marvellous force like personal influence, and used it to corrupt the truth. Man's own unregenerate heart is still, as much as when Paul wrote *Romans*, the root of all his troubles. And do not our own hearts tell us that ? Have we never misused the freedom of our will ? Have we never swerved from the way of Christ ? Have we never turned and forsaken Him and fled, and then stood aghast at our own disloyalty ? We know we have. " All we like sheep have gone astray." Not once, nor twice, but many times, we have broken our pledged word to the Captain of our souls. We have defaced God's image in us, and brought discredit on the blessed name we bear. By many a tragic failure, by many a secret pact with evil, by many a slinking from the field in the day of battle, we have sold Christ. And God has seen it all. We know—how vividly we know—what those eleven men were feeling in their shame !

Again, on their faces we encountered *fear*. Is that not here to-day ? " Will it be our turn next ? " was their thought in the upper room : and people and nations are restlessly, feverishly facing that to-day. Where is security to be found ? Must the weak things of the world live for ever beneath the shadow of the menace of the strong ? Is there any certainty that the things which crucified Christ—envy and pride and force and vengefulness—may not conquer everywhere at last ? Will it be our turn next ? Fear haunts the world, the kind of fear that poisons life and breeds the very things it dreads.

Finally, on the disciples' faces we saw *Christ-forsakenness*. Is that not here to-day ? We have our " Recall to Religion " movements. Why ? Because, on so wide a scale, Christendom has been losing Christ. We have kept Him as a historic memory, but we have lost Him as a living intimate presence. We have kept Him as an object for our veneration and our worship, and we have lost Him as a herald voice to be obeyed. We have kept Him, as the school of liberal theologians kept Him, the greatest leader who ever led the hosts of humanity, the finest teacher who ever taught, the noblest example who ever pointed out the way, the best and highest of all the sons of men : and we have lost Him as God incarnate in the flesh, the invasion into history and humanity of a kingdom, a

4

power and a glory super-human and super-historical, the advent into this confused and helpless world of an eternal grace and truth able to redeem humanity and to make all history new. That is the divine Gospel which our modern humanisms have mutilated. That is the God of limitless power and love we have been reducing to an article in a creed, a remote abstraction, a struggling, thwarted tendency imprisoned in the structure of the universe. That is the living Christ we have been losing. And then perhaps we wonder why our religion lacks verve and vigour and vitality and fire! Is it so surprising? We are like those forlorn disciples, in the desolation of their Christ-forsakenness.

What then? Is this sombre, tragic prospect all the tale? The formidable forces that now grip the heart of humanity in the fell clutch of despair and shame and fear and Christ-forsakenness—have they the last word in the story?

Look and see. We are back in the upper room. But surely—these cannot be the same men! It is quite incredible that twenty-four hours should work such a change. For look at them—their faces shining, their eyes lit up with the light of triumph, their voices throbbing with the emotion of a wonderful discovery, their words ringing with joy and victory. No, these cannot be the same. We must have mistaken our way. We have come into the wrong street. We have lost our bearings in the " black-out " of Jerusalem. We have knocked at the wrong door. This cannot be the place. We were looking for a funeral, not a festival. It is most embarrassing to arrive like this at the wrong house. Let us apologize for our intrusion, and hasten away. Can anyone direct us to the right address? We are seeking the followers of Jesus, the prostrated, brokenhearted, inconsolable followers of Jesus. We are wanting to find Peter and James and John, the pathetic remnant in the house of mourning. Let us begone. But stay! *This is the place.*

And these are the men ! Incredible—yet true. For through the babbling incoherencies of their bewildered joy you can hear two phrases constantly repeated—" Christ is risen ! God has spoken ! " And ever and again they break out irrepressibly into the music of a psalm : " When the Lord turned again the captivity of Zion, we were like them that dream. Then was our mouth filled with laughter, and our tongue with singing : then said they among the heathen, The Lord hath done great things for them. The Lord hath done great things for us ; whereof we are glad."

I say again, there is no natural theology, no mechanistic psychology, which can explain that transition.

What has happened to those four attitudes we encountered in that upper room ? These men's irrevocable despair—God has taken that, and buried it out of sight for ever in Christ's empty tomb ! Their shame and dreadful self-despising—God has taken that, and matched it with His grace and free forgiveness. Their haunting, devastating fear—God has taken that and killed it once and for all, nailing it to the cross. Their desolate Christ-forsakenness—God has taken that, and filled and flooded the aching, empty void with Christ's dear comforting presence, far closer and more intimate than before.

So once again, and for the last time, we turn from that upper room of long ago and far away, and look out upon the human scene to-day and in upon our own sin-scarred, distracted hearts. Why should we go on living on the wrong side of Easter ? Why, in our verdict on the total meaning of life, ignore the one decisive piece of evidence ? God has spoken ! The word from beyond time and history has pealed forth. Grace triumphs. Through the thick darkness omnipotent love and regnant righteousness march out to their sure victory. Christ has risen !

It is the Easter message that holds the answer to this tragic earth's vast need. If this is false, there is no hope for humanity anywhere. If this is true, then all our dreams are true. The power of God that broke the concentrated might of evil in the raising again of Jesus shall yet resurrect the world !

Here is the answer to the four attitudes which dominate our outlook upon life to-day. Our uttermost despair, the poison of a corroding fatalism—Christ risen answers that. For now we know that the Lord God omnipotent reigneth, that already Satan like lightning has fallen from heaven : and " shall not the Judge of all the earth do right ? "

Our shame and self-despising, our human helplessness against the subtle things which corrupt the nature and rot the soul—Christ risen answers that. For now we know that there has appeared on the stricken field of our personal defeat " a second Adam to the fight and to the rescue " : a grace which, having once broken the fast-bound chains of hell, is not going to be baffled by any of the chains that bind our souls in slavery.

Our sin of fear, our dread of the unknown way—Christ risen answers that. For now in the darkest valley shines the radiance of an inviolable hope. If the God who raised up Jesus be for us, who can be against us ? All braggart principalities and powers look puny and pathetic when you have seen the conquering Christ ! " He is my light and my salvation ; whom shall I fear ? He is the strength of my life ; of whom shall I be afraid ? "

Finally, our bitter sense of Christ-forsakenness, the impoverishment of our faith, the coldness of our hearts—Christ risen answers that. For the Resurrection means not only a Christ who defeated death on one memorable day in the long ago : it means a Christ alive for ever—and therefore living now. " Speak to Him, thou, for He hears ! " He is no illustrious name buried in a book or tied in the graveclothes of a dead theology. He is no receding memory, to make you cry—

> " O for the touch of a vanish'd hand,
> And the sound of a voice that is still ! "

The hand is not vanished. It is reaching out to you in love to-day, and one grasp of that all-conquering hand can make you courageous and invincible. The voice is not still. Hark ! Can't you hear it in the hushed temple of your inmost soul ? He is risen. He is here. He is Immanuel, God with us on this His own triumphant day—and God with us for ever.

This—nothing less—is the logic of faith. This is God's decisive answer to the chaos of the world. This—Christ alive from the dead—is the word of the Lord to you. And everything you may ever need is here—hope when all hope seems broken, courage when you are terrified, light when you are in darkness, forgiveness when you have blundered badly, friendship when you are feeling lonely and forsaken, and at the last, a wonderful welcome home, from the Lord of life eternal, when your day has run to sunset, and the evening star is in the sky.

V

THE GOSPEL OF THE ASCENSION

" He was parted from them, and carried up into heaven. And they
worshipped him, and returned to Jerusalem with great joy : and were
continually in the temple, praising and blessing God."—LUKE xxiv. 51–53.
" It is expedient for you that I go away."—JOHN xvi. 7.
" He ascended up on high, he led captivity captive."—EPH. iv. 8.

SUPPOSE you had just been saying Good-bye to someone
whom you loved intensely : you had stood on the quay
at the docks until the ship could be seen no more ; or you
had walked up and down the platform in the station, almost
wishing it were time for the train to go, that this agony of
parting might be over ; or you had taken leave of home,
not knowing what changes might come before the day of
your returning ; or you had watched the last lingering light
of consciousness flickering out from a dear face in the
deepening shadows of the valley of death. Would you feel
like singing then ?

What lover ever sang when parted from the beloved ?
What heart was ever blithe in the moment of farewell ? It
is a grey and cheerless dawn that breaks upon the world
when you have had to say good-bye.

John Wesley has told, in his *Journal*, of his mother's
last hours on earth. " From three to four the silver cord was
loosing, and the wheel breaking at the cistern ; and then
the soul was set at liberty. We stood round the bed and
fulfilled her last request : ' Children, as soon as I am released,
sing a psalm of praise to God.' " That is noble, but excep-
tional. For there are partings that wring the soul with
misery. " O my son Absalom ! my son, my son Absalom !
would God I had died for thee, O Absalom, my son, my son ! "

It is not that last farewell only which shadows life's

gladness and makes the music mute. Where love has welded souls together, all partings are bound to hurt. And when afterwards you go back and walk alone among the familiar scenes, you find them haunted now by ghosts of memory. How can the heart be glad when it is as though the spring had gone out of the year and the sunshine from the sky ? " O Death in Life, the days that are no more ! "

How astonishing, then, to read the words with which St. Luke closes his Gospel ! " Jesus was parted from them. And they returned to Jerusalem with great joy : and were continually in the temple, praising and blessing God." The dearest Friend whom life had ever given them had gone where they could not follow. There had been those last brief, never-to-be-forgotten weeks together, those infinitely precious conversations, and then the final walk along the familiar country road where so often they had sauntered carefree in a past that now seemed infinitely remote : and then—they were alone. They ought to have been desolate and brokenhearted. They ought to have turned homeward with heavy steps and slow, too sad for speech, woebegone with an intolerable repining and regret. They ought to have felt and looked like men bereaved and broken down and forlorn. If they had gone straggling back to Jerusalem that day like disorganized pathetic units of a routed host drifting home from a disastrous campaign, that we could have understood. I want you to realize how surprising are the words that meet you here : " They returned with great joy, praising and blessing God."

There had been a time, indeed, not many weeks before, when the very thought of Christ's departing had sent a sudden shiver through their souls. Had anyone told them then that the day of His going would find them serene and cheerful and rejoicing, they would have spurned the suggestion as monstrous and incredible, not far removed from blasphemy. Knowing how they felt, He had tried to break the news to them quite gently. " It is expedient for you

that I go away." But they had flatly refused to believe it.
Expedient ? Was orphanhood expedient ? Was the wreck
of fairest hopes expedient ? Was disaster for the high
adventure to which they had given their lives expedient ?
Was the pain of lacerated hearts expedient ? What could the
Master mean ?

But now they knew. Now they were questioning no longer.
This farewell was not hope's defeat, but its glorious verifica-
tion. They saw now how true that hard saying of their Master
had been. It *was* expedient. Once they had doubted and
denied. Now they understood. Do we ? In what sense is it
legitimate to say that—for the disciples, for the Church,
and for ourselves—the termination of the earthly ministry
of Jesus and His passing away from mortal sight for ever
were not loss, but clear and unequivocal gain ?

It was expedient, first, for *the spiritualizing of religion*.
This was the reason Christ Himself had given. " If I go not
away, the Comforter will not come unto you ; but if I depart,
I will send Him unto you."

Suppose He had stayed with them. Suppose the Galilean
idyll had been renewed. Suppose the story of His companionship with them had simply been resumed at the point where
it had been interrupted. You can see what would have
happened. They would have remained dependent on His
visible presence. They would scarce have progressed beyond
the rudimentary class in the school of faith. The beatitude
of those who see not, yet believe, would have eluded them.
In every perplexing path of life, they would have counted
upon hearing His dear familiar voice and seeing the reassuring
smile. But faith is not faith, when it needs the aids of sense
to reinforce it : and so it was expedient for them that He
went away.

Do you wish He had never gone ? Have you sometimes
looked back wistfully across the years and envied those who
walked with Christ in Galilee ? John Bunyan tells us that

once, brooding on the story of the calling of the first disciples, he felt a kind of sudden hot resentment that they should have enjoyed a matchless privilege denied for ever to him. " This Scripture kindled fire in my soul. I could seldom read of any that Christ did call, but I presently wished, Would I had been in their clothes ! Would I had been born Peter ! Would I had been born John ! Or, Would I had been by and had heard Him when He called them ! How would I have cried, O Lord, call me also ! " I think we can understand that. I fancy that in some moods we have all found it in our hearts to envy that precious intimacy.

> " Oh to have watched Thee through the vineyards wander,
> Pluck the ripe ears, and into evening roam !—
> Followed, and known that in the twilight yonder
> Legions of angels shone about Thy home."

But that sentiment is the expression not of faith's strength but of its weakness, not of its full development but of its immaturity. " I should like to have been with them then " : yes, but if that gift has been denied us, it is for the good of our souls, for the delivering of our spirits from the bondage of dependence on the visible and tangible, and for the building up of a personal religion which needs no props and supports of external evidence to lean upon, but stands in the strength of the Spirit alone. " I bless myself, and am thankful," declared Sir Thomas Browne, " that I never saw Christ nor His disciples. I would not have been one of those Israelites that passed the Red Sea ; nor one of Christ's patients, on whom He wrought His wonders : then had my faith been thrust upon me : nor should I enjoy that greater blessing pronounced to all that believe and saw not."

There is a type of pseudo-scientific attitude common to-day : it prides itself on its realism, because it will not admit the validity of anything which cannot be apprehended by the senses. Beyond the region of ocular demonstration, it holds, all is imagination and credulity. Faith in the unseen it pronounces rank self-deception. What this kind of mental outlook has apparently never begun to grasp is the crucial fact that the real master-forces of life are all invisible. The Christian who speaks of holding communion with the unseen is not inventing an imaginary world or taking refuge in dreams and fantasy. He is the true rationalist. He is dealing with hard facts. He is recognizing the existence of forces that have been operative from the foundation of the world. " Blessed are they that have not seen, and yet have believed " : there speaks the higher realism. It is this which keeps confidence steadfast and hope undiscouraged even in times like the present, when the outward aspect of the world is overwhelmingly disquieting, and things seen and temporal threaten to obsess and tyrannize the soul.

Hence the passing away of Jesus as a visible presence from the human scene was not negative and tragic, but positive and providential. What might have looked like irreparable loss was in fact essential gain. It was expedient for the spiritualizing of religion. " If I go not away, the Spirit will not come."

Notice, in the second place, that it was expedient for *the universalizing of the Gospel*. Consider how Christianity began. A Child is born to a peasant woman ; a young Man toils at a bench ; half a dozen fishermen suddenly leave their boats and nets ; among a few out-of-the-way villages a fire of religious revival is kindled, flares up, and dies away ; a table is spread for a family meal in an upper room ; in the obscurity of a wooded glade a bowed Figure wrestles in prayer ; on an insignificant hillock a cross is raised ; in a garden a tomb stands empty. It all sounds so local—does it not ?—a tale from an unimportant backwater of history, far removed from the main stream of the rushing years and the surge and thunder of the deeds of men, a sequestered story of long ago and far away, lovely but irrelevant. Yet it is this that in the providence of God has leapt the barriers of the centuries and the frontiers of every nation under heaven. It is this that from its hidden beginnings has stormed the mind and conscience of the world, and pounded at the battlements of ancient prejudice, and broken down like matchwood the stubbornest defences that men have raised against the fire and tempest of its coming.

" A Word came forth in Galilee, a Word like to a star;
  It climbed and rang and blessed and burnt wherever brave hearts are ;
  A word of sudden secret hope, of trial and increase
  Of wrath and pity fused in fire, and passion kissing peace.
  A star that o'er the citied world beckoned, a sword of flame ;
  A star with myriad thunders tongued : a mighty word there came."

It was for this that it was expedient that Jesus went away. While He was with His followers visibly, He could not belong to all the world. While He was ministering to the needy folk of Galilee, He could not be equally the possession of mankind without distinction, barbarian, Scythian, bond and free. Only by departing from the vision of the privileged few could He reign by His Spirit in the hearts of all.

Have you ever considered how many deeds of help and healing Jesus in His earthly ministry had to leave undone ? There must have been ailing folk in Palestine who had none to carry them to the great Physician when He passed their way ; thousands of burdened men and women who never had a chance to see Him or to hear His voice, or to tell Him of their troubles ; villages longing to welcome Him which perforce remained unvisited because Jerusalem was calling and His hour was come. You know how we are apt to fret and become harassed when life grows so busy and our days so full that scores of tasks which we long to be undertaking have to remain undone. To any man with a conscience, that is bound to be a difficult and perplexing experience. What, I wonder, did it mean to Jesus ? For He certainly had it. The cry of suffering humanity was in His heart, yet there were all those multitudes beyond His reach.

If He had been anyone less than Christ, I think it would have driven Him distracted. But like every other burden which He had to carry, this burden too of the things undone was laid at His Father's feet in prayer and in surrender. " My times are in Thy hand " : and the day would come when the closing of this first stage of His ministry would be the opening of another, and it would be given to Him to be no longer the Companion and the Succourer of the few but the Friend of all and the Saviour of the world. It was expedient, for the universalizing of the Gospel, that He should go away : and it is that departure and ascension which have made Christ our own for ever.

> " Shakespeare is dust, and will not come
> To question from his Avon tomb,
> And Socrates and Shelley keep
> An Attic and Italian sleep.
>
> They see not. But, O Christians, who
> Throng Holborn and Fifth Avenue,
> May you not meet, in spite of death,
> A traveller from Nazareth ? "

Notice, in the third place, that it was expedient for *the energizing of evangelism*. Take the magnificent metaphor in which Paul expressed the function and responsibility of the early Church : " Ye are the Body of Christ." Obviously, if their Master had not passed into the unseen, that challenging conception could never have arisen. Had He tarried in their midst, a visible presence, it could never have occurred to them to say that they were Christ's eyes, to look out in compassion on the miseries of men, Christ's hands, to leap out in deeds of mercy and to smite off the shackles from enslaved and helpless souls, Christ's feet, to pursue the lost down the dark labyrinths of sin, and to rescue the perishing and lead them to the light. It took His departure from the human scene to convince them that they were now the agents of His will upon the earth, that to them had been committed nothing less than a summons to reincarnate their Lord, and that upon their answer to that overwhelming challenge the future of Christ's kingdom would depend. Once that tremendous truth had broken upon them, the inextinguishable fire of an authentic passion for souls was kindled. This was the King's business, they now knew, and it required haste. Over land and sea they sped on the errand of salvation. One master-thought possessed them, the proclaiming of God's mighty acts in Jesus ; one ruling passion consumed them, the reconciling of the world. Hence Christ's very departure, which had seemed the ending of the whole adventure, gave it a new impetus and lease of life. It was the motive of their ambassadorship, the energizing of their evangelism.

We who are called by Christ's name are His hands and feet to-day. Forget that, and religion at once degenerates into a lackadaisical, selfish aestheticism. Remember it, and the flame leaps up on the altar. There is nothing so calculated to deliver a Church from trifling and from apathy, and to put fire and passion into its witness to the world, as the discovery of what it means to be Christ's Body. Is there not a lovely legend telling how Gabriel met Jesus at the gate of heaven when the Saviour was returning at His ascension from His mission to the earth ? " What have You achieved ? " the archangel asked. " What results have You left behind You yonder ? " " I have left," replied Jesus, " eleven men who believe in Me." " Is that all ? " demanded Gabriel ; and Jesus answered, " It is all." " But what if they should fail You ? Are You not risking defeat by committing so much to them ? What if their loyalty should break ? " " I know them," responded Jesus, " and they will not fail ! " Nor did they. Can our ascended Lord have a like confidence in us to-day ? We are His hands and feet, His voice to tell the world the riches of God's grace. He counts on us to make His dreams come true. " Thy kingdom come," we pray : and Christ's answer is to bind the responsibility upon our shoulders. " Go, *you*," He bids us, " live the kingdom life

before the eyes of men. Be you the builders of the city of
God ! " If anything should drive us to our knees in penitence,
and then thrust us forth with an indomitable resolve, it is
the knowledge that yonder in the unseen our Lord still says
to us, as long ago He said to Peter, James, and John : " As
the Father hath sent Me, even so send I you." It was expedient that He should go away—for the energizing of
evangelism.

Notice, finally, that it was expedient for *the fortifying of
faith.* This is immeasurably important. Jesus knew the
terrible hazards His cause would have to meet. He foresaw
the deadly menace of the ruthless principalities and powers.
He knew that history, right on to the end of time, would
fling the frightful challenge of the trumpeting success of
fraud and force and arrogant wickedness full in the face of
those who trusted in righteousness and truth and love. Is
not this very thing happening to-day on a gigantic scale ?
How was faith to be fortified to stand the strain ? How was
the assurance to be given that goodness, justice and love
were not abortive, fanciful ideals, " vanity of vanities," as
sometimes to our bewildered minds they appear to be, but
ultimate values destined to prevail, enthroned eternally at
the right hand of power ? One thing was needful—to know
that Jesus, on whom all the concentrated evil of the world
had wreaked its uttermost will, had emerged triumphant and
was at the right hand of God. This, as the disciples came to
see, was the meaning of His going from them. " He ascended
up on high, He led captivity captive."
    For those men, that changed the whole aspect of the
world. Where once they might have lost heart and cringed
in dismal fear, now they could march like conquerors, knowing
that Christ had already conquered. For if evil, at the very
point where it had put forth its maximum force in one
crowning deed of consummate iniquity—its crucifying of
Christ—had met its match, and lost the battle, and been

routed utterly, what more had they to fear ? Or indeed,
what have any of us to fear, even in the darkest days when
criminal wickedness rides prosperously and righteousness
seems trampled in the dust ? Christ crucified and ascended—
there is the ultimate reality : and the gates of hell shall not
prevail against it.

It is a glorious phrase—" He led captivity captive."
The very triumphs of His foes, it means, He used for their
defeat. He compelled their dark achievements to subserve
His ends, not theirs. They nailed Him to the tree, not
knowing that by that very act they were bringing the world
to His feet. They gave Him a cross, not guessing that He
would make it a throne. They flung Him outside the gates
to die, not knowing that in that very moment they were
lifting up all the gates of the universe, to let the King come
in. They thought to root out His doctrines, not understanding that they were implanting imperishably in the
hearts of men the very name they intended to destroy.
They thought they had God with His back to the wall, pinned
and helpless and defeated : they did not know that it was
God Himself who had tracked them down. He did not
conquer *in spite of* the dark mystery of evil. He conquered
through it. He led captivity itself captive.

When you hear a Richard Lovelace singing

> " Stone walls do not a prison make,
>   Nor iron bars a cage,"

what do you say ? You say there is a man who has not
been mastered by his evil fate : he has mastered it. He is
leading captivity captive. When you think of John Bunyan
incarcerated in Bedford gaol, and out of that bitter bondage
bringing the deathless beauty of the *Pilgrim's Progress* ; or
of Father Damien contracting leprosy on his lonely isle, and
actually transforming that dread disease from a crushing
liability to a glorious asset in the service of his Master ; or
of Josephine Butler brokenhearted by a dear child's death,

and making that broken heart a cradle of love for hundreds of unloved lives ; or of Helen Keller, shut in by a midnight of physical darkness, and using that darkness as a holy shrine for communion with the living God—when you think of such as these, what can you say but that they have taken the wrecking circumstances of life, and transfigured them into means of grace and ladders up to heaven ? They have turned the tables on fate. They have vanquished their victors. They have led captivity captive.

How much more is that true of Him who has given us " rest by His sorrow, and life by His death " ! No wonder the Christian Creed, facing the finished work of Jesus, defies the legions of evil to do their worst. Christ's is the victory, the power and the glory : and the doom of all the godlessness, the barbarity, the lying, arrogant unrighteousness which now bestride the world was written on the day when Jesus defeated the powers of darkness once for all and led captivity captive. It was to make this manifest, not only to His disciples but to every succeeding generation, that from His sojourn on the earth He passed to the right hand of God the Father. It was expedient—for the fortifying of faith— that He went away.

Why then art thou cast down, O my soul ? Why art thou disquieted within me ? Hope thou in God ! Defeat the darkness by the vision of the ascended Christ !

> " ' Lift up your hearts ! ' We lift them, Lord, to Thee ;
> Here at Thy feet none other may we see :
> ' Lift up your hearts ! ' E'en so, with one accord,
> We lift them up, we lift them to the Lord.
>
> Above the level of the former years,
> The mire of sin, the slough of guilty fears,
> The mist of doubt, the blight of love's decay,
> O Lord of Light, lift all our hearts to-day !

Then, as the trumpet-call in after years
'Lift up your hearts!' rings pealing in our ears,
Still shall those hearts respond with full accord,
'We lift them up, we lift them to the Lord!' "

VI

THE VOICE THAT WAKES THE DEAD

" Verily, verily, I say unto you, The hour is coming, and now is, when the dead shall hear the voice of the Son of God ; and they that hear shall live."—JOHN v. 25.

THE difference between an ordinary self-centred, mundane existence, and the new career on which Christ launches the soul is the difference *between death and life*. That is the New Testament's reiterated verdict. Without scruple or hesitation, those men lay hold of the most startling and dramatic metaphor within their reach, and use that to describe the difference Christ has made. " We know that we have passed from death unto life." Nor is that simply their unsupported testimony. It stands as Christ's verdict too. " This my son was dead—and is alive ! "

Now the question arises, Can such a use of language be justified ? Take any two men to-day, the one a sincere Christian, the other avowedly irreligious. Clearly there is bound to be a discrepancy in their outlook and philosophy. But have we any right to say—as the New Testament says —that between these two men there is all the dissimilarity that there is between being alive and being dead ? Is that anything more than random talk, a wild exaggeration, a fantastic overstatement bordering on caricature ? Is it not, in fact, a libel and a slander to say that because a man prefers to rub along without religion and to order his existence in independence of God's revelation in Christ, he is therefore dead ? Does it not look as if those writers of the New Testament, carried away with the fervour of the newly converted, have allowed their rhetoric to outrun their logic ?

That may be our first feeling. But maturer reflection will disclose that they are not after all romancing or being theatrical, not striving after effect nor lapsing into crude, naïve hyperbole : they are speaking sober truth. They are accurately transcribing experience. Ask any one who has deeply felt the liberating, vitalizing touch of Christ upon his soul, and he will tell you—" Only then did I begin to live ! "

Consider, for one thing, the appalling aimlessness of so much human life in this modern world. The highroad of life that stretches from the cradle to the grave is full to-day of people wandering about with no sense of a direction or a goal. Hither and thither they keep rushing, restlessly preoccupied, driven to and fro by strong, conflicting hungers and instincts and desires, pursuing now one prize, now another, absorbed in money-making, love-making, war-making, peace-making, career-making—and yet, in spite of it all, dissatisfied, bored, unhappy. Why ? Because the whole thing seems so senseless, un-coördinated, devoid of plan and purpose. And indeed, if a man has no ultimate scale of values to give integration to his life and meaning to his struggles ; if deep within his secret heart there is no throne where certain regnant convictions hold unchallenged and commanding sway ; if his spirit has never been stabbed awake to an eternal vista beyond the world of time and sense ; if there is no recognition of a supreme controlling Hand which even out of the mistakes and tangles of this earth can weave the finished pattern of a perfect righteousness and love ; if " earth to earth, ashes to ashes, dust to dust " is the last word when the brief kaleidoscope of three-score years and ten is over, how pathetically hollow life becomes—

> " Sad as the wind that sweeps across the ocean
> Telling to earth the sorrow of the sea,
> Vain is my strife, just empty idle motion,
> All that has been is all there is to be."

Were the New Testament writers wrong in holding that such a miserably aimless existence was not worthy of the name of life at all ?

There is another kind of deadness besides that of aimlessness : the deadness of formality. " I know thy works," declares the Christ of the Revelation to the Church at Sardis ; " thou hast a name that thou livest, and art dead." If you were to find a Church one day which had no expectancy in its prayers, no warmth and welcome in its fellowship, no fire or passion in its work for the Master, no feeling of being " lost in wonder, love, and praise " before the mighty acts of redeeming grace, no hushed, awed sense of a divine presence in its sacraments, no kindled.blaze of missionary ardour—what would you say of such a Church ? You would say it was dead. And you would be right. It was G. K. Chesterton who vividly depicted the Church " rushing through the ages as the winged thunderbolt of thought and everlasting enthusiasm ; a thing without rival or resemblance, and still as new as it is old." Alas, that the thunder should ever have been stolen, the winged and rushing spirit curbed and tamed and reduced to a harmless respectable docility : " grimly spiritual persons " (to quote Lippmann's scathing phrase) " devoted to the worship of sonorous generalities." Was the New Testament wrong in nailing down formality in religion as enmity to Christ, the very negation and antithesis of the spirit of life ?

But there is a third condition, beyond aimlessness and formality, which the New Testament describes as death. " You were dead in trespasses and sins," declares Paul. We know that in the realm of organic nature, faculties and capacities which are left lying idle and unused inevitably atrophy and decay. So in the region of the soul. Let a man neglect conscience long enough, and conscience will cease to speak. Let him persistently disregard his potentiality for the unseen and eternal, his faculty for God, and little by little that potentiality will be eliminated, that faculty will contract and shrivel up and dwindle away. Let him abandon himself to evil thoughts and habits, and gradually the whole spiritual universe will take its revenge by rendering him insensitive and blind to higher things, incapable of appreciating the beauty of holiness or of discerning the reality of God. " Verily," said Jesus, in one deep, solemnizing verdict, " they have their reward "—they get what they have set their hearts upon, they end up chained to the worthless things they have chosen. They are imprisoned, helpless, and in the dark. " To be carnally minded is death."

What then is to be done ? Take these three conditions of deadness we have observed : how is man to tackle the crucial problem—the restoring of life ? A soul haunted by the aimlessness of existence may seek release by plunging ever more deeply into the whirl of this world's distractions, endeavouring to give vividness and variety and meaning to its experience by adding on one new sensation after another. That was the way taken by Francis of Assisi in his youth : but there was no salvation there. A Church dead in formality may think to resuscitate life by multiplying organizations, by working out elaborate programmes, by increasing the intricacy and efficacy of the machine. That is what every age of the ebb-tide of faith has tried : but never has there been salvation there. A man dead in trespasses and sins may seek to salve his soul by a frenzy of legal righteousness, covering over the inward radical corruption with a veneer of good works and human merit and self-approval. That was the way Paul took, and Augustine, and Luther : but with one voice they cry to us to-day that there is no salvation there. The fact is, there is still one point at which man, in spite of all his other wonderful achievements, stands helpless and baffled and defeated : he cannot create life. Not all the labours of his hands, not all the ingenuity of his brain, not all the passion of his heart, can work the everlasting miracle of revivification and renascence. He may roll away the

stone from the grave : he can't wake the dead.   Yet nothing
else will satisfy.

> " 'Tis life, whereof our nerves are scant,
>   Oh life, not death, for which we pant ;
>   More life, and fuller, that I want."

Is that quest doomed for ever ?

The answer is here : " The hour cometh, and now is,
when the dead *shall hear a voice.*" At the coming of the sound
of a voice, an aimless world, a formal Church, a sin-entombed
soul, will stand up and live !

How often the hearing of a voice has been decisive ! I
think of Samuel, when the evening hymn was hushed and the
temple courts were dark, and suddenly the voice of the Lord
God rang through the silence of the shrine and called the
child by name ; of Isaiah, startled and arrested and challenged to the very depths of his being by a voice from above
the altar, " Whom shall I send, and who will go for us ? "
of the great persecutor of the Church lying prostrate on the
Damascus road in the blinding glory, while the whole world
seemed reverberating with a cry, " Saul, Saul, why perse-
cutest thou Me ? " of St. Augustine in the garden at Milan,
when the voice of one unseen was heard chanting and repeating " Take up and read, take up and read," and he
opened his Scriptures and was converted ; of St. Joan in
the village of Domremy, listening to her blessed angel voices,
like bells at evening pealing ; of Martin Luther, when into
his troubled soul there broke like trumpet tones the cry,
" Play the man ! Fear not death. There is a life beyond."
How often the hearing of a voice has changed the whole
aspect of the world !

" The hour cometh, and now is, when the dead shall hear
a voice." But which voice ? The world is full of clamorous,
conflicting voices. To whose voice must we hearken now ?

Some would tell us that what we need for our regenerating

is the voice of the scientist. Is that true ? Let us indeed
thank that voice for all it has told us of the majesty and
marvel of the universe ; but let us also remember, as Reinhold
Niebuhr has put it, that " science can sharpen the fangs of
ferocity as much as it can alleviate human pain." It has
" won for us powers," declares C. E. M. Joad, " fit for the
gods, yet we bring to their use the mentality of schoolboys
or savages." And Aldous Huxley, in that deeply significant
book *Ends and Means*, is even more outspoken : " We are
living now, not in the delicious intoxication induced by the
early successes of science, but in a rather grisly morning-
after, when it has become apparent that what triumphant
science has done hitherto is to improve the means for achieving
unimproved or actually deteriorated ends." No, the voice
of science may tell us of a thousand mysteries : it cannot
smite death with resurrection !

Shall we hearken, then, to the voice of the moralist, the
philosopher ? His voice will tell us of the road to beauty,
truth, and goodness. He will set out before us in full and
accurate detail a map of the perfect life, a diagram of the
ideal world. But what is the use of a map to a man in a
dungeon as deep as the grave ? What is the good of knowing
the road if we have not got the power or the vitality to walk ?
The moralist can fashion an ethic or promulgate a code.
But confront him with Ezekiel's problem of the dry bones in
the valley of death, and he is helpless : he cannot regiment
them into a marching army, nor breathe into their deadness
the breath of life.

Will the voice of the Church, then, do it ? Here in the
midst of life, thrusting the eternal issues upon a confused,
uproarious world distracted between Vanity Fair and
Armageddon, making its voice stormy in the ears of each
new generation as it proclaims that man shall not live by
bread alone, stands this strange fact, the Church. And sad
will be the world's fate if ever the Church should cease to
care for the souls of men, or the voice of the Church cry

aloud no longer in pleading and in challenge. Yet I do not
find that Peter and John, encountering a poor cripple at the
gate of the temple, cried—" In the name of the Church, rise
up and walk." I do not find Horatius Bonar, in his great
hymn, exclaiming—" I heard the voice of the Church say,
' I am this dark world's Light.' " Let the Church speak out
fearlessly by all means : but it is going to take another
voice than that to bring Lazarus out of the grave in newness
of life !

Are all the voices, then, that keep crying through the
darkness and confusion of this tragic world powerless to help
man at the point of his most urgent need ? One other voice
there is, and its sound is as the sound of many waters. " The
hour cometh when the dead shall hear *the voice of the Son
of God.*" This is the voice, the only voice, which can echo
down into the dark deeps where my spirit lies dead in its
aimlessness, formality, and sin. " Hark, my soul, it is the
Lord ! "

Turn over the pages of your Gospels, and see the wonderful
works of grace effected by that voice of Jesus. It speaks,
and all is done. It cries " Let there be light," and light
appears. Now it rings forth in challenge to an evil spirit,
" Come out of the man ! "—and in an instant the demoniac
is gentle as a child. Now it shouts above the furious thunder
of the storm, " Peace, be still ! "—and immediately there is a
great calm. Now it cries imperiously into the echoing cavern
of the grave, " Lazarus, come forth ! "—and the dead man
steps out into the light, and lives. Truly, " never man spake
like this Man," nor was any voice heard like this since the
making of the world.

Have you ever listened to its tones ? Sometimes it is a
still small voice, like music far away, a whisper of hope when
all is dark, to comfort and encourage and chase the shadows
from your soul. Sometimes it is a trumpet-call, a battle-cry,
a voice no longer gentle and appealing, but masterful and

mighty and impassioned : " Awake thou that sleepest, and arise from the dead, and Christ shall give thee light ! " Sometimes it murmurs, " Come, weary soul, come unto Me, and rest." Sometimes it blazes forth, castigating all lethargy and comfortable complacence, " Son of man, gird on thine armour, and fight ! Rise up, O man of God ! "

But whatever its tones, it tells of life made new. " The dead shall hear the voice of the Son of God ; *and they that hear shall live.*" Out of their tomb you will see them coming, the imprisoned souls long dead in aimlessness, dead in formality, dead in sin—out into the sudden sunshine of the morning, rejoicing in the rich, invigorating tide of strange vitality which now floods all their being, and walking in the light of the Lord. Henry Drummond, at one of his great student meetings in Edinburgh, read a letter he had received from a man who had made utter shipwreck of life, a letter full of hopelessness and bitterness, a terrible revelation of a sunk and ruined soul. It was anonymous, signed with the one word " Thanatos "—Death. And Drummond (as he afterwards confessed) felt then that if ever a man was irretrievably lost it was the writer of that letter. But there was another night, a year or two later, when Drummond was facing a student gathering again. He reminded them of the story he had told of the man who was a moral, social, and spiritual wreck ; and then went on, " Gentlemen, I have in my pocket to-night a letter from ' Thanatos,' which he sent me this week, and he says he is at last a changed man—a new creature in Christ Jesus." Yes, the voice of Jesus is a Resurrection trumpet, and the gift of God is life.

Have you found the life which is life indeed—not just the bleak monotony of an aimless, purposeless existence, not the dust and ashes of a formal creed where the fire of faith has flickered and gone out, not the misery of moral mediocrity and a cowed and hopeless resignation to the hectoring tyranny of sin—but the glorious discovery of what it means to be victoriously, dynamically, spiritually alive ? There is a poem by G. K. Chesterton, called *The Convert*, in which with startling daring he seeks to imagine the first thoughts and feelings of a man literally taken out of the tomb by Jesus and recalled to earth from the world beyond the grave.

> " After one moment when I bowed my head
> And the whole world turned over and came upright,
> And I came out where the old road shone white,
> I walked the ways and heard what all men said. . . .
> The sages have a hundred maps to give
> That trace their crawling cosmos like a tree,
> They rattle reason out through many a sieve
> That stores the sand and lets the gold go free :
> And all these things are less than dust to me
> Because my name is Lazarus and I live."

And that, if you will believe it, is what the Lord Christ can accomplish still—change our whole scale of values for ever, resurrect our spirits from their encircling gloom, and bring from our ransomed souls the cry, " I was blind, and now I see ! I was lost, and I am found. I was dead, and behold, I live—all glory, Christ, to Thee—I live ! "

Will you believe it ? Or are you still, like Nicodemus, haunted by the question, " How can these things be ? " " It would be so wonderful if it were true : but I don't see how it is ever going to happen." But is not the answer to that perplexity lying here before you ? " The dead shall hear the voice "—not of the great Teacher, not of the Jesus of the Galilean road, not of the Man who walked this way before us—" the voice of *the Son of God*," the voice (that is) of death's Conqueror, of One who ever since the dawning of the first Easter day has held all Resurrection power in His keeping, and reigns the Lord of life for ever. Read the very next words following our text, and you will find that made explicit : " For as the Father hath life in Himself, so hath He given to the Son to have life in Himself." Don't you see now how Christ achieves the seemingly impossible ? He can give you life, by imparting Himself to you, by coming into

you, by making His dwelling with you : for He *is* life. That
is the secret. If Shakespeare were in you, what poetry you
could write ! If Beethoven were in you, what music you
could compose ! If Christ were in you, what a life you could
live ! If ? There need be no if about it. You can't have an
indwelling Shakespeare or Beethoven. You *can* have an
indwelling Christ. You can say with Paul, " I live ; yet not
I, but Christ liveth in me." Then indeed the dead soul has
heard the voice of Resurrection. Then your spirit has cast
off all its bonds and come alive ! Then

> " From the ground there blossoms red
> Life that shall endless be."

" The hour cometh," said Jesus. When will it come ?
Have we to tarry for some far-off, divine, incalculable event ?
Have we to loiter helpless till the next nation-wide revival
goes sweeping through the land ? Have we to wait perhaps
till the hour of our departure sets us free ? " The hour
cometh "—if only we knew when ! There is a brief entry in
John Wesley's *Journal*, amazingly significant when you
consider the date, Sunday, 2nd April 1738. Those were the
days when Wesley's heart was as yet unkindled by the fire
from heaven. Here is the entry. " Easter Day.—I
preached in our College chapel on, ' The hour cometh, and
now is, when the dead shall hear the voice of the Son of
God, and they that hear shall live ' " : and then this
plaintive note, " I see the promise ; but it is afar off." No
wind of God was blowing then, no breath of Paradise to stir
his poor dead soul to life. " The hour cometh : but," said
Wesley sadly, gazing down the dim vistas of the trackless
years, " it is afar off." Was it ? You turn a few pages of
the *Journal*, and suddenly, just seven weeks later, the fire
from heaven falls ! Afar off ? " The hour cometh—*and
now is* ! "

We glorify the past, and say, " O had I lived in that
great day when Christ was really here ! " We dream of the

far future, and say " O that we might have lived to see the glory that our children's children will behold, when Christ comes again into His own ! " But why dwell regretfully upon an age that is gone, or envy wistfully an age that is not yet born ? Christ is here ! The Lord and Giver of life is here. The hour cometh—and now is ! " To-day, if ye will hear His voice, harden not your heart." To-day reach out hands of faith, and pray, " Jesus, think on me ! Thou ever-present Saviour, whose name is Resurrection and life, speak with the voice that wakes the dead : shatter the silence, pierce the gloom of my lost worthless soul." And He will work in you the everlasting miracle, the mightiest of all His mighty acts : and you will know the thrill that ran through the morning stars at creation's dawn—because your name is Lazarus and you live !

VII

WHO IS THIS JESUS?

(1) BEHOLD THE MAN

" And when he was come into Jerusalem, all the city was moved, saying, Who is this ? "—MATT. xxi. 10.

ALL the city said it then; and all the world has said it ever since. For nineteen centuries one Figure has haunted the thinking and the conscience of mankind.

If you go climbing among the mountains, you may come occasionally to a lofty pass where the water-courses change their direction. Here a tiny rivulet makes its inconspicuous way to join the rivers flowing eastward : yonder, a few yards off, another begins its long winding journey towards the sunset and the western lands. The raindrops falling on one side of the summit may be carried down to the North Sea, while those on the other merge at last in the Atlantic. You are standing at the watershed, where all the streams divide.

Incomparably the most important watershed in the long history of humanity has been the Incarnation of Christ. At this point, the streams divide. After this, the human course and direction are changed. One Figure has split history in two—so that every event is now dated with reference to His coming, either before or after. In the clash and turmoil of this bitter age in which we live, His influence is still a more dominating thing, His power more to be reckoned with, than the power and influence of any Caesar. For this one Figure multitudes to-day would be glad to die ; and no man who has once seen Him can ever quite thrust Him out of sight again or evade His urgent challenge. " Who is this ? " they asked at the street-corners in Jerusalem long ago : and it is no academic speculation or theological theorizing that renews the question now. It is life, it is history, it is all that is deepest in your experience and mine, that force it inescapably upon us. Who is this Jesus ?

Let us begin our inquiry by setting right in the centre of our minds one fundamental fact : the Christian religion is first and foremost and essentially a message about God. It is not primarily a new ethic. It is not just a gospel of brotherliness and loving our neighbour and accepting the Golden Rule. It is not in the main a philosophy of life or a social programme. Doubtless it includes all that : it involves an ethic, supplies a philosophy, enunciates a programme for society. But basically, it is none of these things. It is not a message about human virtues and ideals at all. It is a message about God.

That message is this—that the living God, eternal, immortal, invisible, has at one quite definite point broken through into history in an unprecedented way. Once and for all, in an actual life lived out upon this earth, God has spoken, and has given the full and final revelation of Himself. In Jesus, God has come.

Such is the dramatic and astounding statement on which the Christian religion is built. Possibly familiarity has dulled its wonder for us : but will you try to realize afresh just how electrifying, how startling, that statement is ? In order to realize it, we must go back to our Gospels and contemplate the picture that confronts us there. Who is He, of whom such amazing things are spoken ?

They tell us that for the greater part of His life He was a working carpenter. His home was in an obscure provincial village. He was born in a stable, adjoining a roadside inn. Wealth and official position He had none. He wrote no books, He fought no battles, the applause of listening senates was never His to command. His friends were mostly as poor as Himself, fishermen and peasants. When He left home and started preaching His own family tried to dissuade Him, thinking and actually saying that He was mad. The theologians and clever people scoffed at what they thought was His illiteracy. The crowds which at first gathered inquisitively to listen to His teaching soon dwindled and vanished away. His own best friends showed signs of doing the same. " Will ye also go ? " He had to ask them ; and at the end, they did desert Him to His fate. He died a felon's death, reviled and execrated, hanging between two thieves. He was buried in a borrowed grave.

But then a strange thing happened. It was rumoured that death had not finished Him. It was reported that He had been seen alive. And then, quite suddenly, His disciples appeared in the streets proclaiming that He had risen. They said He had come back to them. They said the carpenter's apprentice of Nazareth was at the right hand of God in heaven. They said they now saw, what formerly had been hidden from them, that from the first God had been uniquely present in Jesus ; that in that life and death, the unseen had become visible, and the eternal had become historic, and God had become man.

Was it surprising that the world, hearing all that, laughed it to scorn ? The Book of Acts, in its second chapter, records that the first contemporary theory about the apostolic preaching was that these men had been drinking—" full of new wine " : the tale was so incredible. And when from its home of origin in Jerusalem, it began to circulate more widely, acquiring currency in the great cities of Asia and the west, the whole Roman Empire rang with contemptuous laughter, shouts of amused derision.

But the extraordinary thing was this, that neither with laughter nor with force, not with the massive arguments of her philosophers nor by the might of her thundering legions, could Rome stop Jesus. What actually happened was that Jesus stopped Rome, and on the dust and ashes of her broken splendour set the foundations of the empire of God which was to be.

So the question is thrust back upon us with redoubled force : Who is this Jesus ? When the first Christians appropriated the word Lord, Kyrios (the same hallowed name which the Old Testament had reserved for the Hebrew Jehovah), and dared to use it of this Galilean Carpenter ; when those men, strict monotheists as they were, took that astounding and unprecedented step, were they just dreaming, romancing, yielding to the intoxication of a foolish fancy ? Were love and imagination running away with them ? Or was the thing true ?

Some of you will remember the passage in Mrs. Humphrey Ward's *Recollections*, in which she tells how once she met Walter Pater at Oxford. She had thrown off the Christian faith ; and reckoning on his sympathy, she expressed the belief that Christ's day was done. He shook his head, and looked troubled. " I don't think so," he said. " And we don't altogether agree. You think it's all plain. But I can't. There are such mysterious things. Take that saying, ' Come unto me, all ye that labour and are heavy laden.' How can you explain that ? There is a mystery in it— something supernatural."

Even the sceptic has stood troubled and ill at ease before this strange fact of Christ. Here none of his categories seem to fit. His confidence deserts him. There *is* mystery in it.

Now if we try to analyse the mystery, we shall find, I think, that it is threefold—the mystery of a personality, the mystery of a power, and the mystery of a presence.

When I speak of *the mystery of a personality*, I am thinking of the startling coalescence of contrarieties that you find in Jesus. He was the meekest and lowliest of all the sons of men : yet He said that He would come on the clouds of heaven in the glory of God. He was so austere that evil spirits and demons cried out in terror at His coming : yet He was so genial and winsome and approachable that the children loved to play with Him, and the little ones nestled

in His arms ; and His company in the innocent gaiety of a
village wedding was like the sunshine. No one was ever
half so kind or compassionate to sinners : yet no one ever
spoke such red-hot, scorching words about sin. He would
not break the bruised reed, and His whole life was love :
yet on one occasion He demanded of the Pharisees how they
expected to escape the damnation of hell. He was a dreamer
of dreams and a seer of visions : yet for sheer stark naked
realism He has all our self-styled " realists " beaten. He was
the servant of all, washing the disciples' feet : yet master-
fully He strode into the Temple, and the hucksters and
traders fell over one another in their mad rush to get away
from the fire they saw blazing in His eyes. He saved others :
yet at the last, Himself He would not save. There is nothing
in history like the union of contrasts that confronts you in
the Gospels. The mystery of Jesus is the mystery of a
personality.

But it is more. It is *the mystery of a power*. From that
far day when He took a deadly cross, and converted it into
a glorious throne, that power—like a streak of gold—has
marked the centuries. Empires have gone down before Him.
Through His influence, great movements of reform have
swept the earth. In His name, men and women of every
age and race have " wrought righteousness, stopped the
mouths of lions, and out of weakness have been made strong."
He has been the master-force behind the onward march of
men. What Emerson said of Jesus was indeed magnificently
true : " His name is not so much written as ploughed into
the history of this world." Thomas Hardy, near the close
of *The Dynasts*, makes Napoleon say—

> " To shoulder Christ from out the topmost niche
> Of human fame, as once I fondly felt,
> Was not for me."

The one name before which the Anti-God movement of to-day
trembles is the name of Jesus of Nazareth. There is no

6

modern Caesarism which can shoulder Christ off the page of
history, or break His grip on the souls of men.   After
nineteen centuries, we still baptize our children in His name ;
when love and marriage come, His is the blessing we invoke,
and His the altar at which we plight our troth ; when all is
over, it is beneath His cross we lay our dead, and it is in His
message of eternal hope that we find comfort.   Ten thousand
times He has broken the chains of evil habit, and set the
prisoners free.   He has put energy and victory into wasted
lives and souls rotting with sin.   And there are those in this
Church now who would unhesitatingly ascribe "every virtue
they possess, and every victory won, and every thought of
holiness," not to their own resolution or resources, but to the
saving might of Christ alone.   The mystery of Jesus is the
mystery of a power.

But it is still more.   It is *the mystery of a presence*.   In
every age, His own words have been verified anew—" Lo, I
am with you always."   Now notice what this means.   It is
frequently said that it is quite impossible that Jesus should
have any final relevance for the modern mind or for the
social order of to-day.   He was born in the first century.
His environment was totally different from ours.   The quiet
life of a peasant in agricultural Palestine was worlds apart
from the hectic life of a city-dweller in this mechanized,
industrialized age.   We have problems on our hands which
the first century never envisaged.   How should Jesus, born
a Jew, using the categories and thought-forms of His own
age, facing the problems of His own society, still remain
authoritative for us ?

> " The Man upraised on the Judean crag,
>   Captains for us the war with death no more,
>   His Kingdom hangs as hangs the tattered flag
>   On the tomb of a great knight of yore."

But the argument which imprisons Jesus in the fetters
of a particular age and environment and denies His validity
for to-day involves a double fallacy.   It ignores two decisive

facts : the one, that the human heart which Christ addressed
is still the same, the same in its loves and sorrows, its temptations and hopes and passions and defeats—*that* has not
changed ; the other, that in any case we are not harking
back to a dead memory, but encountering the challenge of a
living spirit. This Christ is a present fact, and men know it.
For when we read our Gospels, intending to judge and assess
and pass our verdict on what meets us there, gradually an
extraordinary thing begins to happen : the central Figure
steps out from the page, and stands before our conscience,
and judges us. This is not talking metaphorically or at
random. It is not using language dishonestly. In fact, the
more honest we are in this matter the more vividly do we
grow aware that Someone—not a mere fact of history, not
the moving memory of a mighty life long since passed away,
but Someone alive and present—is meeting us, is refusing
to be held at arm's length or thrust aside, is dealing with us
as only God could deal. This is not romancing. It is a
strictly accurate, unrhetorical account of what actually
happens. It is the assured, irrefragable experience of men
and women in this Church to-day. The mystery of Jesus
is the mystery of a personality, and of a power, and of a
presence.

What, then, are we to say of Him ? What explanation
shall we offer ? Reason and conscience alike demand that
we should attempt some answer. We cannot be content to
leave an unprecedented fact like this unexamined. For the
sake of our own peace of mind, if for nothing else, we must
try to reach a verdict. Who is this Jesus ?

The deeper answer to that question we must hold over
for our next study. We shall consider then whether we
cannot recapture for ourselves the sublime and breath-
taking conviction of the men of the New Testament, that
this Jesus was God manifest in the flesh. But for the present
let us concentrate on getting this one thing quite clear—

that whoever or whatever else He may have been, whatever other name or predicate we may feel impelled to give Him, He was at least *truly and fully man*.

I beg you never to let that go. It is crucial for salvation. If Jesus was not truly a man, if His humanity was in some sense unreal, an appearance or a disguise, if the Figure in the Gospels was an unearthly angelic visitant, a demigod in human shape, the whole doctrine of redemption falls to the ground. Hold on to the full humanity of Jesus !

Many good people are in danger, perhaps quite unconsciously, of losing sight of this essential aspect of the person of our Lord. It is a strange and very significant fact that the first heresy which ever vexed the Christian Church—the so-called " docetic " heresy of the first and second centuries —was not a denial of the Godhead of Jesus : it was a denial of His true manhood. It was an assertion of His Godhead which virtually emptied His manhood of all reality. That attitude is still rife. Even now there are good Christian people who have an uneasy feeling that you cannot emphasize the humanity of Jesus without subtracting from His divinity—which is an utterly erroneous idea. They have been so concerned (and indeed quite rightly concerned) to uphold at all costs the Godhead of Jesus that He is no longer, for them, truly and genuinely human. But I repeat —unless Christ was real man, there is no salvation.

Can there be any doubt as to the witness of the New Testament on this matter ? The Jesus of whom the evangelists tell is veritable man if ever there was one—not some heavenly Titan masquerading as man, but man in very truth. He knew, as we do, what weariness means, and the burden of sheer physical exhaustion : " Jesus, being wearied with His journey, sat thus on the well." His tears at Lazarus' grave were not forced tears, but the real grief of a sensitive spirit. He felt, as we do, the need for friends : what volumes that poignant question in Gethsemane speaks —" Could ye not watch with Me one hour ? " He had to

fight temptation, not only in the desert at the beginning,
but right on to the end of the journey : and it was no sham
fight, no easy, automatic victory, but a real and desperate
encounter, a struggle that made His soul sweat blood.
What He suffered in His body on the cross, and in His mind
and spirit through all the despising and rejecting which
culminated there, was not make-believe or solemn play-
acting, but something so terrible that thought recoils before
it and language fails. " He descended into hell."

No, there is not one shadow of doubt as to the New Testament's witness. From every page of the Gospels there
emerges a Figure whose humanity is unmistakable and
authentic, bone of our bone and flesh of our flesh. I say
nothing about the other side of the picture now. Let it
suffice for the moment to get this one truth piercingly clear
to our own minds and hearts ; and to be able—with the
Roman governor who tried His case at the end—to say,
" Behold the Man ! "

There is a most moving passage in which the great
Russian novelist Turgenev has described how once there
came to him, in a kind of vision, a swift and wonderful
insight into the meaning of the humanity of Jesus. " I saw
myself, a youth, almost a boy, in a low-pitched wooden
church. The slim wax candles gleamed, spots of red, before
the old pictures of the saints. There stood before me many
people, all fair-haired peasant heads. From time to time,
they began swaying, falling, rising again, like the ripe ears
of wheat when the wind in summer passes over them. All at
once a man came up from behind and stood beside me. I
did not turn towards him, but I felt that the man was Christ.
Emotion, curiosity, awe overmastered me. I made an effort
and looked at my neighbour. A face like everyone's, a face
like all men's faces. ' What sort of Christ is this ? ' I thought.
' Such an ordinary, ordinary man. It cannot be.' I turned
away, but I had hardly turned my eyes from this ordinary
man when I felt again that it was really none other than

Christ standing beside me. Only then I realized that just such a face is the face of Christ—a face like all men's faces."

He is true man, this Jesus. Never for a moment must that truth be suffered to grow dim. We dare not—if we have set our hopes upon Him—let this fact go. It is crucial for the world's salvation. Do you see why ? Do you understand why it is so overwhelmingly vital and important to reassert the full humanity of Jesus ? Suppose we were led to conclude that He was not quite human, that He never met us just on our level, that there is no true identity between Christ and our sinning, suffering race, then not only are we robbed of our most precious pattern and example, but what is far worse, we have to say that God has not come the whole way after all, that God has not quite stooped down to the depth of our urgent need nor borne all our human burden : and that means—no atonement, no healing of our mortal wound, no breaking of our bitter bonds. I beg you to realize that that—nothing less—is the issue ; and realizing that to cling, as the New Testament clings, to the certainty of Christ's full humanity, to the glorious, heart-stirring and subduing fact that God, in love for you and me, has indeed come all the way, has started on the level where we are and met us where we live, and borne our earthly frame of dust and clay, that we may wear His immortality.

> " With this ambiguous earth
> His dealings have been told us. These abide :
> The signal to a maid, the human birth,
> The lesson, and the young Man crucified."

We cannot tell, says Alice Meynell, what other forms of revelation God might choose for other worlds. We cannot guess His secret dealings with other dwellers in His wide universe, beyond this wayside planet we inhabit.

> " O, be prepared, my soul !
> To read the inconceivable, to scan
> The myriad forms of God those stars unroll
> When, in our turn, we show to them a Man."

" There is one mediator between God and men, the Man Christ Jesus."

But is that all ? Is that the final word ? In our next study we shall endeavour to press more deeply into the mystery ; until we reach a point where, looking upon this Man, our souls are able to say, " My Lord and my God ! "

VIII

WHO IS THIS JESUS?

(2) BEHOLD YOUR GOD

" In him dwelleth all the fulness of the Godhead bodily."—COL. ii. 9.

THERE was a day when death had darkened the home of that rugged but sensitive soul, Thomas Carlyle. Some one, taking a New Testament, opened it at the Gospel of St. John, and read the familiar words : " Let not your heart be troubled. In My Father's house are many mansions." " Aye," muttered the bereaved man, " if you were God, you had a right to say that ; but if you were only a man, what do you know any more than the rest of us ? "

That incident may well give us our starting-point to-day, reminding us, as it does, that on the answer which we individually give to the question " Who is this Jesus ? " hang for us the most momentous issues of life. " If you were God, Jesus, we can face the darkest hours victoriously ; but if you were only a man, life has us beaten for ever."

Let me recall in a word the path our thoughts travelled in our previous study. We were dwelling on the true and full humanity of Jesus. We saw that from every page of the Gospels there emerged a Figure of real human lineaments —not some heavenly Being disguised or masquerading as a man, but a man in very truth—really tempted, really suffering, really knowing those experiences of conflict and weariness, of yearning and limitation, which are what we mean by being " human." We recognized how crucial this fact was for our Christian faith : for if Jesus does not meet us on our own level, He is no Saviour for us.

But now, supposing all that is granted, we have still not finished with our question. Or rather, it has not finished

with us. He was true Man : but is that all ? He was (as
even unbelievers and non-Christians agree) the greatest Man
who ever lived : but is that the final truth ? Will conscience
and spiritual insight, or even reason and commonsense, be
content to leave the matter there, and probe the mystery
no further ? Are human categories sufficient to explain this
strange phenomenon—this unique personality that confronts
us in the Gospels, this historic power that blazes a track
across the centuries, this living presence that stands and
judges us in the deep places of our souls ? He is Son of man :
but is He simply to be classified with all the other sons of
men ? If not, what name are we to give Him ? Must it
not be at last the name which is above every name ?

Let me say at once that this is a question which can be
settled only from within a Christian experience. I mean
that it is only as we consent to follow Christ and live with
Christ that we can come to know who He really is. It is
well that we should labour under no misapprehensions at
this point. To attempt to demonstrate the divinity of Jesus
—that He is God manifest in the flesh—to a man who has
no inclination for the life of discipleship, and no intentions
of embarking on it, is simply wasted effort : and all our
arguments and discussions, under these conditions, are just
beating the air. That needs to be said, and ought to be
said quite frankly. *It is only from within a Christian experience that the divinity of Christ can be understood.* Let it
not, however, be imagined that to say this is to take refuge
in evasion and give the case away. For is it not true that
in our daily life we are in contact with a whole series of facts
which can be grasped and appreciated only as we yield and
submit ourselves to their influence ? Well then, why should
this rule not hold of our relationship to the fact of Christ ?
Just as you cannot really see the marvellous " Five Sisters "
window at York as long as you stand outside the Minster
—you have to enter and look upon it from within, and then
the matchless profusion of its beauty is revealed ; just as

you cannot appreciate great music at its true value unless you submit yourself humbly and quite deliberately to its influence and its working; just as you cannot understand the deeper reaches of friendship unless you are prepared to make the adventure of trusting yourself to your friend—so you cannot come to a knowledge of who this Christ really is, except from within the life of Christian discipleship. That stands to reason. Some men declare unconcernedly, or even truculently, that they do not believe in Christ. But then, some men have no right to believe in Christ. They have no qualification for believing, no conceivable possibility of understanding the fact of Christ, because they have not yielded to the challenge of the fact. I repeat, therefore, it is only as we follow Jesus, and seek to live with Him, that there can break on us at last the incredible yet inevitable truth of who this Jesus is.

Keeping that in mind, we return now to our question. This Christ is perfect man—but is He more? What name are we to give Him? You would not thank me, I imagine, in this the supreme issue of our faith, for being vague and nebulous and talking generalities. I invite you, therefore, to consider five facts, all pointing decisively to the same overwhelming conclusion : " In Him dwelleth all the fulness of the Godhead bodily."

The first cardinal fact is *the claim Jesus made for Himself*. Do we realize how astonishing and unprecedented this is ? Think of other great religious teachers and leaders who have arisen—Socrates, Buddha, Confucius—and then ask, What was their paramount concern ? Not to fix attention upon themselves, but to win acceptance for their message. " I am nothing," they seemed to say, " the truth is everything. Perish my name, if only the message live ! " But with Jesus and with Him alone, it is utterly different.

He deliberately places Himself at the very centre of His own message. His supreme concern is not to implant some abstract truth in His hearers' minds : it is to win their devotion to His own person. He does not merely claim to have found the answer to all men's needs : He claims to *be* the answer. " Come unto *Me*, all ye who labour, and *I* will give you rest." What other prophet or preacher ever dared to say a thing like that ? If the language were not so familiar, it would simply stagger us with its audacity. Calmly He arrogates to Himself a position transcending all the wisdom and the splendour of the centuries. " A greater than Solomon is here." " Prophets and kings have desired to see those things which ye see, and have not seen them." He declares that at the Day of Judgment the final test will be " Ye have done it *unto Me*," " Ye did it not *to Me*." " Whosoever shall be ashamed *of Me*, of him shall the Son of man be ashamed, when He cometh in the glory of His Father." " He that loseth his life *for My sake*, shall find it." His whole attitude is " God and I." " Before Abraham was, I am ! "

What are we to say about all this ? There are just two alternatives. Either it is the infatuation of an absurd megalomania, or else it is really true. Either these sayings are the preposterous, incredible arrogance of a pathetic and pathological egotism—or else He had a right to say them. You have to choose one or the other : there is no third option. The extraordinary thing is that, while on the lips of anyone else these sayings would sound utterly presumptuous and incongruous and unbalanced, somehow on His lips they sound entirely fitting and apt and just and credible. Who, then, is this Jesus ? One signpost we have found marking the way to an answer—the claim He made for Himself.

The second decisive fact concerns *His sinlessness*. That word indeed is too negative to describe a moral perfection which was always active and energizing ; but the fact stands, on the testimony of friend and foe alike, that this man, alone of all the sons of men, " did no sin, neither was guile

found in His mouth." Read the Gospels, and again and
again you will see His enemies turning the fiercest searchlights
of their hostile criticism upon Him. Can they detect one
flaw in moral character ? Not one, for all their searching.
" In all points tempted like as we are, yet without sin."

Moreover, this stands not only on the evidence of friend
and foe, but on the testimony of Christ Himself. Never
once is Jesus heard confessing sin. This Man whose whole
life was a constant self-identification with sinners, who came
far closer to them than any one else before or since, and
brought them to the mercy-seat of God for the cleansing of
their hearts and lives, never had to bow in penitence nor
plead for cleansing for Himself. How many a lesson He
taught His disciples on the need of praying for forgiveness
every day they lived ! Yet He never needs or asks to be
forgiven.

That fact surely is startling. And it becomes all the
more startling when you consider that it is precisely the
saintliest people in the world who have been most conscious
of their own sin. Read the stories of the saints, the spiritual
history of a Paul, a Thomas à Kempis, a Teresa, and in
every case this fact confronts you—that in proportion as a
soul draws close to God, the more vividly does it realize its
own personal unworthiness. It is the chief of saints who
know best that they are the chief of sinners. The clearer
the vision of God, the deeper the dissatisfaction with self.
That is the universal rule to which all the saints conform.
Does Jesus conform to it ? Ought we not to find that Jesus,
having a unique God-consciousness, had also a unique awareness of sin ? Yes, indeed, if He is just the greatest of the
saints, we should. But if what we find is the exact reverse ;
if here, in this one instance, the rule is broken through completely ; if so far from having a desperate sense of sin, like
Paul and à Kempis and Teresa and all the finest souls of
history, He alone has none ; if He is thus not only different
from all sinners, but different also from all saints—then who

is He ? Who must He be ? The fact of sinlessness is the
second great signpost marking the way towards an answer.

The third decisive fact is this : *Jesus does for men what
only God could do.* Here I am thinking particularly of the
experience of being forgiven. Consider it like this. Suppose
I do something which I know to be wrong. Suppose that
thereupon I " rationalize " my action, finding palliating
circumstances, and justifying myself to my own satisfaction.
Is that the end of the matter ? In my heart of hearts I
know that something else is needed to deal with what has
happened and to right the wrong. For what my act has
done is to throw me out of gear, not only with my better
nature, or with a moral ideal, but with the universe. The
barrier that has been raised is not between my higher and
my lower self : it is between me and God. And that is the
real barrier that must be dealt with. In other words, it is
God who must forgive—else there is no true forgiveness
possible. It is God who must put me right, or else the
wrong remains unannulled. " Thou must save, and Thou
alone."

But now see what happens. This thing which none but
God can do—this divine, supernatural thing—*Jesus does.*

Look at your Gospels. He did it again and again in
Galilee. And, mark you, it was not only that He pronounced
words of absolution—any priest can do that—but it was
this, that He actualized God's forgiveness for those poor
sinful folk, embodied it, " represented, sealed and applied " it
(to use the words of *The Shorter Catechism*) to their desperate,
gaping need ; so that having been with Jesus, they knew
with a sense of amazed, incredible relief that God was at
peace with them, and they with God. And what happened
then in Galilee has been happening ever since. Consult
your own experience. Have not the hours of your deepest
assurance of divine forgiveness been the hours when you
have encountered Christ ? Who, then, is this Jesus ? When

the Pharisees, attacking Him, declared " No one can forgive
sins but God only," and argued that consequently Jesus
must be a usurper and an impostor, their first statement was
perfectly correct. Only God can convey forgiveness : that
is true. And that is what we have to square with this other
unimpeachable fact, that forgiveness is conveyed by Jesus.
Only God can open the gate of the kingdom of heaven :
yet it is certain that for thousands Christ has opened it.
Only God can break the chain of a man's sinful nature : yet
for thousands Christ has broken it. Only God can redeem :
yet I am certain that Christ is my Redeemer. If Christ thus
does for us what only God could ever do, who can He be ?
What other name is possible except God manifest in the flesh,
the fulness of the Godhead bodily ?

The fourth decisive fact is *the universality of Jesus*. It
is worth asking ourselves the question : How do we propose
to account for the unique phenomenon, that Jesus has laid
His spell invincibly upon every century and every race and
upon all kinds and conditions of men ? Aristotle never did
that : he was too Greek, and too academic. Buddha never
did it : he was too typically Eastern. Only in Jesus has
everything local and temporal been transcended by a spirit
universal and eternal.

Look at the first circle of His friends. Peter and John
were, temperamentally, poles asunder : yet in His eyes they
both beheld the answer to their dreams. Consider His early
biographers. Matthew the Jewish taxgatherer and Luke the
Gentile doctor had nothing whatever in common : yet to
draw His portrait for the world to see was, to both men,
the only thing that mattered. Or think of the modern
writers who have toiled to tell of Him—Papini and Bruce
Barton, as different as an Italian mystic and an American
business man could be, Emil Ludwig and Middleton Murry,
and a host of others even in this last decade, of utterly
diverse intellectual background and racial sympathy and

moral ideal, yet all fascinated by this one fact, all drawn by the compulsion of the mystery of Christ! Or pass in review the unbroken ranks of His friends and followers throughout the ages. Who can this be who can grip and captivate the souls of men so utterly different as Luther the Reformer and Loyola the Jesuit, as Francis the friar and Moody the evangelist, as G. K. Chesterton and General Booth, as Cardinal Newman and David Livingstone ? What an amazing universality is Christ's !

> " I see His blood upon the rose
> And in the stars the glory of His eyes,
> His body gleams amid eternal snows,
> His tears fall from the skies.
>
> All pathways by His feet are worn,
> His strong heart stirs the ever-beating sea,
> His crown of thorns is twined with every thorn,
> His cross is every tree."

Could any mortal man thus besiege and lay captive the thinking and the worship of the centuries ? Must not this beleaguering spirit be eternal and divine, the fulness of the Godhead bodily ? The universality of Christ is our fourth significant signpost pointing to the answer.

The fifth and final fact is the most decisive of all. It is *the divine self-verification of Christ in conscience.* For there is a very wonderful thing which happens : you begin exploring the fact of Christ, perhaps merely intellectually and theologically—and before you know where you are, the fact is exploring *you,* spiritually and morally. You begin by dealing with a historic Figure as presented in the Gospels, and gradually you become aware that the ultimate reality and heart of things is dealing with you. You begin by looking for the secret of this Master of life who walked the Galilean road, and piercingly you are made to feel that everything that is highest and holiest and divinest in the universe is looking for you. You set out to see what you can find in Christ, and sooner or later God in Christ finds you.

That is the self-verification of Jesus. That, in every age, has been the ultimate and sure foundation of the impregnable conviction of His divinity. In Christ, the one and only God has come. It is a confession of faith which I am constrained and bound to make, because the more I confront myself with the fact of Christ, the more intensely do I know that the living God is confronting me, demanding —as only God can demand—the entire and utter surrender of my soul. If the final reality of the universe comes to meet me anywhere, it comes to meet me here ; and all I know of God—His nature, attributes and ways of working—has come to me through Jesus. Wherefore, with the whole company of His disciples throughout the centuries to whom the glory of the Word made flesh has been revealed, I, too, can take the sublime, imperishable words upon my lips and say—" This is the fulness of the Godhead bodily. Thou art the King of glory, O Christ ; Thou art the everlasting Son of the Father ! "

In these two studies, we have been facing the fact of Christ, in His humanity and His divinity. But let us not suppose that our quest can ever end in a mere giving of assent to certain truths and propositions. When Saul of Tarsus, in the supreme moment of his life, had received an answer to his first impulsive cry " Who art Thou, Lord ? " immediately and instinctively a second question came— " What wilt Thou have me to do ? " And when from afar we have caught our glimpse of the glory of the Lord, there rises at once and confronts us in the secret place of conscience the inevitable challenge—" If that is Christ, what is our response to be ? "

To that question each of us must find an answer for himself. It will be well if, standing at the foot of the cross, we can give such an answer as that which was given by St. Aloysius long ago :

" O Christ, Love's Victim, hanging high
  Upon the cruel Tree,
What worthy recompense can I
  Make, mine own Christ, to Thee ?

My sweat and labour from this day,
  My sole life, let it be,
To love Thee aye the best I may
  And die for love of Thee."

THE TRIUMPHANT ADEQUACY OF CHRIST

"I am sure that, when I come unto you, I shall come in the fulness of the blessing of the gospel of Christ."—Rom. xv. 29.

SEE Rome and die, says the proverb. It was the dream of Paul's life to see Rome before he died. He was determined not only to see it but to win it for Christ. The little Christian community in Rome was holding on grimly to its precarious, hard-won position, knowing that at any moment the full force of the legions of heathenism might be turned against it. But now Paul was resolved to fling himself into the attack : please God, the forlorn hope would yet become a glorious advance. He had had enough of skirmishing with paganism at its outposts ; he had fought the world, the flesh, and the devil in Syria, Macedonia, and Illyricum. Now the hour had come to assault the pagan principalities and powers at their headquarters, to make the foundations of Cæsar's empire tremble, and to give Christ the throne.

Strange, fantastic hope ! Judged by any rational standards, it was sheer absurdity. On the one side there was the metropolis of the world, the heart of the empire, magnificently proud and regal on her seven hills, ruling with a rod of iron and shaking the earth with the march of her invincible legions ; and on the other side, this little Jew, with his scarred face and his frail-looking body, and nothing at all to offer—no credentials, no testimonials or references from important people, no imposing organization—nothing but what he called his gospel. But then, to Paul, that was simply everything ! " I am sure," he cries, " that when I come unto you, I shall come in the fulness of the blessing of the gospel of Christ." See how he loads his language, how he piles the words up, one on top of the other, till the sentence becomes top-heavy and begins to stagger with its weight of truth—" the fulness of the blessing of the gospel of Christ ! " See how he reiterates and drives home his challenge, four times over ; and every word is another hammer-blow at the powers of darkness, another triumph-shout of the sons of light—" the fulness of the blessing of the gospel of Christ." Here it stands to-day, to tell all the world what true religion is, and what is the saving might of Christianity. Let us take each of the four terms separately ; and let us begin with the last.

"I am coming to you *with Christ.*" Not, mark you, coming with a new philosophy of life, though Rome loved dabbling in philosophy. Not coming with a new political theory, though crowds would doubtless have flocked to such a message. Not coming with a new interpretation of religion, though the intelligentsia would have been immensely intrigued by that. "I am coming to you with Christ," said Paul.

It was not even " I am coming to preach righteousness, temperance and judgment "—the theme of the flaming sermon that made Felix tremble. It was not " I am coming to argue the cause of morality," though God knew Rome was needing that desperately. It was not " I am coming to give you Christianity," though that might have seemed the most natural thing to say. It was none of these. It was this : " I am coming to you with Christ."

If ever there was a man of one subject, that man was Paul. " I determined," he told the Corinthians quite frankly, " not to know any thing among you, save Jesus Christ." " To me," he wrote to the Philippians, " to live is Christ " —life means Christ to me. That was his one theme, given to him straight from God Himself ; and if ever a time should come when that is no longer the central theme of the Christian

Church, then the day of the Church will be finished. The one thing that can justify the Church is a great passion for Christ.

There have been other men who have burned with the same flame as the apostle. I think of Raymond Lull, valiant missionary to the Moslems, with his oft-repeated exclamation, " I have one passion—it is He, it is He " ; of Charles Wesley, singing and helping a multitude of others to sing —

> " Thou, O Christ, art all I want;
> More than all in Thee I find ; "

of C. H. Spurgeon, crying out the secret of his life, " I looked at Him, and He looked at me, and we were one for ever " ; of Alexander Whyte and Marcus Dods in their long Saturday walks together—" Whatever we started off with in our conversations," said Whyte, " we soon made across country, somehow, to Jesus of Nazareth." " We preach always Him," said Martin Luther, describing the message of the Reformers, " this may seem a limited and monotonous subject, likely to be soon exhausted, but we are never at the end of it." If a man should live to be a hundred, preaching twice a day about Jesus, even then he would not be at the end of it. At this moment, in ten thousand gatherings of His people, men are still, after nineteen centuries of Jesus, thinking about Him, telling of His all-sufficient grace, exploring His eternal truth—and still not anywhere near the end of it. Is that not one of the strongest proofs of His divinity ? Any other subject under heaven would have been exhausted long ago : this theme remains bewilderingly rich, everlastingly fresh and fertile. The early Church had a strange name for Jesus. It called Him " the Alpha and the Omega " ; which means, to put it in the language of to-day, that Jesus is simply everything in life from A to Z. There is nothing worth heralding but Jesus. " I am coming to you with Christ," said Paul. The man of one subject !

Now why ? Why this exclusive preoccupation ? After

all, Rome was not wanting this Christ of his : what Rome
was quite definitely wanting was help with certain concrete,
practical problems. There were, for example, problems of
personal relationships—stubborn, intractable problems of
race, and class, and family. The world, rent with strifes and
hatreds and divisions, was needing desperately a truer
brotherhood, a more enduring peace. " I offer you Christ,"
said Paul. Might not the world have retorted, " But you
don't understand ! It is not that we are wanting. Stop being
irrelevant " ? There was, too, the problem of moral control.
A multitude of hearts, torn with the lusts of the flesh, cried
inarticulately for self-mastery. " I offer you Christ," said
Paul. Again, might not the world have retorted, " Man,
you don't understand ! You are right off the track. It is
not that we are asking for. We are wanting self-control " ?
Why, then, with all these different and definite problems in
front of him, racial, social, political, ethical, did Paul keep
harping on the one note—Christ, Christ, Christ ?

Let us set this in the light of our modern situation. Why
keep to the one note to-day ? This is where the critics of
the Gospel strike. " Leave that played-out message," they
demand, " that refuge from hard facts, that pathetic strum-
ming out the one old theme. We don't deny the truth or the
historicity of the story of Jesus : what we do deny is its
relevance to the present world-scene. Let us come to grips
with actualities, and do something. Why all this talk of
Christ ? "

Can we meet that ? Assuredly we can ! They tell us
Jesus is simply irrelevant to-day. We dare to maintain
that Paul's way—" I offer you Christ "—is still, after nineteen centuries, the one and only way of hope. Take our
most pressing problem. Take the frightful difficulty of living
together in the world, the age-long, urgent problem of personal
relationships between man and man, between race and race.
What is the best way to deal with that ? Is it to preach
brotherhood ? Is it to beg and beseech men to love one

another and be friends ? That leads nowhere. And why ? Because it is tackling the problem from the wrong end. But now, suppose you begin at the other end. Suppose you start further back. Suppose that some at least of the toil and energy now being put into the effort to promote brotherhood on a purely natural basis could be turned into another channel altogether. Suppose you bring men face to face with God in Christ. Suppose they feel the impact of Jesus, and come under the spell of Jesus. Why then, the other thing we are after, the brotherhood we long for, begins to come in of its own accord. It comes as a by-product. And thus the problem solves itself. For souls that are in true and vital union with Jesus develop a tone and colour in which brotherhood, so far from being impossible, has become inevitable. Christ irrelevant ? He is the one fully relevant fact in life to-day.

So with all the other problems that vex the heart of this troubled world, our own moral problems included. The weary business of trying, by herculean efforts of will, to eliminate evils and cultivate virtues is always in the long run futile. It is starting at the wrong end of things. The other end is the place to begin—and the other end is the grace of Christ. Here is David Brainerd describing, in that wonderful *Journal* of his, the method of his work among the North American Indians : " I never got away from Jesus, and Him crucified ; and I found that when my people were gripped by this, I had no need to give them instructions about morality. I found that one followed as the sure and inevitable fruit of the other." Yes, indeed ; for Jesus, once known and understood and loved, brings with Him into a man's life a different atmosphere, in which spontaneously the evil things begin to droop and the fine things burst to bloom. Christ irrelevant ? He is as relevant to every one of us, in our deepest and most intimate need, as the daily bread we have to eat to keep ourselves alive.

Christianity, therefore, is right, absolutely right, when it refuses, in spite of a barrage of criticism, to be deflected from the one object for which it exists, which is *to hold up Jesus*. It must be the most hopeless, sterile, soul-destroying thing imaginable to have only arguments, advice, and moral points of view to offer to the world to help it in its troubles ; but to have Christ to offer—a living and accessible and all-sufficing Christ—how different that is, how redemptively effective, how gloriously charged with hope ! " I am coming to you with Christ," said Paul.

Now take the next step. " I am coming to you *with the gospel* of Christ." Gospel, as everyone knows, means tidings, news, good news. Not views, mark you, but news. The substitution of views for news is one of the most damaging and deadening things that can happen to religion. Sometimes the Church itself has become infected by this error, and has been so preoccupied with man's views of God that there has been little time or energy left for heralding God's news to man. What is the news ? " There is only one piece of news I know," said a good woman to Tennyson, when the poet on a journey had arrived at her house and inquired if anything of note were happening, " there is only one piece of news I know : Christ died for all men." " Well," said Tennyson, " that is old news, and good news, and new news." Is that not your own feeling, every time you open your New Testament ? Like the great runner Pheidippides, bringing to Athens the news of the victory of Marathon, those men and women of Jesus were carrying a message from the battle fought out to a finish at Calvary ; and wherever they passed, through city street or highland glen, one cry they had to all they met—" Tidings, good tidings ! The greatest of all good tidings—God and sinners reconciled ! " And hearts by the thousand, hearing it, were thrilled. It was glorious news, the like of which they had never listened to before.

But to-day—" Christ died for us," says H. G. Wells, " do

we care ? " " I suppose Christ did die for the world," says
some one apathetically, " but then it is such an old story,
time-worn and effete. You really cannot blame us if we take
it pretty calmly."

There have been days, thank God, when the news of
Christ meant so much to men that they could not keep their
voices steady when they spoke His blessed name. But we
—well, we do take Jesus calmly, do we not ?—even His
crown of thorns and His pierced hands and His sweat of
blood. Yet in the deepest sense, this fact of Jesus, crucified,
dead and buried, risen and exalted, is news still, tidings
nothing less than startling. And if we are not startled, it
can only be because the meaning of the fact has not been
apprehended.

For think what is involved. Take a saying like this—" I
can do all things through Christ which strengtheneth me."
Take the fact of a man, once broken and defeated and helpless, yet now standing on his feet, with head up, with level
eyes confronting life and danger and furious opposition and
death, crying, " I can do all things through Christ ! " Now
that, in essence, is Christianity. And do you not see that if
that is what Christ is aiming at, and if in spite of it we are
content to plod along our undistinguished road, with things
perhaps holding us down in captivity to-day that were
holding us down ten years ago, then Christ's offer is news
indeed, astonishing and startling news ? Or take the great
cry of Easter morning, " Christ is risen ! Christ is here."
That, again, is Christianity. And do you not feel that if
that is true, then a good many of us have yet to experience
something of what Dr. Dale of Birmingham experienced one
day in his study when he was writing an Easter sermon for
his people ? Half-way through his work, the thought of the
risen Lord broke in upon him as it had never done before.
" Christ is alive," he said to himself, " alive ! " And then
he paused. " Alive ! " he cried again. " Living as really as
I myself am ! " And he got up and walked about, repeating

" Christ is living, Christ is living ! " It had come upon him
with a burst of sudden glory—Christ risen, and alive, and at
his side. And for multitudes of professing Christians that is
news still, startling news. Or turn to the Sermon on the
Mount, calling to us down the centuries to love our enemies,
to go on loving even when spoken against and hurt and misrepresented, to love—as Christ did—right through to the
end. That is Christianity—the belief that this, impossible
as it seems, can veritably by the grace of God be put into
practice. And if that is true—not, as is so often hinted, the
poetic licence of an overheated piety, not something to be
explained away by ingenious commentators or neutralized
by a mass of exceptions, but really true, something which
Jesus intended men to take just as He spoke it and to act
upon, working it into the very fibre and constitution of the
world—then, I say again, over great areas of life to-day His
gospel is news, startling news. Or take what is really the
core of the Christian Gospel, the doctrine of the forgiveness
of sins. That is the distinctive glory of Christianity. But
for so many of us it is still just a doctrine, an article in a
creed, a bit of rather ponderous theological lumber. Yet
here are those people of the New Testament singing and
revelling and ecstatic about it ! Why ? Was that just silly
emotionalism ? That is the last charge that can fairly be
brought against the men of the early Church : their logic
was level-headed and irrefragable. Why, then, were they so
excited ? Because forgiveness means this amazing thing—
the complete and perfect healing of a relationship that
seemed irretrievably spoilt and damaged. It means that
the uneasy, guilty feelings which trouble the mind and
haunt the memory can be utterly transmuted. It means,
for all the penitent, an unconditional new beginning. It
could mean your going away from this Church to-day with
every barrier between God and your own soul completely
broken down. It could mean life's most precious relationship put gloriously and decisively right. It could mean,

where that relationship is concerned, your facing life now without one care in the world. And do you not see that, if this is true (and as sure as Christ died, it is true), then for multitudes to-day it is news, exhilarating, magnificent news?

And yet they tell us that this Christianity is an old story, tried out for nineteen centuries and exhausted! If the Gospel consisted of men's views and notions, that verdict might be right. But the Gospel is not man's theorizing about God: it is God's news to man. And there is no exhausting that. "I am coming to you," said Paul, "with the gospel—the good news—of Christ."

Now take the third step. "I am coming to you *with the blessing* of the gospel of Christ." Here the suggestion is the reaction of religion upon life, its practical effect on the concerns of every common day. It makes life blessed, says the apostle: it lights up a man's whole experience with joy and peace and courage and serenity.

With one voice all the saints proclaim it, that there is no nook or cranny of life which is not crowned with light and flooded with sunshine, no dull stretch of the road which does not grow romantic, no common task or lonely way which is not marvellously transfigured, no human friendship which is not hallowed, no heavy cross which does not begin to shine with glory, when once Christ and His glad tidings have gripped and held the heart.

All the saints have proved it. Paul and Silas proved it, lying with torn backs and bleeding heads in the Philippian dungeon: for even that grim shambles of a place could not quite smother the joy that broke into songs at the midnight hour. Francis of Assisi proved it. Who that has read the story of the Christian centuries does not love St. Francis? And why? It is the man's gallant joyfulness that grips you, the joy which sang its way in beggar's clothes round Italy, earning for him that blithesome and most honourable

name, " God's Troubadour " ; the joy which leapt like fire
from his soul to a thousand others, till tens of thousands
had been kindled at its torch, and a dead Church, feeling
that the winter was past and the time of the singing of birds
was come, broke from its sleep in sudden resurrection ; the
joy which at the last went down into the valley of the shadow
of death singing, and passed singing to the throne of God.
And the secret of it ?   The blessing of the gospel of Christ !
General Booth and the Salvation Army have proved it.   The
driving-power of that great movement which has seen so
many miracles of grace is its indwelling joy, the radiant
overflowing happiness of ordinary folk who, having themselves
been caught by love's strong arms out of the toils of sin,
really know, as a vivid and most personal experience, the
amazing difference Christ can make.   Nor is there one of
us who may not prove for himself, that true blessedness—I
mean real solid happiness, and quietness and poise and dignity,
freedom from nerves and restlessness and the worried,
hectic attitude which is so common to-day, the power of a
spirit genuinely liberated and at peace—is in our grasp,
since Christ is here ;   and that the most burdened heart
amongst us now can go forth from the place of prayer rein-
forced and resolute and calm, and clothed with the gladness
of God.   " I am coming," said Paul, " with the blessing of
the gospel of Christ."

Now take the final step.   " I am coming to you *with the
fulness* of the blessing of the gospel of Christ."   And for some
of us the crux of everything lies here.   We have the blessing
of the gospel of Christ, and we thank God for that—nothing
is going to be allowed to rob us of that ;   and yet, is there
not a dim feeling that we have never quite entered into the
fulness of the blessing ?   Something has come to us from our
religion ;   much that we treasure dearly has come to us out
of the bosom of our Christian faith.   Yet there is something
lacking, some final gift of God unappropriated, some last

step untaken, some deepest secret unprobed. There is many
a man to-day who prays to God in the name of Jesus, and
would feel utterly lost if robbed of prayer : yet there is
something missing. He joins in worship, loves the old hymns,
finds that they help and speak to his need : yet there is
something lacking. He is aware that Jesus can give absolute
victory in the moral sphere : yet he has never been absolutely
victorious. He knows that Jesus can keep the human heart
in the very peace of God : yet he still gets worried. He is
sure that Jesus can raise a man above the clamour of tongues
and the opinions of the world and the things that are apt
to hurt : yet he has never been raised above them. He has
the blessing—but not the fulness of the blessing. And so
the pilgrim soul of him on its march through life lacks
that feeling of release and spontaneity, that steadfastness
and buoyancy and dignity, which God intended it to
have.

Well for him if, like the young man in the Gospels, he
takes his disappointment direct to Christ Himself. " Master,
all this have I done, all these commandments have I kept—
what lack I yet ? " " One thing thou lackest," said Jesus,
and then laid His finger on the one factor never completely
committed to God's charge, the one evaded moral decision.
" Until you have faced this, my friend, and put it right, it is
going to spoil everything for you, and bring a cloud across
the sun ! "

Is this the Word of God to-day to some of us ? One sin
retained, and all the rest of life's glory dimmed in conse-
quence ; one corner barricaded against Christ, and all the
rest reduced in Christian efficiency ; one secret hugged from
God, and a shadow over all the sunshine ; one heavenly
vision disobeyed, and the soul's gloaming gathering in ; one
weak moral compromise accepted, and all the lights of
religion lowered, and the full blessing never known—is that
what Christ sees, looking now at you and me ? Then the
next step lies with ourselves. Down with the barrier !

Away with reservations! Be done with the misery of a divided soul. Offer the whole sacrifice upon the altar of God. So shall we have, no longer an impoverished religion and a deficient moral dynamic, but the living and limitless blessing in the God-created splendour of its fulness.

THE LOVE OF GOD

" With Thy calling and shouting my deafness was broken; with Thy glittering and shining my blindness was put to flight. At the scent of Thee I drew in my breath, and I pant for Thee. I have tasted, and I hunger and thirst; Thou hast touched me, and I am on fire for Thy peace."—ST. AUGUSTINE.

" If you would wish to know how the Almighty feels towards us, listen to the beating of your own heart, and add to it infinity."— LACORDAIRE.

X

THE ROMANCE OF ORTHODOXY

" Then they said one to another, We do not well : this day is a day of
good tidings, and we hold our peace."—2 KINGS vii. 9.

ANY man who at the present juncture announces as his
subject "This is a day of good tidings" must be
prepared for the instinctive, inevitable retort, "What a
singularly inappropriate theme ! And what a lack of sense
and perspicacity and right feeling to choose it at all ! For
whatever may be said about this strange day in which we
live, you certainly cannot describe it as ' a day of good
tidings.' It is a day of tidings so perpetually disquieting and
dismal and downright bad that the only defence against the
almost daily shocks is an attitude of Stoic fatalism. It is a
day of such a dearth of good tidings that people are breaking
down right and left beneath the strain. To quote these
words of Scripture and apply them to to-day, when the
whole world under withering blasts of disillusionment is
suffering from nerves, is simply foolish. A day of good
tidings—for whom ? Not presumably for the hundreds of
thousands of our brothers and sisters who have been robbed
of all human rights, subjected to immeasurable agony, and
driven homeless across the earth ! Not, surely, for any
thinking man upon whose mind and conscience the madness
of the world weighs with a sense of almost intolerable shame.
Here is no time of good tidings ; and the religion which
talks in that vein is simply proclaiming its own irrelevance
and forfeiting all respect. If the Church has not anything
more apposite to say than that, so much the worse for the
Church ! " That, I think, is our first instinctive reaction.

But this is a case where first reactions are wrong reactions.

8

I take this text, not because the Christian religion is an otherworldly quietism, the pursuit of people who are out of touch with contemporary unpalatable realities (for in point of fact, it is anything but that) ; not because the newspapers during the week are gloomy, and it is necessary, for social and national purposes, to provide an antidote on Sunday (please God, the Church will never consent to become a mere appendage of State policy like that) ; not because so many among us to-day are feeling strained and dispirited and " under the weather," as we say, and we want something bracing and comforting and rallying and heartening : not for these reasons do I choose this word of God which says " This day is a day of good tidings," but simply because it happens to be true. I take it because, dark and disheartening and threatening as the human prospect may be, there is something to set on the other side—something, mark you, not less, but more real than the grim concrete actualities that are confronting and confounding us—something in our Christian inheritance which, if we once really understand it, and assess it at its true value, and give it its due weight in our total situation, can counterbalance our fears, and make us even in this desperate time more than conquerors !

I underline that proviso—*if we really understand it*. That is the crucial question : Do we ? Are the terrific, world-shaking implications of the simplest assertions of our Christian creed being properly understood to-day ? Are the two or three central doctrines of our faith—the things to which it is so easy to subscribe almost mechanically—being appreciated in their radical and revolutionary consequences ? On this point, some words of Miss Dorothy Sayers in a pamphlet entitled *Strong Meat* are well worth pondering :—" It is startling to discover how many people there are who heartily dislike and despise Christianity without having the faintest notion what it is. If you tell them, they cannot believe you. I do not mean that they cannot believe the doctrine : that would be understandable enough, since it takes some believing. I mean that they simply cannot believe that anything so interesting, so exciting and so dramatic can be the orthodox Creed of the Church." I am sure that is rightly said. If the basic doctrines of our Christian faith seem to us dull and uninteresting, it must be because we have never grasped their meaning, never begun to envisage their overwhelming consequences for ourselves, for the world, and for mankind's predicament to-day. Once these things are understood— once you face the astounding assertion that " the same God who made the world lived in the world and passed through the grave and gate of death "—once you see that nothing less than that is the creed, the orthodox creed, of the Church, then you begin with a thrill to realize that what Christianity has got hold of, what a genuine Christian lives by, is literally the most " interesting, exciting, and dramatic " fact on the face of the earth, able to burn up all our fears and low-spiritedness and doubt and depression in a great flame of praise and gratitude to God !

Now with these things in mind, will you listen again to the urgent challenge of this text ?   " They said one to another, We do not well : this is a day of good tidings, and we hold our peace." It will help our purpose to recall the original setting of these words. They come from an extra-ordinarily vivid scrap of Scripture narrative, which has been too often neglected. The scene is laid at the gates of Samaria during a siege. Round the walls in unbroken line Ben-hadad of Syria had set his blockading army, and the Israelite garrison was slowly being starved to death. Within the town conditions were appalling—men going about the streets gaunt and haggard, women standing at the house-doors with weakly, puny children clasped in their arms, crowds gathering nightly outside the royal residence clamouring " Bread ! Bread ! For God's sake give us bread ! " And the king, helpless and at his wits' end and stricken by the sight of his people's misery, wore sackcloth next his flesh.

But it chanced that near the city gate there lived a little colony of lepers, four of them huddled together in a wretched hut. If the plight of the besieged populace was bad, theirs was even worse. They had always made a living by begging ; but now, with famine raging, who was going to think of them ? " Why sit we here until we die ? " they said. " If we do nothing, we shall be dead within a week. If we go into the city, the end may come even sooner : for the people there are desperate, and who knows but that they might turn on us and stone us ? We have only one chance now—and that is to go to the enemy camp. There is food in plenty where the Syrians are, and perhaps they may spare our lives : at the worst, they can but kill us."

So in the evening twilight, they stole out of their hut by the gate, and crept down towards the besieging camp. And at every moment they were expecting to be challenged, they were waiting for the " Halt ! Who goes there ? " of the Syrian sentries. But to their astonishment no challenge came. They reached the outermost circle of tents, and still there was no challenge. " What can it mean ? " they wondered. " Is it perhaps a trap, a cunning snare ? " Cautiously they peered into one of the tents. It was deserted. But there, in front of them, were food and drink ; and without another thought the four ravenous creatures fell upon it. Then into another tent—and there, scattered on the ground, as though abandoned by men fleeing in some nameless panic, was a great heap of booty, silver, gold, and raiment. And so from one tent to another—until the startling truth began to dawn upon them : the Syrian army had fled, had vanished to the winds before some swift, mysterious terror of the night, had left everything behind in desperate haste to be gone ! In and out amongst the tents went the four lepers, feasting their eyes upon the plunder ; until suddenly—" Stop ! " cried one of them to the others, " We do not well : this day is a day of good tidings, and we hold our peace. We must get back to the city at once, and tell the great news ! " And

back they went, and told their tale to the watchers at the
gate, and the watchers took it to the king, and the king
ordered out a patrol to go and test the incredible story;
and the patrol returned, and reported that the lepers' news
was true. So ended the terrible siege, and Israel's joy and
relief knew no bounds. " It is the Lord's doing," they said,
" and marvellous in our eyes."

" This day is a day of good tidings, and we hold our peace."
Do you not feel now how cogent that challenge is for us, and
for the whole Christian Church ? Think of the dramatic,
incredible tidings that were committed to the Church once for
all nineteen hundred years ago. What did those men then
preach ? They preached one thing, and one thing only—
and it was not an idea, it was a fact : it was not vague
uplift, or beautiful phrases, or ethical commonplaces, or
theories of life, (these are what Christianity in many minds
is identified with to-day), it was Jesus and the Resurrection.
In other words, it was God's victory—not in hope, and dream,
and fancy, but in history—over all the powers of evil. It
was the discovery that if you crucify justice and righteousness and love, and trample them beneath your feet, they will
certainly rise from the dead the third day. The world to-day
preaches ideologies : here is something better—here is a
fact, and a fact on which every boastful, ironclad ideology
shall yet break itself in pieces.

Think of the story. That the God who made the universe
and sways the stars should take to Himself a human body,
and tread the dusty places of this low earth, not a disguised
divinity, but veritably a man—this is in all conscience
startling enough. But that God should be the jest and sport
of an ignorant, vindictive rabble ; that He, encountering
the concentrated might of the malignant machinations of
the devil, should pass down into the valley of the shadow ;
that He should turn the cross on which they hanged Him,
battered and broken and outwardly defeated, into the supreme

triumph of history, and a throne ; that having tasted the ultimate bitterness and severity of death, He should then break the bands of the grave, and smite man's last enemy, and triumphantly vindicate righteousness for ever ; that all this should be, not man's prodigious dream, but God's historic deed—who, I say, can measure the marvel or the magnificence of that ?

And that is what every one of us claims to believe who is a professing Christian. That is the orthodox creed of the Church—your Church. Men and women, why are we not carried away by the splendour of it ? Why are we not realizing that here is the answer, God's decisive and sufficient answer, to the paralyzing doubts and daunting problems of this present evil age—this unconquerable Christ, this eternal pledge that love and justice and truth are the only unconquerable realities on earth, and that those who scourge them and spit upon them and crucify them shall yet be smitten dumb before the glory of their resurrection ? " We do not well : this day is a day of good tidings, and we hold our peace."

Those early Christians did not hold their peace. Grim and terrifying and demon-infested was that world which they inhabited ; and if we think our prospects to-day are threatening and precarious, theirs were tenfold more distressing. But so full were their hearts of God's great deed in history, so clearly did they recognize its vast and cosmic consequences, so vividly out of earth's blackest tragedy had they seen heaven's glory shining, that joy indomitable was in every word, and the music of a matchless confidence in all their message, as they shared their mighty tidings with the world.

I wonder why we who are their lineal successors—heirs of the same Gospel, and children of the same Resurrection— lag so far behind them in enthusiasm and conviction. So many who bear the Christian name to-day appear to have no notion that enshrined in the very heart of their religion is a fact of such incalculable vitality and force that it can make the pomp of emperors ridiculous and the pride of dictators merely crude and vulgar and pathetic. G. K. Chesterton once declared that " Christianity even when watered down is hot enough to boil all modern society to rags." It might be better to put it more positively and say that the orthodox creed of the Church—that God became incarnate, and walked the earth, and died, and rose again, and turned evil's supreme, most trenchant triumph into its most crushing, irrevocable defeat—contains a potential energy capable of burning up all the dross of men's unrighteousness and of making the whole world new. This day is a day of good tidings : why do we—so unlike those early Christians—hold our peace ? If the Christian fact is so essentially dynamic, why is not our faith in the fact more noticeably contagious ? Why, if we have really been caught by the splendour of Christ, is the world in its contacts with us so little impressed, so far from being inclined to " take knowledge of us that we have been with Him " ? If our personal religion, our individual Christian conviction, is really vital and assured, why is it not proving for others, in this confused, perplexing age, a hiding-place from the wind of doubt, a covert from the tempest of mental and moral bewilderment, the shadow of a great rock in a weary land ?

Is it because there has begun to creep into our own souls some doubt about the relevance of the Christian facts in a blatantly non-Christian world ? Is it because prayer, and devotion, and the sense of the unseen look poor and frail and puerile—things almost to be ashamed of—when you set against them the massive logic and clever arguments of the sceptics ? Is it because we have been reading Joad and Russell and others who challenge with incisive criticism the very bases of the faith by which we claim to live, until faith is intimidated and conviction paralyzed by the thrust and impressiveness of the attack ? It is well, doubtless, that we should be aware of the arguments which are being launched

by trained minds against the Christian position to-day,
arguments which have often a wealth of literary charm and
logical skill to support them, and the weight of imposing
names behind them. But it is well also to remind ourselves
that Christianity has nothing to fear intellectually, any
more than it has to fear ethically and spiritually, from the
forces of the opposing camp. Its creed makes sense of the
universe, as the dreary theories of the sceptic never can.
And why should we, when some latter-day opponent appears,
forget the witness of the saints of two thousand years ?
Must we suddenly grow ashamed of Paul, and Irenaeus, and
Augustine, and Aquinas, and Luther, and (for the great line
of succession of defenders of the faith runs down to our own
day) Chesterton, and Charles Gore, and John Oman, and
Hugh Mackintosh, men intellectually the equals of, and
spiritually whole worlds beyond, any of the modern heralds
of agnosticism now writing ? Why should we forget that all
down the ages there have sprung from the bosom of the
faith lives of incredible loveliness, characters of supernatural
quality, men and women—some of them of dazzling distinction, many utterly obscure—whose intensity of God-consciousness, whose serenity of mind in the face of crushing,
desperate trouble, you simply cannot explain apart from
the fact of Christ ? Read the latest and wittiest exposure
of the defects and irrationalities of the Christian faith : then
go back and read Augustine's *Confessions* or Bunyan's *Grace
Abounding*. Does not that fusillade of clever scepticism look
strangely unimportant and even tawdry now ? How un-
convincing are all the discussions about prayer compared
with the light on the face of a man who has truly prayed !
How unsubstantial are the arguments of all the sceptics who
have ever lived, when there breaks upon your ears that
thunderous chant of the saints of every age : " Therefore
with angels and archangels, and with all the company of
heaven, we laud and magnify Thy glorious Name ; evermore
praising Thee, and saying, Holy, holy, holy, Lord God of

hosts, heaven and earth are full of Thy glory : Glory be to Thee, O Lord most High ! "

I know what men say, challenging the deepest and dearest convictions of our faith. But the other day there came to me a letter from China. It was written by the wife of a young missionary doctor. God had blessed them greatly in their labours there, and had given them two dear children to make glad their home. But typhoid came, and the young doctor was taken, and this letter was written two days after his death. " As you know," it said, " these years have been ones of perfect joy, perfect understanding, perfect love, and I praise God with all my heart for His great gift to us of such love." A little later, it added this : " I cannot begin to understand—but I know *our* love for our little ones, and that God's love is infinitely greater—I can only trust that love." If you confront yourself with the question, On which side does error lie, and illusion, and unreality—with the spirit which penned that letter, or with the self-confident negations of the materialist and sceptic ?—immediately with all its strength the deepest instinct of your soul replies, Not with the writer of the letter ! Set such artless, moving sentences as these, and the faith inspiring them, over against the most formidable challenge of the spirit of denial, and they not only hold their own—they reduce that challenge to impotence and bring its most close-knit arguments to silence.

Let us reiterate it : we are not building, in our Christian religion, on fancies and the stuff of dreams, but on proved and tested fact. " On Christ, the solid rock, I stand." In Christ, crucified, risen, and alive for ever, God has acted, and still acts decisively ; and at the name of Jesus every knee shall bow. This we believe, and this we hold, and this we know ; and there are no good tidings in all the world so mighty or so marvellous as this. Therefore I say, we do not well, if in this day of such tidings we hold our peace !

Can you imagine a biological research student, who discovers the cure for some dread disease which has long scourged the human race, keeping that discovery to himself, concerned above everything else to safeguard it as his own possession and to make a fortune out of it ? You cannot imagine that —unless, indeed, the man's conscience were dead. It is against the ethics of the kingdom of science to hold up any discovery which is likely to bless the world and bring relief to suffering humanity. And it is against all the ethics of the Kingdom of God to hold up the discovery of a Redeemer. If you know Christ, if ever Christ has been strength to your weakness, comfort to your sorrow, light to your darkness, "God's presence, and His very self and essence all-divine" in hours when heart and flesh were failing you, and grim unanswered questions stood knocking at your door—if He, the Sun of righteousness, has risen upon you then with healing in His wings, you hold in your possession the very tidings for which this world in its pathetic plight is waiting. Never was there a time when the need was greater that every Christian should be witnessing vigorously, by life and deed and character, to the relevance and the redeemership of the Christ whose name he bears. Send the good tidings on !

I daresay there were some in the Israelite garrison in Samaria who thought the four lepers quite mad when they burst in with their strange story of the nocturnal flight of the besieging army. "Don't listen to such tales!" they exclaimed. "These men are not to be trusted—they are fools!" And the bearer of God's good news must be prepared for a like retort to-day. Let not that, I beg you, impede your witness. If you have seen Christ regnant at the cross ; if you have watched God in that supreme act turning the devil's flank, and changing what looked like irreparable disaster for the campaign of His Kingdom into the instrument of its complete and final triumph ; if from the intimacies of personal experience you can speak of " my gospel," and can say "His grace avails for me"—then, at all costs, you must bear your witness. There are worse things in this world than being reckoned a fool for Christ's sake ; and even those who call you that will secretly be feeling the impact of your conviction, and will be haunted by an uneasy distrust of their own self-sufficiency and irreligion. Therefore—send the good tidings on !

For, finally, remember this—that a personal religion which remains individualistic and unshared soon loses its own freshness and glow and certainty ; whereas a faith which goes forth witnessing confirms itself, and gathers strength and vigour and momentum. To go on holding your peace, when good tidings are in your heart, is eventually to reach a point where even for yourself God's mightiest works seem drab and common and unmeaning. To tell the good tidings out and to share them with the world that needs them is to keep the flame of wonder and adoration continually alive and burning on the altar of your own spirit. Therefore —send the good tidings on.

If the Church were witnessing with all her might, and in all her members, to the things which she most surely believes and by which she lives, how incalculable might be her achievement in this perplexed, distracted generation ! If we, the children of Zion whose captivity God has ended, had our mouths filled with singing for the gladness of that great deliverance, what threatening shadows might be scattered, what dark and dreary places flooded with the blessed light of hope ! If every professing Christian were a veritable ambassador of Christ, how the royal banners of His Kingdom would go from strength to strength, conquering and to conquer ! This is a day of good tidings. One thing is needful. The world cries for it. Honour claims it. Christ commands it. Send the good tidings on !

XI

NEVERTHELESS !

" No chastening for the present seemeth to be joyous, but grievous :
nevertheless afterward it yieldeth the peaceable fruit of righteousness."—
HEB. xii. 11.

" We have toiled all the night, and have taken nothing : *nevertheless
at thy word* I will let down the net."—LUKE v. 5.

" Without were fightings, within were fears. *Nevertheless God.*"—
2 COR. vii. 5, 6.

HAVE you ever considered how great an element of
paradox there is in our human life ? The facts of life
have a disconcerting way of confounding our careful theories,
throwing out our calculations, contradicting our generaliza-
tions. Just when we think we have found a formula to fit
the facts of life, something unpredictable and eccentric
turns up, and makes our neat, ship-shape logic look absurd.
Just when we think we have established the rule, we discover
a host of exceptions.

" Just when we are safest, there's a sunset-touch,
A fancy from a flower-bell, some one's death,
A chorus-ending from Euripides,—
And that's enough,"

enough to embarrass our precision, and to dynamite our
dogmatism, and to play havoc with the axioms which we
had thought quite water-tight and comprehensive and
secure.

I mean that no sooner have we fixed on one aspect of life,
and nailed that down, and said " This certainly is true,"
than there crops up some other aspect, apparently directly
contradictory to the first, and we have to say " But this also
is true." Life is a thing so fair and lovely and sublime :
but it is also true that there is an element in it unspeakably

cruel and bitter. Human nature is such a godlike work of art, a divine amazing masterpiece, only " a little lower than the angels " : but it is also true that man is such stuff of clay, so easily devil-ridden, so prone to forget the angels and to sink lower than the beasts. Christ's yoke is easy and His burden light : and yet it is the hardest thing in all the world to be a Christian. God foreknows the future, and sees the end from the beginning : yet the human will is free. We are to bear one another's burdens : yet every man shall bear his own burden. We are citizens of the world, members of an earthly society, with all the ties and responsibilities which that involves : yet our citizenship is in heaven.

Life is full of this kind of paradox, this inescapable tension between opposing aspects of our experience. You can't card-index life. You can't pigeon-hole truth. You can't hope to get the mystery of it tied up into a neat little formula, with no loose ends anywhere.

People are always attempting to do that. The human mind has a passion for systematization. It hates loose ends. It wants to have everything docketed and tabulated and tidy It has an ingrained tendency to seek a snug, compact philosophy.

But it is a vain quest. Life is too big and complex for such treatment. There will always be awkward, intractable factors turning up, to take our confident theorizings by surprise ; always an element of paradox to derange the symmetry of our logic. The truth is, life is so constructed that at its heart there is a great " Nevertheless ! " We study the facts, and draw deductions, and arrive at conclusions, and feel that we have found and formulated the truth ; but then life itself with a sudden thrust and challenge intervenes. " All that may be true," it seems to say to us, " your state-ment of the facts may be sound and unexceptionable ; never-theless there is this ! "—and with that it sets down something that seems daringly, almost violently, to contradict our previous position—" there is this to reckon with ! " That is the element of paradox in life, the mysterious zig-zag of truth ; and it is this, when you come to think of it, that gives our life on earth its danger and zest and glory.

Here in the Scripture passages which I have set together we have three suggestive instances, illustrations of this divine, dramatic " Nevertheless ! "   " Nevertheless afterward ! "   " Nevertheless at Thy command ! "   " Nevertheless God ! "   I think it will repay us to ponder each in turn.

Take the first.   Here is this writer to the Hebrews.   " No chastening for the present seemeth to be joyous, but grievous: nevertheless afterward it yieldeth the peaceable fruit of righteousness."   This is what might be called *the Nevertheless of a transformed experience.*

What are we to understand by " chastening " ?   It means the whole range and extent of life's stern discipline, all the hard and difficult things that test the faith by which we live. It means the darkness in which we stand when some of the familiar and comforting lights have gone out.   It is what happens when plans fail, and dearest desires are frustrated ; or when health gives way ; or when homes are broken up, and good-byes are said ; or when some secret unshared burden weighs upon the heart ; or when the world goes mad, and chaos comes again ; or when death parts two souls that loved as David once loved Jonathan.   It is all the darker side of life ; and when this man says that " no chastening for the present is joyous, but grievous," he is surely right.   For these things hurt.   They mystify.   They search the soul, and leave deep scars behind.   It is no use being merely jaunty about the mystery of life, or saying, " Cheer up ! It doesn't matter."   It is not faith, it is folly, to suggest that trial and suffering are illusions.   There is no virtue in pretending that darkness is not sometimes terribly black and eerie, or that brutal facts are not brutal.   Chastening is not joyous.   It is grievous.

It can be so grievous that some are turned by it to bitter-

ness. " Why should this be tolerated ? " they demand,
arraigning the government of the universe. " Why does God
allow it ? What have I done to be treated so ? " And they
fall victims to self-pity, and resentment, and a brooding,
smouldering depression.

But here in this epistle is a man whom quite desperate
trouble has utterly failed to embitter. He has found the
secret of victory, and serenity, and strong unbroken self-
mastery. Do you ask him what his secret is ? Here is his
answer—" Nevertheless ! " " Life's discipline may hurt
and grieve : nevertheless afterward "—and with that, out
of the very heart of his trouble he brings a prize more fresh
and fair and lovely than the unhurt, untroubled life can ever
show—" nevertheless afterward it yieldeth the peaceable
fruit of righteousness," it wins as its harvest the strong
peace of a quiet mind, and the tranquillity of an upright
soul.

You must have seen it happening—here a man grappling
with crushing, overwhelming misfortune, and bringing back
from that battlefield of the soul a new sense of the real issues
of life, a new poise and dignity of bearing, a new awareness
of unseen, infinite resources ; there a woman imprisoned in
the long bondage of wearing illness, and developing out of
that experience a tenderness, a loveliness of spirit, a communion with the unseen, which seem to turn that sickroom
into a temple and a shrine.

Nevertheless afterward ! So trouble is transformed, and
they who sow in tears reap in joy, reap the rich harvest of
a deep, inviolable peace. I am not suggesting, of course,
that this wonderful transmutation of pain and suffering into
beauty and blessing happens inevitably or universally. We
may quite well miss it altogether. We may travel through
the dark valleys, and come out unblessed. The harvest
in life and character belongs only to those who are prepared
immediately to let God in upon their problem or their sorrow,
setting their own trouble in the light of the cross where

Christ bore all the troubles of the world, and showing themselves eager and resolute to co-operate with the divine plan
and will. Theirs—theirs alone—is the rainbow arch across
the storm. They only know the secret of the Lord.

Let us turn now from the writer to the Hebrews to Peter
the disciple. Here is another decisive Nevertheless. " We
have toiled all the night, and have taken nothing : nevertheless at Thy word I will let down the net." This we shall
describe as *the Nevertheless of an unquestioning devotion.*

Consider what Christ was asking. He was asking something that on the face of it looked utterly unreasonable. " Let
down your nets for a draught." But had they not been
doing just that very thing for hours without success ? Had
they not been scouring the sea backwards and forwards, to
and fro, through the long hours of a weary night ? Anyone
who understood anything about fishing would have known
that if the hours of darkness had yielded nothing there was
not the remotest chance of a catch now when the waters
were shimmering in the morning sun. And those disciples
were expert fishermen, and knew all the science of their
craft. What could Jesus be meaning ? " Master, we have
toiled all the night, and have taken nothing ! "

So many of us, unlike Peter, never get beyond that.
" Look at the world—we have toiled all night to reconstruct
the world on a basis of brotherhood and freedom, and international honour and straight dealing, and safety for our
children ; and after all that, the iron age of blood and
barbarism returns. Look at the Church—we have toiled
all night for a revival of religion as in the day of Pentecost,
toiled for the hope of the fire of the Gospel running irresistibly
through the earth and burning up all our hampering divisions,
our pitiable formalities, our second-hand loyalties, in a great
flame of fellowship in Christ : but oh, how the vision tarries,
how remote the glory of the dream ! Look at our own hearts
—we have toiled all night to drive our own lives straight and

true through the tangles of this tempting world, to build a
character that would be secure and resolute and strong, to
take from life the comfort and assurance of having achieved
something solid and enduring and substantial ; and what
have we to show for it ? The same old disappointing mediocrity, the same weak yielding before the hectoring voices of
besetting sin, the same monotony of defeat. We have toiled
all the night, and have taken nothing ! " So many of us never
get beyond that.

But hark to Peter ! " Master, we have toiled all night
and taken nothing ; nevertheless "—and the man, as I see
him, was on his feet, and his voice was ringing, and his eyes
shining—" nevertheless at Thy word I will let down the net ! "
It did not matter that the advice seemed totally unreasonable,
it did not matter that all his fisherman lore was dead against
it : it was the word of Jesus, and nothing else counted
compared with that.

Nevertheless at Thy word ! Can we look into the eyes of
Christ, and say the same ? Can we say it when His commands
to us appear unreasonable, all against our natural instinct,
interfering even with our cherished ambitions and plans for
our career ? Why does Christ sometimes make things so
dreadfully difficult for His servants ? Why should a
Schweitzer have to cut his career in two, and go to Central
Africa ? Why should the human heart be expected to
" contend for the shade of a word and a thing not seen with
the eyes," instead of settling down and relaxing and being
comfortable, and leaving things to take their course ? Why
should a man have to keep aiming at the ideal of the Sermon
on the Mount, when it has been proved to him by repeated
defeats that he cannot hope to reach it ? What is the good
of getting back into the old boat, at the old place, with the
old net, when you have toiled so long in vain ?

That is the natural language of the heart. But the man of
faith is the man who can cancel all that out with one ringing,
decisive " Nevertheless ! "—the man who, encountering the

9

most stubborn, recalcitrant facts, can achieve that paradox of faith, can stand there before his God and cry " Let the world say this or that, let all human wisdom mass its arguments and reasons : nevertheless at Thy word ! " Give Christ a faith like that, and anything—any undreamt, stupendous miracle—might happen even now.

Pass on just once again. We have listened to the writer to the Hebrews, and to Peter the disciple. We have heard the Nevertheless of a transformed experience, and the Nevertheless of an unquestioning devotion. Let us listen finally to St. Paul. Here is the crucial, crowning instance of the paradox, the most defiant, dramatic Nevertheless of all. " Without were fightings, within were fears. Nevertheless God ! " This is *the Nevertheless of a direct divine revelation*.

Here was this lonely servant of Christ, confronting his grim and desperate situation, wrestling with life. ' " Without were fightings." That meant the assaults of paganism, the mailed fist of a totalitarian State battering at everything the Church held dear, the threat of destruction and ruthless extermination hurled at the dreams and hopes of the saints of God. " Within were fears." That meant the man's own consciousness of personal inadequacy, his aches of memory and gusts of shame, his sense of being the most appallingly earthy of earthen vessels, and the unworthiest of all the unworthy servants of the Lord. The man's prospects, to all seeming, were pitiful, his plight desperate and pathetic. He ought, by all the rules, to have been a nervous wreck. He ought to have cried " I'm beaten," and given up the unequal struggle. He ought, humanly speaking, to have blown out the protesting light of his soul, in bitterness and disillusionment. He ought to have taken up his pen, and written, " Without were fightings, within were fears, therefore hope died within me, and the dark night of unbelieving fatalism claimed me for its own." Of course he ought ! But to this man in the darkest hour there had come one flash across the midnight ; and here, in the light of that great vision, he springs to his feet, breathlessly flinging defiance at the menace of the facts, bluntly contradicting the logic of the natural with the thrust and invasion of the supernatural. "Without were fightings, within were fears. Nevertheless God ! God comforted me." And so—magnificently—he sounds the trumpet-note of victory.

Can you rise to that final, decisive Nevertheless ? God knows we are all of us needing it to-day. Without are fightings, principalities and powers setting themselves in battle array against the most sacred standards of our life, doctrines of naked materialism and brute force laughing to scorn the spiritual values of the faith of Christ. And within are fears —fears of our own deficiency of inward resource, fears of a break in our faith when the real test comes, fears of the unknown future and the dim and menacing way. Can we, recognizing the fightings and the fears, fling these two shining words right in the wretched lowering faces of them all— "Nevertheless God " ? Darkness may cover the earth, and gross darkness the people—nevertheless God ! The powers of evil may cynically strike a pact together, as Herod and Pilate became friends on the day of Calvary—nevertheless God ! Faith may tremble at the assaults of devastating doubt, and heart and flesh may faint and fail—nevertheless God ! Can you rise triumphantly to that ?

There was a day in Martin Luther's life when the road grew suddenly dark and threatening, and death seemed very near. "The Pope's little finger," thundered the Cardinal legate, " is stronger than all Germany. Do you expect your princes to take up arms to defend you—a wretched worm like you ? I tell you, No ! And where will you be then ? Tell me that !—where will you be then ? " " Then, as now," cried Luther, " in the hands of Almighty God ! " That is the victory that overcomes the world.

Can we, facing the fightings and the fears, around, within, rise to it ? Others have achieved it in days more terrifying than our own. Our own forefathers achieved it on the scaffold and at the stake. The Lord Jesus Christ achieved it in Gethsemane. " Let this cup pass : nevertheless Thy will, Father, not Mine, be done." Think of that, and know you are not alone when trouble comes. Reach out of darkness, and feel the pressure of a more than human hand. Stand up in the might of Christ, and bid defiance to your fears. " Nevertheless God ! " And the rest will be music, and a march to victory.

XII

GOD AND THE FACT OF SUFFERING

(1) The Burden of the Mystery

" Have mercy upon me, O Lord, for I am in trouble."—Ps. xxxi. 9.
" Now is my soul troubled ; and what shall I say ? "—John xii. 27.

IN that strange medley of a book, *Sartor Resartus*, no
passage is more vivid or dramatic than the description
of Carlyle's philosopher gazing out from his high attic across
the city at midnight, and musing upon the age-long mysteries
of life and death, love and suffering, hope and misery. Down
beneath him and all around, the dark streets stretch away,
where half a million human beings are herded and crammed
together—the joyful and the sorrowful, men dying and men
being born, some praying and others cursing, women laughing,
others weeping, " all these heaped and huddled together,
with nothing but a little carpentry and masonry between
them," a kind of microcosm of humanity gathered there
beneath the covering of the vast, indifferent night. " But
I," he concludes, " I sit above it all ; I am alone with the
Stars."

Is God like that ? How many troubled hearts there are
to-day in which that terrible suspicion has begun to rear
its head ! God seems so remote, so high above this low
earth's welter and confusion of suffering and darkness and
unsolved questions crying out vainly for an answer. Was
Celsus, the formidable antagonist of the Church in its early
days, perhaps right when he bluntly characterized the
Christian doctrine that " God takes an interest in man " as
being " an absurd idea " ? Was Euripides right, when in his
great drama, *The Trojan Women*, he drew that most moving
picture of Queen Hecuba, broken-hearted and widowed and

childless, with all her world in ruins around her, while the gods on Olympus are too absorbed in other things to hear her bitter cry, or even to notice her where she lies prostrate before them in the dust ? Is God like the divinities of Tennyson's *Lotos-Eaters* ?

" For they lie beside their nectar, and the bolts are hurl'd
Far below them in the valleys, and the clouds are lightly curl'd
Round their golden houses, girdled with the gleaming world :
Where they smile in secret, looking over wasted lands,
Blight and famine, plague and earthquake, roaring deeps and fiery sands,
Clanging fights, and flaming towns, and sinking ships, and praying hands."

" I sit above it all ; I am alone with the stars." Is God like that ? From Rachel weeping for her children to Jesus suffering on His Cross, from the Trojan queen in her hour of desolation to every troubled heart or home throughout the world to-day, there rises the insistent question, "Why should this happen ? Why should these troubles come ? My God, why hast Thou forsaken me ? "

There are so many forms of trouble in this world—physical, mental, emotional, spiritual ; and the challenge which they severally and collectively present to faith is so radical, that one craves passionately to be able to let in some light upon the darkness. Certainly no one who takes life seriously can escape the necessity of confronting this problem and coming to terms with it in his own soul. It will be worth while, therefore, in this and the three succeeding talks, to concentrate our thoughts upon this matter which so deeply concerns us all.

Right at the outset let me say this—that if there is one subject in which the use of any language that is merely facile and conventional must be reckoned as a positive offence, it is this subject of the mystery of suffering. Stock phrases, for instance, like " the nobility of pain," " the uplifting influence of suffering," are very easy to use, but may simply prove that the one who uses them has never grasped what the real problem is. Would you go to someone in trouble and say to him piously, " Ah but, friend, consider how good this is for your character " ? Would you try to heal his wound with tags of commonplace counsel like " Take courage ; it might have been worse," or " Don't worry : it may never happen," or " It's a long lane that has no turning " ? All that may be true enough ; but it has scarce begun to come in sight of the real problem, and it is certainly not within shouting distance of the Christian answer. The one thing that is quite inexcusable in this whole matter is to be complacent and platitudinous. For when we approach this mystery, we are treading on holy ground. To take but one instance, here are some sentences from a letter which Earl Grey, after his wife's death, wrote to a friend. " I am having a hard struggle. Every day I grasp a little more of all that it means. Just when I have got my spirit abreast of life, I feel and understand more sorrow and sink again. Sometimes it is like a living death ; and the perpetual heartache, which has set in, wears me down." Surely in face of troubles like that, it would be far better to be silent than to say things trite and commonplace. Can any attempt indeed to interpret the dark enigma be other than utterly inadequate ? Yet even so, one must try to find light enough to walk by. God willing, our quest may not prove quite in vain.

Let us, to begin with, be quite clear that in this matter we are not dealing with any merely theoretical conundrum or dilemma. The problem of suffering is urgent and practical —relentlessly so. It is forced upon us from three directions.

First, *history* forces it on us. Why, for instance, does God ever permit the unspeakable sufferings and horrors of war ? Why, in the name of all that is righteous and true, should this fair earth be desecrated and defiled by such foul and monstrous iniquities of barbarity, persecution, and intoler-

ance as have been witnessed in these days in which we live ?
You see, the problem of suffering is no longer a thing that
can be left to the theorizings of philosophers and theologians,
or to the meditations of the aged and infirm : it concerns us
all, directly and even violently, in this generation. Very
specially it concerns the youth of this generation. There is
no thinking young man or young woman who is not grappling
with it. History is forcing it upon us.

Second, *life* forces it upon us. Walk through the wards
of a great hospital. Why should there be disease germs ?
Why should a baby be born blind, or, even worse, insane ?
Why should the innocent suffer ?   Why are there slums ?
Why is Nature " red in tooth and claw " ?   Why are there
earthquakes, famines, volcanoes ?   " You know," cries a
young man in one of Hugh Walpole's greatest novels, " you
know there can't be a God, Vanessa. In your heart you must
know it. You are a wise woman. You read and think.
Well, then, ask yourself. How *can* there be a God and life
be as it is ? If there is one He ought to be ashamed of Himself,
that's all I can say." Life forces the question upon us.

Third, *our own experience* forces it on us. For suffering
includes not only physical pain, but all the troubles, disappointments, bereavements, frustrations, to which the
human spirit is heir, all the swift desolating calamities that
crash their way through our hopes and dreams, all the slow,
subtle disillusionments that steal the heart out of life. It is
this aspect of experience, far more than any merely speculative
doubt, which is the real threat to faith. Trouble brings many
lives face to face with spiritual crisis. How will they react ?
The answer to the problem of suffering must be no abstract
answer in terms of words, but a concrete answer in terms of
life. For it is life that forces the problem upon us.

Now this leads us to the next point—and it is essential
that we should get this clear, for it is vitally important, yet
often overlooked. Have you noticed that *the first thing*

Christianity does to the problem of suffering is to heighten and accentuate the difficulty of it ? In fact, it is precisely our Christian faith that creates the problem. There is no real problem of evil for the man who has never accepted the Christian revelation. He may recognize indeed the fact of suffering : but only to the believer is suffering a mystery. For, you see, only the Christian says " God is love " : therefore, it is only he who has upon his hands and heart the terrible task of squaring the dark, tragic things in life with such a daring declaration of faith. So, in a sense, it is a far worse problem for the believer than for the unbeliever, precisely because of his asseveration of the love and sovereignty of God. For if there is no God—just a dead mechanism of a world—then obviously there is no reason why these dark and evil things should not happen. They are simply there ; there is nothing to explain. But if you assume a God of light and love, then the question grows acute, and the burden of the mystery becomes heavy. We do well to face this fact quite frankly, that the first thing Christianity does with the problem of suffering is not to solve it, but to heighten and accentuate it.

But having said that, we are entitled to go on at once and add this—that if the unbeliever escapes the problem of evil which is so real a mystery to the Christian, he immediately finds himself encountering another problem which for the Christian is no mystery at all, namely, the problem of good. It is certainly hard to explain why, if God is love, there is so much suffering in the world. That is the believer's problem. But I submit it would be even harder to explain why, if there were no God, nothing but a dead, unspiritual universe, there should be such facts as self-sacrifice, and reverence, and nobility, and heroism, and men who will die for their conviction of the right. That is the unbeliever's problem. And I am sure it is harder and more insoluble than the other.

Some of you will remember a fragment of conversation from John Galsworthy's *Maid in Waiting* : the girl Dinny is talking to her mother, Lady Cherwell. " I suppose there is an eternal Plan," she says, " but we're like gnats for all the care it has for us as individuals." " Don't encourage such feelings, Dinny," says her mother, " they affect one's character." " I don't see," replies the daughter, " the connection between beliefs and character. I'm not going to behave any worse because I cease to believe in Providence or an after life." " Surely, Dinny——" " No ; I'm going to behave *better* ; if I'm decent it's because decency's the decent thing ; and not because I'm going to get anything by it." Whereupon her mother asks, " But why is decency the decent thing, Dinny, if there's no God ? " That is the ultimate problem. Why, out of an unspiritual universe, should spiritual facts have arisen ? Why is decency the decent thing, if God is a dream ? Where did the beauty of a Beethoven sonata come from ? Why should Captain Oates have walked out into the blizzard to die, like a hero, for his friends ? The unbeliever's scheme of things will allow no answer except that all the loveliness of life, all the fine and noble and heroic things, are—as Bertrand Russell has put it candidly—" the outcome of accidental collocations of atoms," and all the order of the universe the product of blind chance. That, to me, sounds as sensible as to say that you could take a bag full of single letters of the alphabet and throw a few handfuls of them up into the air anyhow, and they would fall down in the form of a Shakespeare sonnet or the prologue of St. John. The thing is absurd ! Let me put it like this. I, as a believer in God, have to face—as the unbeliever does not—the mystery of the existence of evil. I admit that. But here is the other side of it : the unbeliever has to face—as I, who believe in God, do not—the mystery of the existence of good. And his problem is definitely more insoluble than mine.

Let us, then, take courage and face this problem bravely. I suggest that our next step must be to clear the ground by setting aside once for all certain attempted solutions of the problem which cannot be allowed to stand. I am going to mention three such solutions to you now. You will observe that in each case an element of truth is present—for otherwise they could scarcely have been so vigorously sponsored throughout the centuries. But few things are so dangerous or misleading as a one-sided truth.

First, we must reject the solution *that all suffering comes from God*. The element of truth, of course, in that statement is that God has created His world in such a way that sin and suffering are possibilities. But to hold, as some good people do, that God is the direct and immediate cause of everything that happens, and therefore the cause of all the evil things that happen—that kind of rigid determinism, that almost mechanical predestination, affronts our moral sense, and makes nonsense of the fact of human freedom. I am not going to dwell on this now. May I just remind you of Dr. Samuel Johnson's wise retort when someone, carried away by the logic of a rigid theory of predestination, had virtually denied human freedom? " Sir," said the good Doctor, " we are free, and we know it, and that is an end of it." The first familiar solution of our problem must fall to the ground.

Second, we must equally reject the doctrine *that all suffering is due to sin*. The element of truth in that is that all sin does undoubtedly produce suffering in one form or another. Indeed, it would be true to say that it is the sin and folly and bungling and selfishness of men, in history and down the ages, which are responsible for a vast amount of the suffering in the world to-day. To take but one modern instance, how much of the international plight and confusion of recent decades, with all the tragic consequences of suffering for the individual, were due to mistaken policies which failed to reflect the true spirit of Jesus ? Can there be any doubt that if, at certain decisive points in history, there had been a more resolute attempt to take the ethics of Jesus seriously, to accept them heartily and to act upon them, much of the chaos and bitterness which the world has seen could have been avoided ? It is true, in other words, that all sin involves suffering. But what I want you to see is that it is not true to turn that round the other way, and suggest (as some unthinkingly do) that all suffering is due to sin, as if a man's troubles were necessarily punishments, indications of some flaw in his character.

I am sure it is important to say this quite emphatically ; for I have met people, good people who, if some great trouble comes into their life, are made perfectly miserable by the thought that it must be due to some special sin. " What have I done that this has happened to me ? " But you can't equate character and suffering in that way. Thank God, you need not do it ! Long ago, for instance, when some parts of the Old Testament were written, the idea was that piety and prosperity were in direct proportion to each other, and that, therefore, to be visited by trouble and adversity was a sure token that you had been guilty of sin. " Whatsoever he doth," sang the psalmist of the righteous man, " shall prosper. The ungodly are not so : but are like the chaff which the wind driveth away." That, you remember, was precisely the position of Job's friends. There was Job, a mass of suffering. Therefore, said they, he must have sinned terribly : let him confess his sin, and perhaps God would remove his suffering. That was the old orthodox idea. But it was far too simple to be true. It could not fit the facts of life and of experience. And what makes the Book of Job such a vivid drama is that all through it you can see the suffering man grappling with that false, misleading solution of the mystery, protesting against it, refusing to believe the facile theory of an equivalence between suffering and character, and finally, with agony and travail, wrestling his way through to a deeper and truer answer to his problem. But we can bring in a greater witness than Job. Let us listen to Jesus speaking. " There were present at that

season some that told Him of the Galileans, whose blood
Pilate had mingled with their sacrifices. And Jesus answering
said unto them, Suppose ye that these Galileans were sinners
above all the Galileans, because they suffered such things ?
I tell you, Nay. Or those eighteen, upon whom the tower
in Siloam fell, and slew them, think ye that they were sinners
above all men that dwell in Jerusalem ? I tell you, Nay."
That is plain enough. Here you have it on the authority
of Jesus that it is a false simplification to say that all suffering
is due to sin. And there was another day, you remember,
when Jesus and His disciples met a man who had been
blind from birth : and the disciples asked Jesus (notice the old
rigid idea of an equivalence between sin and suffering coming
out again almost instinctively), "Master, who did sin, this
man, or his parents, that he was born blind ? " And the
answer was—" Neither hath this man sinned, nor his parents."
Therefore, my friend, if you have been vexing your soul with
the idea that some suffering of yours is necessarily a punish-
ment visited on you by God because of sin, it is Christ who
has given me authority to bid you put that dreadful thought
away. This is the second false solution of the mystery of
suffering which we must resolutely set aside.

Finally, we must reject the theory *that all suffering is an
illusion*. The element of truth here is that a good many of
our pains and troubles are in the mind mainly. They are
mentally conditioned. They can be traced back to familiar
and ascertainable psychological causes. They are not
objectively real. We conjure them up ourselves. It is our
mental attitude that creates them. No doubt many troubles
are like that. But what exaggeration to say that all suffering
is of this kind ! Think of the dark tragedies in the earth at
this moment—ruined homes, oppressions of the weak by the
strong, cries of orphaned children, squalid slums, defeats in
business, disappointments in love, broken hearts—is all
that mere appearance ? Are such sufferings a phantasm of
the mind ? Mark you, if they are, then all the heroisms

men and women have produced in facing sufferings such as
these have been unsubstantial and quixotic. Will you say
that ? Were the martyrs at the stake playing a game ?
Was Jesus in His Passion week just acting ? Is the good
fight of faith mere make-believe ? Will you go to a man who
has lost a limb in an accident, and say to him, " Buck up,
old fellow, it isn't real " ? Or to a desolate mother who has
lost a child, and say, " Your suffering is in the mind only—
you'll get over it " ? There are systems of thought to-day,
modern theosophies, whose gospel is that all suffering is an
illusion. I say these systems are an affront to the intelligence
and an offence to the heart. I have seen a child crying over
a broken toy as if its heart would break. Is that trouble an
illusion ? Only one with no understanding of childhood
would dream of saying that. It is real—and it matters.
And we poor humans, with our broken pathetic toys and
desolating sorrows—are we imagining things ? Do you
think God would allow His children to go on indefinitely
being mocked with an age-long illusion, being deceived and
made tragically unhappy by what was nothing more than a
figment of their own foolish, fevered imagination ? What
a poor, ungodlike jest ! To say that all suffering is illusion
would be like asking a man who had just lost his wife to come
to the theatre, or suggesting to someone who is desperate
with a guilty conscience that all he needs is a game of golf.
No, you do not dismiss the challenge of the mystery of
trouble with a wave of the hand, nor with the easy verdict
of a superficial optimism which says, " The thing is unreal."
It is as real as the stones that killed Stephen, as real as the
nails they drove into the flesh of Christ. This third familiar
explanation we must unhesitatingly reject.

What, then, are we to say ? The search for a solution
must be continued. This present study has been in the
nature of a clearing of the ground for something more positive
to follow. It may be, of course, that we shall find there is
no complete and final answer to the mystery of suffering. It

may be we shall have to confess that to understand the mystery fully, we should require to look out upon life with the eyes of God Himself. In other words, we may be led to conclude that there will always, to the very end of the day, be need for an act of sheer naked faith. If that is so, we need not be ashamed. Faith requires no apology. And in any case, if it is faith in God which creates the problem (as we have already seen reason to maintain), it is surely understandable that it is only faith in God which is going to answer it.

In our next study I invite you to consider some beams of light upon the darkness of the mystery. " If I from my spy-hole," wrote Robert Louis Stevenson, " looking upon a fraction of the universe, yet perceive some broken evidences of a plan, shall I be so mad as to complain that all cannot be deciphered ? " I think the attempt to solve the enigma is rather like learning a foreign language. You read a page, and you understand perhaps only a word or two here and there. But you do not on that account say—" This book is nonsense ! It has no meaning." You say, " Because I recognize a word here and there, I am sure all the rest makes sense. And one day I shall understand." Yes, even now there are traces of a plan, beams of light flung out athwart the darkness. It is these that we must now try to follow. And it may be we shall come to see our darkness, if not dispelled, at least redeemed and robbed of all its fears by one light, far steadier and brighter than all the rest : the light of the love and victory of God on the face of Jesus Christ.

XIII

GOD AND THE FACT OF SUFFERING

(2) LIGHTS IN THE DARKNESS

" Who is among you that feareth the Lord, that walketh in darkness
and hath no light ? let him trust in the name of the Lord, and stay
upon his God."—ISA. l. 10.
" Unto the upright there ariseth light in the darkness."—Ps. cxii. 4.

THERE is a very moving scrap of conversation near the
beginning of the *Pilgrim's Progress*. Poor burdened
Christian had met Evangelist, and begged for help and
guidance. Whereupon Evangelist pointed to the far distance,
and asked, " Do you see yonder wicket-gate ? " And
Christian looked, and shook his head, and answered " No."
Then Evangelist tried again. " Do you see yonder shining
light ? " he asked. And Christian peered away to the far
horizon, and noticed something—one spot that seemed not
quite so dark as all the rest ; and he answered, " I think I
do." " Keep that light in your eye," said Evangelist, " and
go up directly thereto, so shalt thou see the gate."

I fancy that if some one inquired of you or me, " Do you
see the answer to the riddle of life and the mystery of
sorrow ? " we should have to answer, as bluntly as Christian
did, " No, I don't see it." But if the inquirer went on to
ask, " Do you see any points of light, any places where the
darkness of the mystery is not quite so dark as elsewhere ? "
some of us, with Christian, would reply, " I think I do."
It is some of these beams of light that I invite you to consider now. It may be that if we keep them before us and
trust their guiding, we, too, may " see the gate." For the
darkness in which we walk is not impenetrable gloom ; and
the night—thank God—has stars.

The first beam of light is what I would call *the beneficence of inexorable law.*

It is perfectly clear that a good deal of the tragic element in life is due to the working of certain uniform principles which govern the universe. There is the law of gravitation, for instance. That law means that a child who wanders too near the edge of a precipice may be killed ; that an aeroplane whose engine fails may crash. But the point to notice is this —that the same laws which are responsible for so much human suffering are also the indispensable sources of most of the things that make life worth living.

Does it not begin to lighten at least the burden of the mystery when we grasp that ? The fact of the matter is that even though the physical laws of the universe may often work out tragically for human beings, yet for all that we would not choose, even if we could, to live in a world without these laws : for then our predicament would be infinitely worse than it is now.

Gravitation, as I have said, may mean the death of a child or the crash of an aeroplane. It may mean scores of accidents and disasters every day. But remember this : without gravitation, you could not walk along the street, you could not travel in a train, you could not launch a ship, you could not span a river with a bridge. Life would simply become unlivable.

Or think of fire. It is an inexorable property of fire that it gives out heat. And that very property may mean some day that a hundred people, trapped in a blazing building, are burnt to death. What then ? Do you wish that fire would not behave like that ? Then it would cease to be fire, and all its tremendous contribution to human welfare and well-being would be lost. You can't have it both ways.

Take even grim facts like earthquakes and volcanoes. It is hard to discover any trace of beneficence there. But the fact is that the very forces which occasionally produce these

10

devastating outbursts are the same forces which, working continually beneath the earth's surface, make and keep this planet habitable for the sons of men.

You cannot have all the assets of life, and refuse its liabilities. The uniformity of Nature, the inexorableness of law, may cause us tragic sufferings : but if Nature were not uniform, if law were not inexorable, we should not be here at all, either for happiness or for woe, for life would be impossible. Here is how the late Canon Streeter illustrated the point. The pressure of law, he suggested, is "like the immovability of the touch-line, without which there could be no game, though it would at times be vastly convenient to an individual player if by a miracle the line would approach or retire a yard or two." Picture that wing three-quarter racing down the touch-line with the ball. The opposing back comes out to tackle him. How opportune it would be for the man with the ball if the line were movable—if it would suddenly bend back in the nick of time, and let him past ! And yet you can see that it is on the rigidity of the touch-line that the whole game depends : there could be no game without it. So in the serious business of life. Sometimes it would facilitate things vastly for the individual player, for you and me, if the laws of Nature would bend back and let us dodge them. We all wish fervently that they would do that sometimes. And yet, can't you see that it is upon the absolute fixity of that line, the rigidity of that law, that the whole game depends ? What kind of a universe would it be in which Nature were erratic and capricious ? What kind of a world in which the law of gravitation operated one moment, and not the next ? It would be a madhouse of a world. Of such a world Othello's cry would be strictly true, " Chaos is come again." It would be quite impossible to get ahead with the business of life. The rigid laws of God's universe may hit us sorely sometimes ; but if that is the price we have to pay for being delivered from the terrifying alternative, every soul of us would say " It's worth the

price ! " Robert Browning knew what he was talking about
when he cried " All's love yet all's law ! " There, then,
shines our first beam of light upon the mystery—the beneficence of inexorable law.

The second beam of light is what St. Paul described as
our membership one of another.

There is no question that much of the innocent suffering
in this world is due to the fact that we are all so inextricably
mixed up together. If one man plays the fool, a dozen, or
a score, or a thousand may be ruined. If one country breaks
faith, the whole world may be plunged in cataclysm. That
is manifestly true. But over against it you have to set this
countervailing consideration, that the very fact—our mutual
interdependence—which is responsible for so much of the
sheer tragedy of life, is also responsible for life's greatest
glory.

And again I ask you—does it not begin to lighten the
burden of the mystery when you realize that even if this
corporate relationship of mankind is the cause of half our
troubles, there is not one of us who would choose, even if he
could, to stand outside that relationship, for then our human
prospect would be infinitely darker than it is ?

Perhaps some one says, " I do not agree. I should be
much better off, standing for myself alone ! Why should
life compel me, willy-nilly, to be intermeshed, bound up in
the same bundle with thousands of other people, and to be
involved in all their blunderings and follies and futilities ?
Why should I not break away, and stand isolated, free,
master of my fate and captain of my soul ? "

But wait a moment. There is another side to it. Suppose
you got your way. Suppose that this troublous and highly
dangerous fact of being members one of another were eliminated. Suppose you were an isolated unit. Then certainly
you would escape hundreds of the things you suffer now.
But think what you would lose ! Think what you owe to

this perilous fact of belonging to the human fellowship. The bread you eat, the clothes you wear, the coals you burn, the scientific discoveries you use, the books you read, the medical help you call in when you are ill—they have all come to you through other men's labours. All the assets of the infinitely complex human relationship are yours. So again I say—you must not try to have it both ways. This fact of mankind as a brotherhood is double-edged : you cannot accept the assets, and disown the liabilities ; you cannot share the blessings, and shirk the risks. And if it came to be a choice between having a place in the corporate fellowship, with all the sufferings which that entails, and contracting out and standing on your own in naked isolation, there is no sane man who would hesitate one moment. " It's worth the price," he would say, bowing his back to humanity's burden, " it's gloriously worth the price ! " Clear through the midnight darkness of the mystery gleams this steady light : our membership one of another.

The third beam of light which shines out for me is *the wisdom of the divine impartiality.*

Look at it like this. Most of us would say that the real crux of the whole problem of evil, the cruel sting of the thing, is the absolutely indiscriminate way in which trouble falls on saint and sinner alike. It aims its blows with appalling indifference at those who deserve them and at those who do not deserve them in the least. There was an earthquake in India. It knocked down a mission-house, and left standing —just a few doors down the street—an opium-den. In that mission-house, for years, souls of men and women had been getting saved : in the opium-den, for years, souls had been getting damned. Yet the earthquake destroyed the mission, and spared the den. And we want to ask, Why ? Why should it not have been the other way round ? Would it not be a better universe if we could be sure that virtue would reap its appropriate reward, and vice its appropriate pain ?

It is this dreadful indifference that is the problem, this
appalling impartiality that baffles us! What are we to
say of a world which enthrones a Herod, and crucifies a
Christ ?

Let us go to our New Testament on this point. What has
the Gospel to say about it ? At first sight, the Gospel has
very little comfort to give. It does not say that, if a man
follows Christ, his business will not go bankrupt. It does
not suggest that, if two parents believe sincerely in God,
death will never rob them of a child. It does not hold out
a promise that, if you are a religious man, there will always
be supernatural intervention to lift you out of every tight
corner—like the *deus ex machina*, the " God from the
machine," of the old Greek plays. Jesus once told a story
about two houses, the one built by a wise man, the other by
a fool ; and Jesus said that on both these houses—which
meant, on both these lives, the saint's no less than the
sinner's—" the rain descended, and the floods came, and the
winds blew and beat." And our puzzled hearts cry, Why ?
Would it not be a far juster and diviner world if evil got its
deserts, and goodness went immune ?

But think again. Would it ? I am sure that on second
thoughts you will see that a world like that would be definitely
less divine, far more trying, than the actual world in which
we live to-day. For it would mean that the laws of the universe would have to be suspended or interrupted every time
a good man was in danger or in difficulty ; and that (as we
have seen already) would simply lead to chaos. Moreover
(and this is even more crucial) an inevitable corollary of a
universe in which penalties and rewards were invariably
dealt out in direct ratio to vice and virtue would be the de-
spiritualizing of religion and the ruin of character. For if
a Christian escaped the troubles that visit other folk, if
religion " got you off," you can see what would almost be
bound to happen : religion would become a kind of gigantic
insurance policy—a commercial transaction, a *quid pro quo*

—and you would have people paying the premium for the sake of the insurance. And that would be the ruin of religion and character for ever. No, far better that troubles should come, and darkness descend, and the heavens crash and fall, than that righteousness should be sought for any reason save for righteousness' sake alone. That is another star, shining aloft to illuminate our darkness—the wisdom of the divine impartiality.

There is a fourth beam of light we can discern : *the awakening of the conscience of humanity.*

It is of vital importance to get this clear. Must we not believe that one main function of the fact of the suffering which we encounter all around us is to be a perpetual challenge to us to be up and doing, to be co-operating with a burden-bearing God, and to be giving ourselves in consecrated service for the healing of this broken earth ? If the sight of suffering is indeed having that effect upon us, then the sorrows of those who suffer will not have been in vain : they will have contributed something positive. For they will have helped to stab the human conscience broad awake, and to send us out crusading for a better and happier to-morrow, and for a world nearer to the mind and will of God.

I think, for instance, of facts like poverty, unemployment, and war, and of the cruel agonies which these entail. Now if poverty, unemployment, and war were the will of God, then of course we should simply have to accept them. There would be no call for us to do anything about them, or to stir a finger to remove the sufferings they bring. But if these things are not the will of God at all, but simply the product of human bungling and selfishness and sin, and if accordingly God's mind and programme for the race is that they should one day be banished from the earth, then clearly we are not meant to lie down under them and accept them with resignation. Every man, woman and child who is enduring anguish to-day from the results of poverty, unemployment, or war is

contributing something to the total challenge which comes
to us like an urgent divine summons and incentive, to get
on with the work of world-rebuilding.

For consider. What do we expect to happen ? Do we
suggest that because poverty, unemployment, and war are
clearly contrary to the will of God, therefore God Himself—
without waiting for anything else—should suddenly intervene
and remove them ? But surely what is involved in the very
fact on which we have already dwelt—the fact that God
deliberately chose to make His children a fellowship and not
separate units—is that He means us to be the agents of His
purpose, and the channels of His providence to one another.
It would be wrong for a father to do all his boy's homework
for him, while the boy idled and played. And it would be
deleterious and disastrous if our Father in heaven were to
solve all our troubles for us, and land us in the New Jerusalem,
while we sat looking on. No, God's work waits upon the
awakening of man's conscience, and the dedicating of his
heart and hands in willing service.

Mark you, this assertion does not (as some timidly protest)
dim the glory of God by hinting at a failure in omnipotence,
a slur upon the divine sovereignty. For the fact is that it is
God Himself who, in His sovereign wisdom, has chosen to
have it so.

Hence we may say that those who suffer need never feel
that their pain and grief and trouble are quite negative and
unmeaning. They are doing the work of God by getting the
conscience of mankind awake. In that sense, the sufferers
of to-day are bearing the burden for the unborn generations
of to-morrow ; the cross they carry now is contributing to
the final liberation of the race ; their vicarious Via Dolorosa
is the highroad to the city of God. " Let Thy work appear
unto Thy servants, and Thy glory unto their children."
That is a real light on the darkness of the mystery.

We have thought in this connection of poverty, unemployment, and war ; but there is one fact we dare not miss out,

the grim fact of sickness and disease. "Why," we ask,
"does God allow that? Why does He permit the things
which are everyday occurrences in our hospitals? Why
does He not come in, and by one word of His mouth heal all
those dreadful ills and disabilities to which the flesh is heir?
Clearly they cannot be His will, for on almost every page of
the Gospels you see Jesus fighting the scourge of disease,
and refusing to be resigned to it. And if it is not His will,
why does He not remove it now?"

It may not be all the answer, but it is part of the answer
at least—that here, as in the other cases of poverty, unemployment, and war, God means *us* to be the messengers of His
providence to others. Here as there, God's will waits upon
the arousing of the conscience of His children. It is safe to
say that if the conscience of the world were sufficiently
awakened to spend on the constructive, glorious work of
eliminating disease and promoting health one-twentieth
of what the world is actually spending now on the negative
and horrible work of creating implements of death and
devastation, nearly all the scourges of sickness and disease
which are baffling us to-day would be gone from the earth
in a decade. Certainly we have no right to blame God for
not removing sickness and disease, as long as man goes on
destructively squandering the very resources for their
removing which God has put into his hands. Let us pray
rather that the conscience of humanity may be awakened
and aroused. Let us thank God for every token of that
awakening we encounter. With the vast spectacle of the
world's suffering confronting us, let us resolve before God
that we at least shall be broad awake to our responsibility,
realizing our function as mediators of His will and providence
to our fellow-men. And let us meanwhile recognize that all
the tragedies of this earth—by challenging the conscience
of humanity—are making a positive contribution to the
redeeming of the world; and that those who suffer and who
sorrow are fellow-labourers with God in the bearing of that

age-long cross by which at the end of the day all sufferings shall be mended and all sorrows lose themselves in perfect joy. This is our fourth beam of light—the awakening of the conscience of humanity.

There for the present we must leave it. Nothing has been said as yet about a fifth light, perhaps the greatest of them all, namely, the power of sorrow and trouble to chisel the spirit and beautify the character and deepen the whole tone of life. Something of that we shall see in our next study.

Yet must we not admit quite frankly that if these gleams of light we have been noticing were all the answer that could be given, if the very best one could do for a soul in trouble were to dwell upon the beneficence of inexorable law, our membership one of another, the wisdom of the divine impartiality, and the awakening of the conscience of humanity —if that were the sum-total of the comfort to be offered, one would hardly have the heart to dwell upon it at all? For what men and women want most in the hour of trouble is not an answer to a problem, but a power to carry them through. And indeed, even if the best and most completely satisfying solution of the mystery of suffering were available, that would not alter the fact that the actual suffering itself —the grim reality in experience—would still be there to be endured.

So we begin to see that there is a deeper question than Why?—namely, How? The ultimate demand is not " Why has this happened to me? " but " How, seeing it *has* happened, am I to face it? " And when you see that, suddenly the New Testament comes right in. The New Testament is not much concerned about Why?—for it knows that that is not the basic question. But it is desperately and magnificently concerned about How? It does not offer you a theory and an explanation : it offers you a power and a victory.

Thus far in our study we have been lingering in the forecourt of the Temple, for even the forecourt is not without its message for mind and conscience. But now we must press right in, until we reach the Holy Place ; and there we shall see, coming forth to meet us, God's answer—when we lift our eyes and gaze upon a cross.

XIV

GOD AND THE FACT OF SUFFERING

(3) Wearing the Thorns as a Crown

"Son though he was, he learned by all he suffered."—Heb. v. 8.
(Moffatt.)

LET me set down two incidents, as giving the keynote for our thoughts to-day.

In one of George Macdonald's books, there is a woman who has met a sudden sorrow. " I wish I'd never been made!" she exclaims petulantly and bitterly : to which her friend quietly replies, " My dear, you're not made yet. You're only being made—and this is the Maker's process." The other incident is from a play of Ibsen's. " Who taught thee to sing ? " one of the characters asks another. And the answer comes—" God sent me sorrow."

Here, then, we come in sight of this lovely and momentous fact—that in the making of the soul, and in the producing of life's deepest and profoundest harmonies, suffering has a positive and creative function to fulfil. This is the truth which Elizabeth Browning, in a sonnet entitled " Perplexed Music," has beautifully expressed—

> " We murmur,—' Where is any certain tune
> Or measured music, in such notes as these ? '—
> But angels, leaning from the golden seat,
> Are not so minded ; their fine ear hath won
> The issue of completed cadences."

Let us recall the path our thoughts have travelled up to this point. We passed in review three familiar solutions of the mystery, which respectively trace all suffering back to God, to sin, to an illusion in the human mind : and each of

147

these we rejected, as being inadequate to meet the facts.
Then we went on to ask whether, even if the darkness lingered,
we could not at least discern some beams of light to penetrate
the shadows ; and four such beams we found—the beneficence
of inexorable law, the significance of our membership one
of another, the wisdom of the divine impartiality, and the
awakening of the human conscience. We agreed that, while
much of the tragedy of life is clearly due to the inexorable
working of the laws which govern the universe, and to the
fact that in the great human family we are all so inextricably
mixed up together, and to the indiscriminate and impartial
way in which trouble falls on saint and sinner alike—we
agreed that we would not choose, even if we could, to live
in a world whose laws were not thus rigid and dependable ;
nor in a world where we could stand as isolated units, instead
of being members one of another ; nor in a world where God
favoured the righteous, and exempted good people from
trouble, and so made religion an insurance policy for those
who would pay the premium. We saw that in a world like
that our predicament would be far worse than in this actual,
present world about whose government we so readily and
perhaps so unthinkingly complain. Finally, we decided that
it was a main purpose of the sight of suffering to stab the
conscience of humanity awake, and to constrain us to realize
our function as agents of God's providence to our fellow-
men. These four beams of light in the darkness we discovered.

But now, as we continue on our road towards the final
Christian answer, there is a fifth light which flashes out
before us : and I cannot but believe that, in speaking of
this, one must be speaking to all. It is the gift which suffering brings to character, the contribution trouble makes to the
moulding and shaping and beautifying of the soul. Even of
Jesus it stands written that " He learned by all He suffered."

You will be aware that in pondering this deep matter we
are standing on holy ground, and dealing with experiences
most intimate and sacred. Here our thoughts begin to

converge upon the very heart of the mystery. Let me endeavour, for the sake of clarity, to take the truth which emerges at this point of our inquiry, and cast it into the form of three propositions.

The first is this. *It takes a world with trouble in it to make possible some of the finest qualities of life.* You do not need to be an art connoisseur to realize that it is an essential of a good picture that there should be shadow in it as well as light. You do not need to be a Bach or a Beethoven to understand how a discord can add excitement and beauty to a harmony. Now life is like that. If there were no risk and danger in life, where would fortitude and chivalry be? If there were no suffering, would there be compassion? If there were no discipline and hardship, would we ever learn patience and endurance? Construct a universe with no trouble in it, and immediately you banish some of the finest qualities in the world.

It is possible to go even further and say, If there were no fierce temptations, where would righteousness be? If there were no demons of darkness to be fought, where would be moral fibre or the thrill of victory? " My temptations," said Martin Luther, " have been my masters in divinity," and there is many a man to-day who could say the same. Do you remember William James' comment on the famous picture by Guido Reni in the Louvre which shows Michael with his foot on Satan's throat? " The world," mused James, " is all the richer for having a devil in it, *so long as we keep our foot upon his neck* "—a daring thought indeed, but you can see the truth behind it. It is the truth of which the apostle James had caught sight when he cried, " Count it all joy when ye fall into divers temptations." Relax life's discipline, remove its hardness, and who among us would be safe? Eliminate from our environment every element of difficulty and toughness and recalcitrance, and spiritual degeneration will not be long postponed. We know our own hearts well enough to realize the truth of this. And so, in the words of a fine poem by Aubrey de Vere—

> "Count each affliction, whether light or grave,
> God's messenger sent down to thee; do thou
> With courtesy receive him; rise and bow;
> And, ere his shadow cross thy threshold, crave
> Permission first his heavenly feet to lave;
> Then lay before him all thou hast."

If life is a warfare in which there is no discharge, an unceasing vigilance, a road beset with dangers, often rough and arduous and thorny, often darkened and obscure, always winding uphill steeply right on to the journey's end—let us not grumble and complain and indulge in petulant self-pity: let us rather thank God for it. For that is how souls are made. It takes a world with trouble in it to make possible some of the finest qualities in life.

Our second proposition is this. *It takes a world with trouble in it to satisfy man's demand for a dangerous universe.* I am sure the human heart's instinct for adventure is a real factor in the situation. We do not merely accept, because we can no other, the fact of a world which has the potentiality of trouble in it: we positively ask for it. From Abraham going out with the morning in his eyes, to Madame Curie wresting from Nature the secret of radium; from a little company of men in an upper room proposing to turn the world upside down, to Albert Schweitzer in his African forest, or the cancer-research student in a biological laboratory—the passion for adventure haunts the human spirit. Man knows that a hazardous universe is better far than any lotus-land of flabby and monotonous ease.

You will remember Aldous Huxley's picture, in *Brave New World*, of such a land, where all the harsh and cutting actualities of life have been magically cancelled out, and the intrusion of pain and trouble is unknown. "It is Christianity without tears," proudly declares the Controller, explaining

his secret. " But," cries another voice, " the tears are
necessary. You get rid of them. You just abolish the slings
and arrows. It's too easy. I don't want comfort. I want
God. I want poetry. I want real danger. I want freedom."
" But," says the Controller, " you'll be very unhappy." " I
claim," retorts the other, " the right to be unhappy ! " That
is a real instinct of the human spirit. Did not Lessing, the
great philosopher, declare that if God came to him, offering
in His right hand the whole of truth, and in His left the
search for truth and all the toil and travail and mistakes of
the search, he would choose the left and say, " Lord, give
me that ! "—not the finished article, but the zest and tang
and danger of the quest ? Did Sir J. M. Barrie not say on
one occasion, speaking of his youth—" The greatest glory
that ever came to me was to be swallowed up in London, not
knowing a soul, with no means of subsistence, and the fun of
working till the stars went out " ? And did not a greater
than Barrie cry—

> " I would hate that death bandaged my eyes, and forbore
>   And bade me creep past.
>   No ! let me taste the whole of it " ?

That is a native element of the human spirit. " The kingdom
of heaven," exclaimed James Denney, " is not for the well-
meaning : it is for the desperate ! " And when we chide
and censure God for creating a world which contains so many
possibilities of grief and suffering, let us remember that there
is that within us which craves risk, and that it takes an environment with trouble in it to satisfy man's demand for a
dangerous universe.

The third proposition is this. *It takes a world with trouble
in it to train men for their high calling as sons of God, and to
carve upon the soul the lineaments of the face of Christ.* Have
you ever watched a child facing one of those minor, desolating
tragedies, the breaking of a favourite doll, or the loss of some

precious childish treasure ?   What utter, overwhelming grief !
The whole world, to the child, looks black.   But you who
take that little one to your arms, to comfort his sad tears
away, know that his pitiful little calamity is not all loss and
darkness : for that is just life beginning those incomparably
important lessons which can be learnt no easier way.   And I
think that often the great Father of us all, looking down at
the griefs and troubles and heartbreaks of us, His little
children, knows—even while He takes us to His everlasting
arms to comfort us—that our day of darkness is not, as we
may think, sheer rack and ruin, but irreplaceably profitable
for the growth and making of the soul.

There was a startling thing that a professor of music in
Vienna said about a pupil of his own.   " She is a magnificent
singer," he said, " and yet there's just something lacking in
her singing.   Life has been too kind to her.   But if one day
it happened that some one broke her heart, she would be the
finest singer in Europe ! "   A crude, even callous, way of
putting it :   yet was there no truth there ?   Has it not
frequently been pointed out that the word " strain " has a
double meaning ?   It means stress, suffering, trouble ;   but
it means also music, it means song.   Is there a connection ?
Life says there is.   Has not all the world's greatest literature,
for instance, sprung from what Ernest Raymond has called
" the hurt of highly sensitized souls " ?   And have not all
the saints been heard praising God for the hour of midnight
and of tempest ?   " I have known," said Ralph Erskine,
lying racked with pain, " more of God since I came to this
bed than through all my life."   " The darkness," exclaimed
Kagawa of Japan, describing what it felt like when he thought
he was going blind, " the darkness is a holy of holies of which
no one can rob me.   In the darkness I meet God face to face."
And here is this amazing statement in *Hebrews*, surely one
of the most daring summaries of the life of Jesus ever penned :
" Son though He was, yet learned He by all He suffered ! "

Now it is here, I suspect, that there lies the clue to this

striking and astonishing fact—that the problem of evil is
raised far more often by the spectators of life than by the
actual combatants. You will nearly always find that the
loudest voices railing against providence and the universe—
the voices which keep crying out noisily " How can there be
a God, and life so tragic and unjust ? "—belong to the
spectators of life's sufferings, and not to the sufferers themselves. You will hardly ever find that the great sufferers
are the great sceptics. Quite the reverse. It is the spectators
—the people who are outside, looking on at the tragedy—
from whose ranks the sceptics come : it is not those who are
actually in the arena, and who know suffering from the
inside. Indeed, the fact is that it is the world's greatest
sufferers who have produced the most shining examples of
unconquerable faith. It is precisely from the company of
the sons and daughters of affliction that the most convinced
believers of all the ages have sprung. Who are the men whose
names stand on the dramatic roll-call of the faithful in
Hebrews ? Are they men whose days were happy and
unclouded and serene, souls for whom the sun was always
shining and the skies unvisited by storm or midnight ? If
any one imagines that such is the background of faith, let
him listen to this—" They were stoned, they were sawn
asunder, were tempted, were slain with the sword, destitute,
afflicted, tormented ; they wandered in deserts, and in
mountains, and in dens and caves of the earth." That,
declares the New Testament, has been in every age faith's
grim heredity ! And it is not from sheltered ways and quiet,
sequestered paths, it is from a thousand crosses, that the
cry ascends—" Hallelujah ! For the Lord God omnipotent
reigneth." " The bird on the branch," wrote Kierkegaard,
" the lily in the meadow, the stag in the forest, the fish in
the sea, and countless joyful people sing : God is love ! But
under all these sopranos, as it were a sustained bass part,
sounds the *de profundis* of the sacrificed : God is love."

What can be the reason ? Must it not be this, that

II

suffering initiates the soul into secrets which the mere onlooker
can never know ?   Here at any rate it is not true to say
that the spectators see most of the game.   They see less than
half the game.   They see the clouds and darkness and mystery
and tragedy, and so they bombard heaven with their petulant
accusations, and shout at God their resentful " Why ?   Why ?
Why ? "   But the sufferers themselves are not like that :
they are not caring to raise the question, for they have
made discoveries—through their sufferings—which are better
than any answer.

> " I walked a mile with Pleasure.
>   She chattered all the way,
> But left me none the wiser
>   For all she had to say.
>
> I walked a mile with Sorrow,
>   And ne'er a word said she ;
> But, oh, the things I learned from her,
>   When Sorrow walked with me ! "

I want you to verify this from your own experience.   If
some recording angel of God were to visit all our homes
to-day, and were to ask us individually to name the experiences which have blessed and taught us most, the influences which have brought the greatest enrichment to our
spirits, would it be the happy, carefree hours that the majority
of us would mention first ?   Surely that angel's book, when
he had finished with his task, would tell a very different tale.
It would tell, of course, of enrichment brought by God's
great gifts of love, and home, and nature, and the beauty of
the world ; but page after page there would be to tell how
trouble, and difficulty, and bereavement, and bitter disappointment, and hopes frustrated, and dreams that flickered
out and died—all the things which hurt and leave a mark—
had brought blessing by imparting new depth, new insight,
to the soul.   And these words that stand written in our text
of God's first-born child Jesus, God Himself may be using

as He looks upon others of His children here to-day : " Son though He was, yet learned He by what He suffered."

Is not this the great transfiguring discovery, that pain can be creative ? You do not just have to bear it negatively : you can use it positively. You can force it not to subtract but to add on something to your total experience. You can take what has all the appearance of being an ugly implement of destruction, and transform it into the loveliest weapon in all your armoury for the good fight of faith. This is what that modern saint von Hügel meant when he spoke about " grasping life's nettle." You can realize, like Paul, that the " thorn in the flesh," the thing which you feel inclined to call (as he did, to begin with) " the messenger of Satan to buffet me," is really not that, but Christ's own angel in disguise. By the grace of God, you can compel the darkest, bitterest experiences to yield up their hidden treasures of sweetness and light. And be very sure of this—no sorrow will have been wasted, if you come through it with a little more of the light of the Lord visible in your face and shining in your soul.

Suppose you had the power to turn back the pages of the volume of the years and make a new beginning ; suppose that the recording angel came to you to-day and said, " Here is your life—I am going to let you go back ten years, twenty years, forty years, and start all over again," what would you say ? Would you ask that the sorrows and hardships you have had should this time be eliminated ? No, surely not : for these things away, how much poorer you would be ! Leave it to Omar Khayyám and all his tribe of hedonistic sentimentalists to rail at " this sorry scheme of things," and to want a world with only pleasure in it and all the suffering left out ; leave it to them to talk in their histrionic and even hysterical way about "shattering this sorry scheme of things to bits and remoulding it nearer to the heart's desire." If " man's chief end " is to be pleased and petted and made comfortable, then Omar Khayyám was right.

But God has greater business in hand with you and me than that poor miserable ideal ; and if the world were nearer to the heart's desire, it might be further from the soul's salvation.   Don't think the trials and troubles are meaningless : one day you are going to look up into the face of God, and thank Him for every sorrow that drove its cruel ploughshare through your soul, and for every tear you ever shed.

> " The cry of earth's anguish went up unto God,—
>   ' Lord, take away pain,—
> The shadow that darkens the world Thou hast made,
>   The close-coiling chain
> That strangles the heart, the burden that weighs
>   On the wings that would soar,—
> Lord, take away pain from the world Thou hast made
>   That it love Thee the more.'
>
> Then answered the Lord to the world He had made,
>   ' Shall I take away pain ?
> And with it the power of the soul to endure
>   Made strong by the strain ?
> Shall I take away pity that knits heart to heart
>   And sacrifice high ?
> Will ye lose all your heroes who lift from the flame
>   White brows to the sky ?
> Shall I take away love that redeems with a price
>   And smiles through the loss,—
> Can ye spare from the lives that would climb unto mine
>   The Christ on His Cross ? ' "

No, God knows best ; and the true Christian reaction to suffering and sorrow is not the attitude of self-pity or fatalism or resentment : it is the spirit which takes life's difficulties as a God-given opportunity, and regards its troubles as a sacred trust, and wears the thorns as a crown.

Finally, let this be added—that the loveliest thing of all about the creative attitude towards suffering is that, if you are able to rise to it, not only do you develop your own character (for that might be a subtle form of spiritual egotism), but you become a source of blessing and of strength to others.

There is nothing on earth more beautiful to see than suffering transmuted into love. To say that the bitter cup can be drunk heroically is no more than every brave man knows already : but to say that one soul's hurt and suffering can distil out life and strength and healing for others—that is the everlasting miracle. But it happens. Do you remember how wonderfully it happened in the experience of John Bright? Richard Cobden called on his friend at Leamington one day, and found him in the depths of grief and despair. " All that was left on earth," said Bright afterwards, describing that bitter hour, " all that was left of my young wife, except the memory of a sainted life and our all too brief happiness, was lying still and cold in the room above us." But " after a time Mr. Cobden looked up and said, ' There are thousands of homes at this moment where wives, mothers, and children are hungry. Now, when the first paroxysm of your grief is past, I would advise you to come with me, and we will never rest till the Corn Law is repealed ! ' " And so John Bright's desolating sorrow was transmuted into loving service of others. Is it not a blessed thing to know that your own sorrows, if you deal with them creatively, can be changed and transformed into a love that will lighten the burden of the sorrows of the world ?

" If you deal with them creatively." " Yes," some one will say, " but that's just the difficulty. How am I to do it ? I see now that suffering is not so much a problem to be explained as a challenge to be met : but how am I to meet it ? There's the rub. By what power am I to emerge as victor over every evil thing that threatens to defeat me ? Unless you can tell me that, all you have been saying is left hanging in the air. It is true enough as far as it goes—but in the last resort it is not explanations I am wanting : it is power to ' stand in the evil day, and having done all, to stand.' "

I think you are right to make that demand. And I believe that to that quest there is no answer save one. The only answer that can ultimately suffice is God Incarnate on a cross, facing there in His own person the very worst that suffering and evil have ever done upon the earth : Christ reigning from that deadly tree, confronting the powers of darkness at last with the startling discovery that what they in their pride had deemed to be a smashing and decisive blow against the empire of light and love was destined to work out to their own undoing and disaster, and to their final irrevocable defeat. For still He comes to us, this Christ victorious over all the mystery of suffering and evil, and offers to make His triumph ours.

That will be the theme of our next, concluding study—that cross of victory, " towering o'er the wrecks of time," shattering the chains of despair and oppression of spirit in which man has been bound captive by the tyranny of the mystery of evil, and flooding the darkest valleys of his earthly pilgrimage with the authentic light of heaven.

XV

GOD AND THE FACT OF SUFFERING

(4) The Cross of Victory

"In all these things we are more than conquerors through him that loved us."—Rom. viii. 37.

THERE was a day when Thackeray was walking out the Dean road to the west of Edinburgh, with three companions ; and as they went, they passed a quarry, and saw, standing out against the sky above it, a great wooden crane —just like a cross. Whereupon Thackeray stopped and pointed, and murmured one word : "Calvary." Then they moved on, all suddenly grown silent, and pondering deeply.

Why did Thackeray do that ? Why should a novelist in the eighteen hundreds, and not a very spiritual one either, hark back instinctively to that death on the Judean hill long ago ? Why should a Roman gallows, and the strange Man who hung there, haunt the imagination and the conscience of the race ? How is it that we to-day, when the whole world is being shaken, are able without any sense of incongruity to sing—

"In the Cross of Christ I glory,
Towering o'er the wrecks of Time " ?

It is because man, in the depths of his spirit, has always been conscious that there, in that cross, God has spoken, and eternity has intersected history. It is because we know that, past all our fumbling human attempts to answer the problem of evil and suffering, here is *God's* answer. Here, if anywhere, is the clue to solve the riddle.

Indeed, I doubt whether, apart from the cross, any of the other interpretations that we can find is ultimately of much

avail. Think of the various beams of light in the darkness
which we have already noticed. They are certainly there,
shining through the midnight of our doubt and perplexity,
real hints and indications of a purpose and a meaning behind
the mystery. But leave out the cross, and will any of these
lights, or all of them together, prove adequate in the hour
of need ?

Will it comfort a bereaved mother, grief-stricken by the
death of a child, to be told about the beneficence of inexorable law, or the wisdom of the divine impartiality ? These
things may be true, as indeed they are : and a world in which
these things are facts, even though it may sometimes involve
tragedy for the individual, is undoubtedly—when you take
a total view—a better and happier place than any world
could be without them. But will it meet that broken-hearted
mother's need to go and tell her that ? Will that make her
" more than conqueror " ? Or again, if you have a friend
who is racked with fearful suffering, a martyr perhaps to
rheumatoid arthritis, will you talk philosophically about
the splendour of a dangerous universe and the providential
purposes of pain ? Or if there is someone who has come
through a shattering emotional crisis, some terrible disappointment which has left life bleak and empty, will you
go to such a one and point out the creative function of trouble
in producing character ? Is that the best that you can do ?
Frankly, I should not like your task.

Moreover, there are further difficulties. For instance, I
can quite well imagine some one wanting to argue like this :
" You say that suffering can make a positive contribution
to life. You say it can bring enrichment to the soul. Well
then, if that is so, why should we try to remove it ? If the
thing brings blessing, why work for its abolition ? Better
leave things as they are, and not meddle." Such an argument,
it is clear, might become a dangerous opiate, lulling the
human spirit into a false resignation and a pious acquiescence
in all manner of evil things. Yet the logic of the argument

seems sound enough. Is this perhaps a place where logic
breaks and goes to pieces on the facts of life ?

Or take this other difficulty, which comes from a totally
different direction. Even if we agree that God's aim is to
produce character, and that in this realm there can be " no
gains without pains," we are still left with the question
whether God could not have brought His sons and daughters
to the same goal by some less tragic road. It is not the fact
of suffering that baffles us, for we can see that we need it :
it is the frightful excess of the thing which seems so cruel and
senseless and superfluous. If God intends man's sanctifica-
tion, why could He not have thought out some kindlier way ?
Surely it ought not to have been beyond the divine inventive-
ness to do that ! Why should a man or a woman who is
already a saint have to suffer fiendish agonies ? If some one's
whole world is wrecked by a tragic bereavement, or an
accident which cripples for life, or an incurable illness, or a
defeat in love, might not such a one, hearing that these
things are the price of character, cry out " It's not worth the
price " ? Or if the nations go to war, if the cruelty of man
brings a new cataclysm upon the earth and millions are
driven into the valley of the shadow, it would be perfectly
true to say that such suffering was the price of God's gift to
man of the freedom of the will : whereupon might not some
one quite legitimately retort, " God's gifts at such a price
are too dear—nothing is worth a price like that " ? It is not
suffering that is the mystery : it is the superfluity of it that
baffles us. Leave out the cross—and will all the other beams
of light in the darkness lead you very far ?

There is still another difficulty. We talk about suffering
producing character. But it is perfectly obvious that it does
not always have that effect. It does not necessarily and
inevitably sanctify. Sometimes its effect is the exact reverse.
Sometimes it embitters. That gallant fighter, Robert Louis
Stevenson, dying of incurable illness, cried—" Sick or well,
I have had a splendid life ! " There was a soul whom pain

had ennobled. But how different the reaction of John Keats in one of his low, peevish moods : " Lord ! a man should have the fine point of his soul taken off to become fit for this world." It is no use talking of the beneficent influence of pain, as though the thing worked automatically : it doesn't. Take this deeply significant confession, from Vera Brittain's *Testament of Youth*, describing the legacy of war. " ' That's the worst of sorrow,' I decided, ' it's always a vicious circle. It makes one tense and hard and disagreeable, and this means that one repels and antagonizes people, and then they dislike and avoid one—and that means more isolation and still more sorrow.' " The fact is that in different lives suffering produces strangely different effects. One man loses his wife, and the loss makes him far more tender and gentle. Another faces the same loss, and it makes him hard and sullen. One woman has a great sorrow, and it turns her to God. Another passes through a similar experience, and she is never seen inside a Church again. It is all very well talking about the blessed ministry of trouble ; but it does not always end in blessing. St. Paul declared, " All things work together for good " ; but he knew better than to leave it at that. He never suggested that all things work together for good invariably and unconditionally. He said—" All things work together for good, *to them that love God*." What we have to recognize is that trouble in itself is neither positive nor negative, it is neutral : whether it is going to become positive or negative depends on the human reaction. Some, like that fine spirit Katherine Mansfield, have the grace to use it creatively. " I do not want to die," she wrote near the end, " without leaving a record of my belief that suffering can be overcome. For I do believe it. Everything in life that we really accept undergoes a change. So suffering becomes love." That is the positive reaction, forcing trouble to yield up its hidden, potential store of blessing. But we do not always rise to that, do we, when trouble comes ? " In all these things we are "—what shall we say ? " More than

conquerors " ? Would God it were true ; but alas, how often
our negative reaction baulks even His will to bless !

Now you see the crucial point we have reached. Decisively
this fact emerges—that man's main concern with the dark
fact of suffering is not to find an explanation : it is to find a
victory. It is not to elaborate a theory : it is to lay hold
upon a power. Even if you possessed the answer to the
riddle, even if you had it written down to the last detail and
could say, " There is the full and final explanation of the
problem of pain," that would not be enough, would it ?
For the pain itself would still have to be borne. That, in
the last resort, is the real demand of the human spirit—not
the explaining of this thing, but grace and help to bear it.
And that is why God gave us Christ.

Open your New Testament. On every page of it you see
the living God coming towards you, and holding out in His
hands—not a ready-made answer to the vexed questions of
the mind, but something better and diviner far—a liberating,
reinforcing power for the soul ! And this is why all the other
beams of light converge at length upon a cross. Towering
out of the dark it stands—God's everlasting answer to the
quest of all the world.

See how the cross transforms the age-long mystery. What
does it tell about the fact of suffering ?

It tells you that *God is in it with you.* We are so apt to
think of God as standing outside the sufferings of this world,
apart and aloof in the untroubled serenity of heaven. " In
this world," said Bacon, " God only and the angels may be
spectators " : and that is the implicit idea in many minds—
a spectator God, dealing out pains and chastisements to His
children, to see how they will react. But when I look with
unveiled eyes upon the cross ; when I grasp that the Sufferer
hanging there is not just another martyr dying for his faith,
but God incarnate, " love divine all loves excelling " ; when
I set that cross against the background of Christ's own

tremendous word, "He that hath seen Me hath seen the Father "—then my heart makes answer to those who speak of a remote spectator God, "You are wrong! God is not outside the tears and tragedy of life. In every pang that rends the heart of man, woman, or little child, God has a share. In every dark valley of trouble and suffering, God is always present."

One of the most moving scenes in English literature comes at the end of Dickens' *Tale of Two Cities*. The carts were rumbling through the thronged streets of Paris to the guillotine. In one of them there were two prisoners : a brave man who had once lost his soul but had found it again, and was now giving his life for a friend, and beside him a girl—little more than a child. She had seen him in the prison, and had observed the gentleness and courage of his face. "If I may ride with you," she had asked, thinking of that last dread journey, "will you let me hold your hand? I am not afraid, but I am little and weak, and it will give me more courage." So when they rode together now, her hand was in his ; and even when they had reached the place of execution, there was no fear at all in her eyes. She looked at the quiet, composed face of the man beside her, and said, "I think you were sent to me by Heaven."

What is the Christian answer to the mystery of suffering ? Not an explanation, but a reinforcing presence, Christ to stand beside you through the darkness, Christ's companionship to make the dark experience sacramental. "Yea, though I walk through the valley of the shadow of death, I will fear no evil : for Thou art with me "—and I think, Jesus, nay, I know, you must have been sent to me by Heaven.

"Look! " rang out the cry in the Book of Daniel, "Did we not cast three men into the furnace ? But now there are four ! Who is that other ? How comes He there, in the midst of the fire ? Is it a spirit, or an angel ? What if it should be God ? God walking there in the flame, to guard and save His own ! "

How different suffering becomes to those who have seen that vision ! It is not just that God knows, and sympathizes with you in your troubles, as any close friend might do. For He is so much closer than the closest friend. He is *in* you. And therefore your sufferings are His suffering, your sorrow His sorrow. Now that is true of all God's creatures. Just think what God's burden of suffering must be, when the pains of all the world are in His heart ! No man who has once grasped this will ever again rail at Providence for being unkind. All our loud accusations and complainings are silenced and grow dumb before that vision of the immeasurable agony of God.

But remember this : if God is in it with you, sharing your suffering, it is also true that *you are in it with God, sharing His redemptive activity and His victory.* It is by the travail of the soul of Christ, by the age-long sufferings of God, that the world is moving on to its ultimate redemption. " With His stripes we are healed." Hence what suffering does, when it comes one day to you, is to give you a chance to co-operate with God. Every soul that takes its personal griefs and troubles, and offers these up on the altar alongside the sacrifice of Jesus, is sharing constructively in that eternal passion of God by which all humanity shall at last find healing and peace. It is as though God said, in the day of darkness, " Here, my child, is something you can do for Me ! Here is your little share in the burden which I have been carrying from the foundation of the world and must carry till the day break and the shadows flee. Here is your part with Me in the age-long cross I bear." The man to whom that voice has spoken is trebly armed for the fight.

You must have noticed how often it happens that men and women who have met great tribulation in their own life come out of that experience with a wonderful new equipment for the service of God and their fellows. They reach the world's heart irresistibly where others only grope and fumble. The real healers of the wounds of mankind are those whose

own peace has been bought at a price, behind whose understanding and compassion and strong calm there lies some tale
of Peniel, some deep, ineffaceable memory of a valley of
shadow, and a lonely way, and a grim wrestling in the dark.
Mary Webb's lovely poem " A Factory of Peace " describes
it well :

> " I watched her in the loud and shadowy lanes
> Of life ; and every face that passed her by
> Grew calmly restful, smiling quietly,
> As though she gave, for all their griefs and pains,
> Largesse of comfort, soft as summer rains,
> And balsam tinctured with tranquillity.
> Yet in her own eyes dwelt an agony.
> ' Oh, halcyon soul ! ' I cried, ' what sorrow reigns
> In that calm heart which knows such ways to heal ? '
> She said—' Where balms are made for human uses,
> Great furnace fires, and wheel on grinding wheel
> Must crush and purify the crude herb juices,
> And in some hearts the conflict cannot cease ;
> They are the sick world's factories of peace.' "

If from one soul's hurt and conflict the balm of healing and
of peace can thus be distilled out for others ; if pain can be
transmuted into power ; if, under Christ, our sacrifices can
be taken up into His eternal sacrifice, and can be made
creative and redemptive—shall we still rail at life when it
grows hard, and brood bitterly upon its cruelty and injustice ? " Most gladly will I rather glory in my infirmities,
that the power of Christ may rest upon me."

God is in it with you, and you are in it with God—that
is the message of the cross on the mystery of suffering. And
that message means victory. There was victory at the cross
for Christ : and God wants you to know that there can be
victory at every cross for you. Will you try, for a moment
ere we close, to focus the picture and get the crucified figure
of the Christ right into the centre of your thoughts ? What
do you see ? It looks, at first glance, pathetically like defeat.

It looks like the intolerable climax of all the pathos of the
world. Here suffering and sorrow and the tragic element
in life seem to blot out our fragile hopes for ever. " O
Sacred Head, sore wounded, with grief and shame weighed
down ! " But you do not see the cross aright at a first glance.
You have to gaze and gaze again. And those who do that
make a marvellous discovery. They see, not Christ the
pain-drenched Sufferer, but Christ the mighty Victor. They
see the blackest tragedy of this earth becoming earth's most
dazzling triumph. Their cry is no longer—" O broken,
bleeding Victim, Thou mournful sacrifice ! "—not that, but
this : " O Jesus, King most wonderful, Thou Conqueror
renowned ! "

You have never truly begun to see the cross till you have
seen that. Is there not a wonderful sense of mastery, right
through the Passion narrative ? Listen to His own words :
" No man taketh My life from Me. I have power to lay it
down, and I have power to take it again." Is there not
royalty in that ? The irony of the situation was that Caiaphas,
poor blinded self-deluded creature, thought that he held the
reins and was the master-figure on the scene. " I have
power to lay My life down," said Jesus. Is that defeat ?
See Him marching steadfastly to Jerusalem. Mark well
His strong ineffable serenity through the last crowded,
terrible days. Watch His bearing before Pilate. See Him
on the cross refusing the drug they offered, that no atom of
the anguish should be evaded. Hark to the ringing shout
that broke upon the darkness : " It is finished ! " Is that
defeat ? Yes, it is : but not Christ's defeat—certainly not
that ! But the defeat of suffering. The defeat of the mystery
of evil, and of all the dark tragic powers of life—and Christ's
victory ! Thou art the King of glory, O Christ—Thou
Conqueror renowned !

" But what has all this to do with me ? " you ask. " Christ
may have conquered in the day of trouble, but my battle has
still to be fought—and what help is there in Calvary for me ? "

Surely the answer is clear. If evil at its overwhelming worst has already been met and mastered, as in Jesus Christ it has ; if God has got His hands on this baffling mystery of suffering in its direst, most defiant form, and turned its most awful triumph into uttermost, irrevocable defeat—if that in fact has happened, and on that scale, are you to say it cannot happen on the infinitely lesser scale of your own life by union with Christ through faith ? If you will but open the gateways of your nature to the invasion of Christ's Spirit, you will do as He did, and " lead captivity captive." " In all these things," wrote one who had tested the promise of God to the hilt in the worst tragedies of life, and therefore had a right to speak, " in all these things "—these desolating, heartbreaking things which happen to the sons of men, these physical pains, these mental agonies, these spiritual midnights of the soul—" we are more than conquerors," not through our own valour or stoic resolution, not through a creed or code or philosophy, but " through Him that loved us "—through the thrust and pressure of the invading grace of Christ.

That is the only answer to the mystery of suffering : and the answer is a question—Will you let God in to reign ? The answer is not a theory. It is a life. It is a dedicated spirit, a fully surrendered soul. That is the one finally valid answer. May God make that answer ours !

XVI

WHEN GOD'S PEACE GUARDS THE DOOR

" Never be anxious, but always make your requests known to God in
prayer and supplication with thanksgiving ; so shall God's peace, that
surpasses all our dreams, keep guard over your hearts and minds in Christ
Jesus."—PHIL. iv. 6, 7. (MOFFATT.)

" NEVER be anxious," says St. Paul. An easy thing to
say : a terribly difficult thing to practise ! If this is
to be made the test of our personal Christianity, how many
of us will come through with flying colours ? " 'Tis not
dying for a faith is so hard," says one of Thackeray's characters, " man in every age has done that ; 'tis the living up
to it that is difficult, as I know to my cost." So when Paul
comes to us, amid the rush and fever and fret and difficulty
and distraction of our common days, and bids us never be
anxious, we feel inclined to say, " Come down to earth !
Who can live up to that ? "

What scores of familiar anxieties get woven into the
pattern of life ! Here is a business man, worried almost to
breaking-point by the uncertainty of the future. Here is a
parent, troubled and perplexed by the differences in outlook
between one generation and another. Here is a home where
some one is lying ill. Here is a man who has been out of
work for years, and is feeling now that he is not wanted, and
is of no use at all to any one. Here is another who is half-
killed with overwork. Here is a girl who has set her heart
on some fine and noble vocation out in the world, but she is
needed at home, and the door of opportunity seems closed.
Here is a young fellow with high ideals, and he is beginning
to realize how much moral compromise the world tolerates
and even demands, and how difficult it is going to be to keep

12

his ideals untarnished. Here is a student at the University worrying about a career. Here is a soul tasting the full bitterness of being lonely. Here is another facing a difficult task with limited resources. Here is one afraid of death. Here is another even more afraid of life. There seems no end to the anxieties which are woven, as by the hand of fate, into the texture of life's pattern.

Yet here is Paul calmly advising us, " Never be anxious." I think our first instinctive reaction would be to say : " This man does not know what he is talking about. If he can't say something more helpful than that, he might at least hold his peace and not mock us ! "

Perhaps some of those Philippians, whom Paul is here addressing, may have felt like that. For it needed strong nerves—to live the Christian life in Philippi. It was like living on the edge of a volcano. Persecution was in the air. The atmosphere was tense with hostility. At any moment, subterranean forces might flare up overwhelmingly. Yet he dared to say, " Never be anxious," apparently expecting them to take him at his word, and to rise to it. What an optimist ! What a mocker !

Yes, it would have been mockery, *if the man had stopped there*. That is where Stoicism puts the full stop. When Stoicism has said a thing like that, it has no more that it can say. " Keep calm. Be brave. Be passionless. Never be anxious." And that is all. Not a word more. But where the Stoic ends, Jesus Christ begins. There is no full stop there in Christianity. The Christian gospel runs right on. " Never be anxious, *but* "—and then comes the secret of the defeat of anxiety, the strategy of the saints, the method by which the victory that seemed impossible is put within our grasp—" but always, in everything, make your requests known to God in prayer and supplication with thanksgiving." That is the authentic apostolic way with every trouble and every worry in the world. *Bring God into it*. Get the horizons of the divine around it. Undergird it with the love of Heaven.

Note Paul's language. Note that significant " always," in everything. Has it ever come home to you with the force of a personal discovery that you can talk to God about absolutely anything—anything whatever that is burdening your secret soul—that that, indeed, is what God desires, not stereotyped prayers daily following a beaten track, nor vague generalities skimming the surface of the real difficulty or problem, but your most intimate confidences about everything ? There is an Old Testament historian who tells how once Hezekiah the king received a disturbing letter from one of Sennacherib's envoys. It was the kind of letter to send a man off his sleep for nights. But Hezekiah, says the narrative, having read it, " went up into the house of the Lord, and spread it before the Lord." And whatever the invading anxiety is, you can always do that with it. It is a marvellously healing thing, to take God into your confidence about everything.

But look at Paul's strategy again. " Prayer and supplication *with thanksgiving* "—that, standing as it does in a message about worry, is mightily significant. When you are feeling fretted and unhappy, says Paul in effect, when life is doing its level best to thwart your plans and defeat your hopes, pause and remember the lovely things on the other side, all God's troops of stars amid the darkness. Turn over the page to the credit side of the account. Do you mean to tell me, asks the apostle, that that side is a blank ? Or that there are only one or two trivial entries there which do not really count at all ? Look again ! Why, even when life is at its worst, that credit side is loaded and packed full with mercies. " Bless the Lord, O my soul, and forget not all His benefits ! " Forget not you are His debtor for every breath you draw ; His debtor for life and intellect, and memory and hope, and the courage to endure ; His debtor for day and night, and the wind on the heath, and the light of sunset skies ; His debtor for every moment of insight, every clasp of the hand of a friend, every atom of beauty in the world around you, every experience of forgiveness at the foot of the cross of Jesus. Be sure you see to it, says Paul, that you face your difficulties and frustrations in the light of your mercies and blessings, " in prayer and supplication—with thanksgiving."

All the saints are with him there. There was a brave servant of Christ of a former generation, Allan Gardiner of Patagonia. His life as a missionary was a record of terrible sufferings and privations ; and he was found at last lying dead on the shore beside an upturned boat. And there, where it had fallen from his hands, was his diary, telling of the hardships he had been through, the hunger and thirst, the wounds and loneliness. But the last sentence, some words pencilled scarce legibly before the dying hand could write no longer, was this : " I am overwhelmed with a sense of the goodness of God." Everything was lost— home, love, and human fellowship, and now life itself was going : and yet, on the very edge of the last silence—" overwhelmed with the goodness of God ! " And shall we say we have nothing to thank God for ? Take life even at its most hurting and most difficult : have we no cause for praise ? "Always," says Paul, " in prayer and supplication—with thanksgiving."

Now I think we can see just how the release from anxiety is achieved. It comes along three lines.

First, *prayer sets things in true perspective.* We are too near our own problems to estimate them correctly. Just as an artist, working on some wide canvas, has to stand back now and again and view it from a distance, so you and I, if we are to keep our proportions right, have to stand back occasionally from the noise and bustle of life into that healing silence which is the presence of the eternal God. "At last," cried an old saint in an hour of victory, " I have made firm my staggering soul ! " That is what prayer does—steadies the jaded nerves, lifts the fevered spirit into a calmer, ampler air, brings a blessed silence in the din of life's conflict, and

makes you sure, as nothing else can do, that the eternal God
—who is the deep, central peace of the universe—is your
refuge, and that underneath are the everlasting arms. So
prayer makes firm the staggering soul. It sets things in their
true perspective.

> " Breathe through the heats of our desire
>   Thy coolness and Thy balm ;
> Let sense be dumb, let flesh retire ;
> Speak through the earthquake, wind, and fire,
>   O still small voice of calm ! "

Second, prayer achieves release from anxiety *by bringing
our will into line with God's will.* Am I misreading the
situation when I say that a major cause of the restless,
unsatisfied feeling and of the frictions that spoil the soul's
serenity is simply this—that our will and God's will are
speaking with different voices ? God's will says, " Do this " ;
and our personal inclinations say, " No—do that ! " And,
of course, that means dispeace and civil war within. But what
happens in prayer is that we take our life and deliberately
put it under God's command. We say " No " to self, and
" Yes " to God. In our own degree we do what Jesus did
that dark night in the garden, when again and again He
prayed the quiet, deliberate words, " Not what I will, but
what Thou wilt." To do that may mean some kind of
Gethsemane for us, as it meant for Him ; but on the further
side of such praying I think we shall always find—what
Jesus found—a wonderful sense of release and liberation,
and a serenity which the world is powerless to destroy.

In the third place, prayer achieves release from anxiety
*by liberating within us new resources of power for handling the
difficult business of living.* Life is not easy to manage, and I
dare say we have all had days when we have felt hopelessly
inadequate ; and it is a nervy, anxious task confronting
complicated situations with deficient interior reserves. At
such times life is apt, as we say, to " get on top of us " ;
and—like Isaiah, crying, " Woe is me, for I am undone "—

we feel tragically ineffective and futile. But what happens
when you pray—if it is true prayer—is that you are con-
necting yourself up with an unseen environment charged with
creative power ; and down the connecting-line of prayer the
infinite energies and resources of that unseen world come
flowing into your own life : so that now—again like Isaiah
—you can confront the hardest task, the most difficult
situation, not indeed with a sense of self-sufficiency, but with
a grateful knowledge of God's adequacy, and can say " Here
am I : send me ! "

> " Lord, what a change within us one short hour
>   Spent in Thy presence will avail to make !
>   What heavy burdens from our bosoms take ;
>   What parched grounds refresh, as with a shower ! . . .
> Why, therefore, should we do ourselves this wrong,
>   Or others, that we are not always strong ;
>   That we are ever overborne with care ;
>   That we should ever weak or heartless be,
>   Anxious or troubled, when with us is prayer,
>   And joy and strength and courage are with Thee ? "

Now observe how Paul proceeds. " So shall God's peace
keep guard over heart and mind." What a lovely phrase
it is—God's peace ! It means the very peace that dwells
in the heart of God Himself. Nothing less than that is the
promise. It shall " stand as sentry " to your soul. The
word he used was military ; and it must have had a special
force for his readers. For Philippi was a Roman colony, and
there was a garrison in occupation ; and many a time his
readers had watched Roman soldiers mounting guard, and
the sentinels patrolling the gates. That, declares the apostle,
with his vivid imagination, is what the peace of God will do
for you, once you really possess it in your heart. It will
guard the entrance. It will hold the fort against every
threatening intruder.

If you accept that picture, then inner peace is a very
different thing from what many people imagine. It does

not mean escaping the battle, or having a comfortable lotus-land to dwell in. It does not mean " O for the wings of a dove, for then would I fly away and be at rest ! " It does not mean that the Christian, any more than any one else, is promised exemption from the troubles and difficulties and disappointments of life. It does not mean that. It certainly did not mean that for Paul, with his floggings and stonings and shipwrecks and imprisonments, and the daily care of all those worrying churches. It did not mean that for Jesus, despised and rejected and cut off from the land of the living. Not for a moment does it suggest that in return for our prayers or piety God will deal out preferential treatment, or give us an easy passage through the troubles and tangles of life. But it does mean this far more glorious thing —that when troubles come, as come they must, the central citadel which is the soul shall stand inviolate, for God Himself will garrison it, and God's peace guard the door.

Such is the victory of the God-centred life, and such its strong, ineffable serenity. It " passeth all understanding," says Paul. You may have seen it, he means, on the face of a friend who has found it ; you may have watched its transforming influence at work in one life here and another there ; but you cannot realize its power or blessedness until you have it for your own possession. For it surpasses all our dreams.

Have we reached that stage yet, I wonder ? I dare say there are a good many of us who would confess that we have had hours when the peace of God was a reality, and then we have lost it again. Perhaps for days or months on end we possessed it : and then, disappointingly, it vanished from our grasp. Well, even our defeats can be of value, even our breakdowns of serenity can teach us something. This vital lesson they can teach us—that the peace of God is not something to be captured once for all : it is something requiring to be recaptured all over again every day. It is achieved, not by one big, spectacular resolution, but by a daily re-surrender of life to God, an ever renewed grip of the only Hand that can hold us upright and keep us safe.

This is why Paul closes with the words " in Christ Jesus " —" the peace of God shall guard heart and mind *in Jesus*." For there is the ultimate secret—not fine resolutions, but contact with a dynamic, radiant Personality ; not laborious efforts at self-improvement, but the transfiguring influence of a friendship with the noblest, strongest, and most understanding Friend in all the world. If only we would start each day with Jesus, reaching out from the dust and darkness of this low earth to clasp the hand of our Friend, the ever-old, ever-new miracle would happen once again, and our restless hearts find rest and healing in the invincible peace of God.

THE COMMUNION OF THE HOLY GHOST

" I think it is possible on earth to build a young New Jerusalem, a little new heaven of this surpassing love."—SAMUEL RUTHERFORD.

"Some seek a Father in the heavens above;
    Some ask a human image to adore;
    Some crave a Spirit vast as life and love;
    Within Thy mansions we have all and more."
                                        GEORGE MATHESON.

XVII

THE MOTHER OF US ALL

" Walk about Zion, and go round about her: tell the towers thereof. Mark ye well her bulwarks, consider her palaces; that ye may tell it to the generation following."—Ps. xlviii. 12, 13.

" Our feet shall stand within thy gates, O Jerusalem. Jerusalem is builded as a city that is compact together."—Ps. cxxii. 2, 3.

" If I forget thee, O Jerusalem, let my right hand forget her cunning. If I do not remember thee, let my tongue cleave to the roof of my mouth; if I prefer not Jerusalem above my chief joy."—Ps. cxxxvii. 5, 6.

" I John saw the holy city, new Jerusalem, coming down from God, out of heaven, prepared as a bride adorned for her husband."—Rev. xxi. 2.

THERE are some words in our language whose very sound has the power to bring troops of memories thronging into our minds. There are certain place-names which unroll immediately before us the living pageant of history. Such a word, for example, is Athens. You have only to mention Athens to set men dreaming of the glory that was Greece, of the deathless achievements of the Hellenic spirit in the realms of beauty, culture, and romance, of the miraculous forward thrust and momentum which the Greek mind gave to the slow evolution of man's conceptions of truth and freedom and fidelity and the dignity of the soul. Such a word, again, is Rome. You have only to mention that name to conjure up a vision of the majesty of law, the drive and dynamic of an incomparable genius for ordered rule and government, the welding together of a turbulent mass of heterogeneous, divisive elements into a solid and enduring unity. What sounds of marching legions, of laden caravans of commerce rolling in from all the ends of the earth, of the felling of forests and the cutting of the great roads, of trumpets and battlesongs and the praise of famous men, lie in the one word Rome !

But there is another name which across the centuries has struck deeper chords and awakened stronger emotions in the human breast than either Athens or Rome : and that is Jerusalem. Into that word there have passed the most intimate and poignant loves and longings of unnumbered men and women, the aspirations of a host of nameless saints, memories that gather in from family altars where our own fathers in God have prayed, and thoughts that often lie too deep for tears. We may never have left the town or hamlet of our birth, nor stirred beyond our native shores : and yet most surely our feet have stood within the gates of Jerusalem, and our eyes have marked her bulwarks, and her palaces and towers. Here is our true citizenship, here our spiritual home ; and of Zion it shall be said, " This man was born in her."

Consider for a moment what Jerusalem meant to the Jew himself. Think of the associations and the sentiments which that dear name carried with it. It stood, first, for *history*. Jerusalem, to the Hebrew mind, meant David the shepherd-king, the man after God's own heart, and Solomon in all his glory, the builder of the temple ; and Hezekiah who had seen the terrible tide of Sennacherib's invasion roll thunderously up to the very walls of the capital, only to be halted there, and scattered in one memorable night, as by the dramatic judgment of the Lord. It meant the discipline and heartache of the years of foreign domination, when the chosen people passed through a seven times heated furnace of oppression, and the glory seemed to have departed. It meant the thrilling hour of national resurrection, when the captive daughter of Zion arose from the dust, and put on her beautiful garments, a queen once more. All the magnificence and sorrow of ages past, all the hope for years to come, were for the Jewish patriot gathered up and centred in the word Jerusalem. " Walk about Zion, and go round about her : tell the towers thereof. Mark ye well her bulwarks, consider

her palaces ; that ye may tell it to the generation following."
Jerusalem stood for history.

But more than that, it stood for *religion*. It stood for
worship. For Jerusalem meant the temple, and the temple
meant God. However far the wandering Jew might roam
around the world, that temple on the hill, like a spiritual
magnet, drew his thoughts continually ; and when Daniel
in Babylon knelt to say his prayers, the window of his room
was open towards Jerusalem. Young men saw visions, and
old men dreamt dreams ; and of all the visions and the
dreams, the dearest and the best was this—a day when the
roads of the world would be full of pilgrim hosts, not Jews
only but men and women of every nation under heaven, all
singing the songs of Zion, all praying for the peace of Jerusalem, as they set their faces towards the temple, for the sake
of Zion's God. Jerusalem, to the Hebrew mind, meant
religion.

But once again, it stood for *home*. There is no literature
in the world in which the sentiment of home, and the desperate
weariness of homesickness, speak so poignantly as in the
Bible. The Jew was so often a man with nowhere to lay his
head, envying the foxes their holes and the birds of the air
their nests, and crying out in the bitterness of his soul for the
hills of his native Judah and the familiar landmarks of the
dear city of God, so dream-haunted, so steeped in sacred
memory ; just as an emigrant on the vast Canadian prairie
might see again in dreams " the lone shieling on the misty
island," and hear the sound of the sea on a Hebridean shore ;
or just as a wanderer in a far country might reach one day
the very breaking-point of misery and loneliness and desolation, and cry " I can endure it no longer, I will arise and go
to my father ! " All exiles speak a universal language.

" Blows the wind to-day, and the sun and the rain are flying,
   Blows the wind on the moors to-day and now,
 Where about the graves of the martyrs the whaups are crying,
   My heart remembers how ! "

That is Robert Louis Stevenson, dreaming of the home of
his fathers and the land of his birth. But it was a Jew to
whom it was given to express once for all time, and for every
exiled soul, the passion of home and all the plaintiveness of
parting, the intolerable yearning of the heart, saddened by an
irrevocable farewell—" By the rivers of Babylon, there we
sat down ; yea, we wept, when we remembered Zion. We
hanged our harps upon the willows in the midst thereof. For
there they that carried us away captive required of us a song :
and they that wasted us required of us mirth, saying, Sing us
one of the songs of Zion. How shall we sing the Lord's song
in a strange land ? If I forget thee, O Jerusalem, let my right
hand forget her cunning "—and then the pent-up emotion
of the man breaks through restraint at last and surges out
vehemently, almost violently, in words of unbearable pathos
—" if I do not remember thee, let my tongue cleave to the
roof of my mouth ; if I prefer not Jerusalem above my chief
joy." That is not rhetoric, or fine writing, or poetry with an
eye to effect : it is a sob wrung from the heart by life's
immemorial pain.

> " Jerusalem, my happy home,
>   Would God I were in thee !
> Would God my woes were at an end,
>   Thy joys that I might see ! "

History, religion, home—all these, for the Hebrew mind,
were gathered up into the name Jerusalem. Nor did it mean
less for Christ Himself. You will remember that there are
just two places in the Gospels where the evangelists tell us
that Jesus wept. Once it was at the grave of His friend
Lazarus ; and once when, coming round the shoulder of the
Mount of Olives, He saw the city of David spread out before
Him in the sunshine, and stood gazing at it with eyes dimmed
with a sudden mist of tears. " He beheld the city," says the
evangelist, " and wept over it "—tears of infinite tenderness
and compassion, and of bitterest regret for what might have

been. " O Jerusalem, Jerusalem, how often would I have gathered thy children together, and ye would not ! " Dear as the springtime to the earth, dear as remembered love in lonely days—so dear was Jerusalem to the heart of the Redeemer.

But what of ourselves ? Has all this any relevance to our own life, in this actual sinning, struggling, warring world ? Surely the significant fact is this, that everything that Jerusalem meant for the Jew has now passed into the very blood of the race. The actual city which Jesus saw from Olivet we may never have set eyes upon : yet the world's heart turns thither as the needle to the pole. We too have walked those streets where in ancient time the feet of Jesus went ; we have dreamt those dreams and sung those songs of Zion, and inscribed our names on the burgess roll of her free citizens ; we, too, have seen the sun flaming down behind the battlements and ramparts of the city of God. People who scarce ever moved from the village where they were born have died with this dear name upon their lips ; and St. Paul was speaking for you and me no less than for his own contemporaries when, in his letter to the Galatians, he flung out the magnificent sentence—" Jerusalem which is above is free, which is the mother of us all ! "

In particular, I ask you to observe that this name gathers up into itself three of the deepest constituent elements of our nature.

The first is *the hunger for God*. I am quite sure that the cares and problems which infest our human life, the incessant pressure of its difficult demands, would soon end in suffocating and stifling the soul within us—were it not for this, that daily we can open our windows towards Jerusalem. That instinct for God burns within us, and will not be denied. And even if sometimes it may seem dead and buried, even if in some lives the winds of doubt and denial may appear to have blown out the light for ever, even if there is nothing

left but the cold grey ashes of an unbelieving materialism, a
heart invulnerable to all spiritual influences and immune
from the invasions of divine grace, even then (this is the marvel
of it, and the boundless hope) there is no saying when that
dead thing within may resurrect itself, and go crying for the
God who is its home ! For as Jerusalem haunted the dreams
of the Jew, so we are all God-haunted spirits.

And the blessed thing is this, that there are none of our
human defences—not self-sufficiency, not deliberate prayer-
lessness, not iron walls of depression and despair, not even
downright flagrant sin—none of them which can guarantee
infallibly to keep God out. Believe me, the crucial fact
about your nature and mine is not the desperate limitations
that vex and thwart and shackle us, it is not the awful
solitude in which we sometimes seem to stand, it is not the
tyranny of moods or the obsession of inferiority or the burden
of defeat : the crucial fact is the capacity for God with which
we have been born, which not " tribulation or distress or
persecution or famine or nakedness or peril or sword " or
shame or sin can ever finally eradicate. " If I forget thee,
O Jerusalem." But I can't ! For God will not be suppressed.
God haunts, disturbs, tracks down at last, confronts me with
a cross. And there, there only, can my restless, hungry
heart find peace. " He loved me, and gave Himself for me."

Beyond this hunger for God, there is a second deep
constituent element of our nature connoted by the word Jerusalem, namely, *the craving for the fellowship of a beloved
community*. Man was never made to stand alone. He was
made for fellowship. He knows that without fellowship he
is a poor creature, only half alive. He needs the society of
his brethren. Even in his religion, yes, in his religion more
than anywhere else, he feels the necessity of breaking down
his isolation, of standing with others, as he turns his face
towards the challenge of the ultimate mysteries of life and
death and eternity. He wants a satisfying community of
kindred minds. He wants the kingdom of heaven. He

wants the city of God. He wants—for this is what it comes to, however derisively he may deny it—he wants the Church.

So it was when William Blake dreamt his dream of " building Jerusalem in England's green and pleasant land." So it was when John of the Revelation brought his book to a close with a vision that has moved and warmed and thrilled the hearts of men and women ever since : " I saw the holy city, new Jerusalem, coming down from God, out of heaven, prepared as a bride adorned for her husband." And so it is to-day wherever—over against the world, challenging the world, refusing to identify itself with the prevailing voices of the world—stands the Christian community, the nucleus and earnest of the new world-order that is to be. It matters not how plain the buildings where the little company gathers for its worship, it matters not how many flaws and imperfections a sneering critic may detect : wherever two or three are met in Christian fellowship, there is the city of God. There is the kingdom of heaven already in action. The critic, entering the door of some humble meeting-house or chapel, and looking superciliously around at the bare walls and the little group of toil-worn, undistinguished men and women, may say—" What have I come to ? There is nothing here of worth or interest." If only his blind soul could see ! " Ye are come unto Mount Zion, the city of the living God, the heavenly Jerusalem, and to an innumerable company of angels, and to Jesus." What matter though the outsider notice only that the shrine is poor, and the faces dull and ordinary, and the words of worship stammering and broken ? Christ sees the shining Bride He loves eternally : the new Jerusalem flaming down from God, all-glorious out of heaven.

Finally, there is *the instinct of immortality*. That is the last deep element of our nature symbolized by the name Jerusalem. We have an intuition that death, when it comes to us one day, will not destroy or render void one atom of our essential being. We have a strange impregnable conviction that death cannot stop us, that we shall go right through it

13

and out at the other side, and that beyond the dark valley
there will be the sunshine of an eternal morning. Long
before Shakespeare had ever penned a line or put his famous
soliloquy on death and the beyond into Hamlet's mouth,
there was a Christian monk in a French monastery, Bernard
of Cluny, who with far deeper insight saw behind the darkness
of the grave, and spoke not of an " undiscovered country
from whose bourne no traveller returns," but taught the
Church to sing—

> " O sweet and blessèd country,
> The home of God's elect !
> O sweet and blessèd country,
> That eager hearts expect ! "

Mere sentiment ? When Bernard wrote " Jerusalem the
golden " eight hundred years ago, the world he saw around
him was rotten to the core, and ripe for doom, and plunging
back to chaos and primeval darkness : and the hearts of the
faithful remnant, Christ's pitiful minority, looked wistfully
beyond earth's miseries and sorrows, and grew homesick for
heaven. Is the instinct of immortality, then, mere sentimental
otherworldliness ? The nostalgia of the weak and cowardly ?
On the contrary ! It is the virile faith of the heroic and the
strong. It is the true essential realism. Let your blind
worldling say what he likes : we *are* strangers here, and exiles,
and pilgrims of eternity. This is not our rest ! The earth is
too narrow to hold us. Our citizenship is in the heavenly
Jerusalem ; and in our Father's house are many mansions.

> " Jesus, in mercy bring us
> To that dear land of rest,
> Who art, with God the Father
> And Spirit, ever blest."

XVIII

NO BORROWED CREED

" That which was from the beginning, which we have heard, which we have seen with our eyes, which we have looked upon, and our hands have handled, of the Word of life ; (For the life was manifested, and we have seen it, and bear witness, and shew unto you that eternal life, which was with the Father, and was manifested unto us ;) That which we have seen and heard declare we unto you, that ye also may have fellowship with us : and truly our fellowship is with the Father, and with His Son Jesus Christ."—1 JOHN i. 1–3.

ONE of the greatest achievements of English music in the realm of oratorio is " The Dream of Gerontius," by the late Sir Edward Elgar. At the end of the original score of the work, which has been presented to the Oratory at Edgbaston, Birmingham, Elgar wrote these words—" This is the best of me ; for the rest, I ate, and drank, and slept, and loved and hated, like another ; my life was as the vapour, and is not ; *but this I saw and knew* ; this, if anything of mine, is worth your memory." There was the great composer's testimony that the music of that mighty work was given to him by direct inspiration ; that it laid hold upon him coercively and creatively and irresistibly, a first-hand, authentic revelation of the eternal beauty and pathos at the heart of things.

" This I saw and knew." When a man speaks like that, the world is bound to listen. And my purpose to-day is to ask, Can we speak thus of our religion ? Can we, in an age when subtle forces are striving to undermine the bases of conviction, when specious voices are busy whispering and hinting that the faith we so much prize is nine-tenths credulity and bad logic and wishful thinking and muddled reasoning, when ethical axioms which once held the field unchallenged are widely repudiated, and beliefs which seemed inviolable find themselves fighting for their life, and even religious people grow uncertain in their attitude and vague about their witness and excessively problem-conscious—can we, in such an age, stand up and confront the whole world with the irrefragable assurance of an authentic, first-hand experience, and say of our religion, what Elgar said of his music, " This I have seen! This verily I know " ?

It is particularly important that we should face ourselves with this question at the present juncture : and that for two reasons. The one is this. Our religion is going to make absolutely no impact whatever on the world in which we live and move and have our being, is going to leave not the faintest impression on the paganism around, unless it is our own assured possession. There is nothing infectious about a second-hand faith. If you have borrowed a creed, accepted it on hearsay, you will never set another soul on fire with it. " If the trumpet give an uncertain sound, who shall prepare himself to the battle ? " If Christ's people are hesitant and doubtful about fundamentals, where is the dynamic for a crusading Christianity to come from ? There are some fine words of John Ruskin's in *Modern Painters* which come to mind. " The greatest thing a human soul ever does in this world is to *see* something, and tell what he *saw* in a plain way. Hundreds of people can talk for one who can think, but thousands can think for one who can see. To see clearly is poetry, prophecy, and religion—all in one." What the world supremely needs to-day is an army of men and women who, whether they say it with their lips or not, will unmistakably declare it by the light in their eyes and the serenity of their spirits and the decision of their bearing : " Here stand I ! I can no other. For this I have most surely seen ! This God revealed by Christ I know."

But if this matter is urgent from the point of view of the

impact of our faith upon the world, it is urgent also because
of the trials, frustrations, disappointments, and disasters
which our own souls are almost bound to meet on their
journey through this life. And if perchance the thought has
crossed your mind that to dwell upon the urgency of religious
vision and a first-hand faith is to wander off into abstractions
and irrelevancies, I beg you to think again. There is nothing
which is more dead on the mark at this moment. The fact
is, the hour may come when everything about you—your
happiness, your grip and self-control, your resilience and
tenacity, your very sanity and reason—will depend on
precisely this thing which you are calling irrelevant, the
degree to which you have built up, or have failed to build up,
an assured and vital faith. When Paul, writing to his Galatian
converts, penned the most moving words, " My little children,
of whom I travail in birth again until Christ be formed in
you," do you think he was just being rhetorical and declama-
tory and sentimental ? No, what made him feel and speak
like that was his piercing sense of the inadequacy of a vague
and indeterminate faith amid the strains and stresses of this
menacing world, his passionate longing to see those people
whom he loved secure in the possession of an experience
compelling and incontrovertible and decisively their own. It
was the thought—" They must realize God through Christ !
Else life will beat them in the end. They will never be able
to stand it ! " " How wilt thou do," cries Jeremiah, " in
the swelling of Jordan ? " And since none of us knows how
soon, for him, for her, some hour of terrible testing may
arrive, nor how desolating the experience may be, how deep
the waters to be crossed and how dark the night to be
endured, it is the most urgent of all concerns that each of
us should reach a point where we can say—" Here at least
is something that will never fail me ! This master-fact I
have seen. This spiritual reality I have encountered. This
God I know. And on a rock He has set my feet ! " Where
others collapse before the strain of life, that man will

stand undaunted in the grimmest days, victorious to the end.

> " Ay, tho' Thou then shouldst strike him from his glory
>   Blind and tormented, maddened and alone,
> Even on the cross would he maintain his story,
>   Yes and in hell would whisper, I have known."

I ask you to observe that this is the constant note of the New Testament. They are not dealing in speculations and views and ideas, those men. Every one of them could say what Jesus said to Nicodemus : " We speak that we do know, and testify that we have seen." They are not weaving an abstract theosophy : they are telling how God got a footing in history. They are not saying, " Come, and we will explain the speculative processes by which we have reached our idea of the divine nature." They are saying, " Come, and we will tell you what God has done for our souls." Take John in this epistle. He does not start off by saying, " We think we have found an adequate philosophy of religion," or " We suppose God must be like this," or " We have been told that redemption means that," or " It is rumoured that God has revealed Himself." His message is totally different. " That which we have heard with our own ears, seen with our own eyes, handled with our own hands, declare we unto you ! "

This is crucially important. It means that Christianity is not just another beautiful speculation on the mysteries of life ; not a theory of spiritual values, or a vague mysticism, or a dialectic about our ethical duty. It is historic fact. It is the eternal world of spirit intersecting, at a definite point of time, and in certain decisive events, this actual world in which we live. It is God visibly and dramatically and redemptively in action, on the plane of history and amid the hard and often tragic realities of human existence. " The life has appeared," says John. " The Word was made flesh."

" And we have seen it." That is what made those men irresistible. That is what carried their Gospel like fire around

the world. It was not mainly what they said. Eloquence
and rhetoric were the least of it. Not every one of them could
write an eighth of Romans or a thirteenth of First Corinthians.
Even a Paul and a John were bitterly conscious that they
were but stammering and stumbling when they tried to
deliver the message, dazzled and bewildered by the glory
of the facts they had to tell. But what vitally gripped and
held the world when the followers of Jesus began to move
out from Jerusalem to the uttermost parts of the earth was
the patent fact that they were not guessing nor romanticizing,
but speaking what they had seen and known, yes, and living
in a way which revealed, more plainly than any words, that
they were men under orders from a higher power, souls under
the authority of a direct, first-hand encounter with the
living God. That is what arrested the world, and built the
Church.

Perhaps some one feels—"That may be all true, but it
does not solve my difficulty. No doubt to those men the
Christian faith may have been intensely personal, an immediate apprehension : but how can it ever be that for me ?
All very well for them to say, ' This we have seen, this our
hands have handled, this we know.' I wish I could say the
same ! And I do recognize that for the practical facing of
this desperately difficult life, with all its possibilities of
sudden vicissitude and trouble and disaster, there can be
nothing on earth so steadying and reinforcing as a proved
and tested experience of God which is vivid and alive. But
how can I get it ? There is no point in what you have been
saying, unless you can tell me that."

I will tell you now. You can get it precisely as those men
of the New Testament got it. And how was that ? By
personal experiment. By the actual process of facing life
with Christ. Take any of your religious problems—the
existence of God, the reality of providence, the assurance
of forgiveness, the power of prayer : in every instance, the

experiment of facing life with Christ can transform a vague half-belief into a burning, shining certainty !

Consider, for instance, the fundamental matter—the existence of God. How did those fishermen and artisans, those tradesmen and taxgatherers, become so superbly God-conscious, so magnificently sure that eternal love was on the throne ? It was the product of the impact made upon them, day in, day out, by the personality of Jesus. This, they came to realize, as they lived with Him and saw His matchless grace and truth, was what all life was meant to be. This was a disclosure of what must lie at the very heart and centre of the universe. In other words, this was God encountering them. You want to be sure of God ? Can you not make the same personal experiment still ? Believe me, you can. By prayer, by steeping yourself in the Gospels, by facing life with Christ, you can pass beyond the religion of rumour and report and inherited tradition, and meet God face to face. " I have heard of Thee by the hearing of the ear : but now mine eye seeth Thee ! "

Or take the question of providence. So many of us are confused and hazy and uncertain about that. But here is Paul emphatically affirming " We know that to them who love God all things work together for good." We do not hope it, or wish it, or dream about it : we know it. How did he know ? Personal experiment again. In all that turbulent, unresting life of toil and controversy and danger, of shipwreck, stoning and imprisonment, of being misrepresented by colleagues, slandered by reputed friends, and vilified by foes, he had tested this thing out. He had walked the troubled roads with Christ ; and at the end, " I know that all things work for good," he cried, " I have proved it ! " Can you not do the same ?

> " O make but trial of His love !
> Experience will decide
> How blest are they, and only they,
> Who in His truth confide."

Or take the forgiveness of sins. Have our own eyes seen, our own hands handled, that ? Have you ever wanted to shout aloud with the authentic rapture of the forgiven and the free ? " No," you say, " I have not. All that is mere dead doctrine to me. I can't get thrilled about it. It leaves me cold." But here is Peter in the Acts, preaching forgiveness with a passionate, lyrical intensity. Why ? Because one morning he had stood on the beach, after an awful night of guilt and shame, and had heard a voice saying " Simon, son of Jonas, lovest thou Me ? " And though his first impulse had been to cry " Is this a dream ? It can't be real ! It is too good to be true "—he had dared to put it to the test, and had found life suddenly transfigured, and all things made gloriously new ! Can you not do that ? By the grace of God, you can. That which our own eyes have seen, declare we unto you !

Or once again, take prayer. What volumes have been written about the problems and perplexities of prayer ! How are we to get past all those obsessing and inhibiting doubts and difficulties to a joyous intimate assurance of prayer's essential worth ? There is only one way. Personal experiment. We endlessly debate such questions as, Is prayer rational ? Does it really work ? Can it be effective in a world of rigid law ? But long ago there was a psalmist who at one stroke cut through all that to the very root of the matter : " In the day when I cried Thou answeredst me, and strengthenedst me with strength in my soul ! " The man had tried it, and he knew. And you and I have God's own promise : " If any man open the door, I will come in." When the Spirit of the Lord came in like a great flood at Pentecost, it was because men, by prayer and supplication, had been opening wide the door. Have you tried that ? " Now I believe in prayer," you will be able to say, " not because others have told me about it, but because I have proved through prayer how God can make the weakest more than conqueror ! "

I need not illustrate further. It is abundantly clear that a vivid, self-authenticating experience of the basic facts of the Gospel was no monopoly of the men of the New Testament. What their eyes saw, ours, too, may see. What their ears heard, ours too may hear. What their hands handled, ours too may touch. And we can say, with a conviction no whit less strong or assured than theirs, " I know whom I have believed ! I know I have passed from death to life ! I know the Gospel is the power of God unto salvation ! This is no borrowed, threadbare faith. It is proved experience, my own, my very own ! "

If you and I can reach a faith like that, then let the threatening future bring what it may, one thing is certain —our souls shall not go under ! Come the four corners of the world in arms, come night and darkness and crushing blows of sorrow, our spirits shall win through unbroken, and our feet shall stand upon the rock.

But do remember this : that kind of personal certainty, that vital first-hand experience of God in Christ, comes only through a great personal venture. You cannot prove that those men of the New Testament are right, or share their blessed discovery, unless you are ready to risk giving every atom of your personality, body, soul, and spirit, to Christ's command. I began by quoting Sir 'Edward Elgar : " This I saw and knew." I want to end now by saying that what lay behind that crowning moment of vision and inspiration was Elgar's utter self-abandonment to the relentless demands of his art. And before you and I can say of the deep things of religion, " This I have seen, and know," one thing must happen—an act of costly, sacrificial self-surrender to the will of God in Jesus.

I put it to you : have we loyalty enough, and intrepidity enough, for that ? He is so determined, this Christ, to take all, or nothing. He binds His claims upon us utterly. His love is more implacable than all the force of men. Our human frailty devises half-measures, and cries " O Christ, inexorable and relentless, haunt me no more, but give me back my peace ! " But if we have once seen Him, never in this life will He let us off. That is why Christianity is sometimes such an agony, and sometimes such a glory. I have quoted Elgar : let me finish by quoting another of the greatest artists of all time, who worked with a different medium, Thomas Carlyle. When Carlyle was in the throes of composing his *French Revolution*, he wrote to his friend Emerson. I doubt if the anguish and the thrill of self-surrender to a great task have ever been more forcibly expressed. " That beggardly Book hampers me every way. To fling it once for all into the fire were perhaps the best ; yet I grudge to do that. It is impossible for you to figure what mood I am in. One sole thought. That Book ! that weary Book ! occupies me continually. For the present, really, it is like a Nessus' shirt, burning you into madness ; nay, it is also like a kind of Panoply, rendering you invulnerable, insensible, to all *other* mischiefs."

There stands the cost—the sweat and agony—of being a dedicated spirit. Are you prepared for that—with Jesus ? For He asks nothing less. The strain of such a self-commitment is immense, the travail of soul terrific. But it is worth it. For beyond it there is born the faith which sees, and knows, and overcomes the world. Truly our fellowship is with the Father, and with His Son Jesus Christ.

XIX

THE RELEVANCE OF THE UPPER ROOM

A COMMUNION MEDITATION

"And he said, Go into the city to such a man, and say unto him,
The Master saith, My time is at hand ; I will keep the passover at thy
house with my disciples. And the disciples did as Jesus had appointed
them ; and they made ready the passover. Now when the even was
come, he sat down with the twelve."—MATT. xxvi. 18–20.

TO that upper room of many memories our thoughts return
at every Sacrament season. We see the Master and
His friends reclining at the Holy Table. We sense the quiet
intimacy of that mystic fellowship. We hear the rise and fall
of the dear voice as it speaks its never-to-be-forgotten words
of parting and solace. We finger lovingly the precious pages
of St. John, burdened with the prayers and promises of that
immortal hour. We think of the generations of men and
women who have nourished their devotional life and revived
their thirsty souls at those unfailing springs—" Let not your
heart be troubled. In My Father's house are many mansions." " I will not leave you comfortless : I will come to
you." " Peace I leave with you, My peace I give unto you."
" I am the true vine, and My Father is the husbandman."
" Abide in Me, and I in you." " These things have I spoken
unto you, that your joy might be full." To that upper room
of long ago and far away, that quiet sanctuary amid the clash
and clamour of the world, the heart of Christendom continually returns. Here, if anywhere, is holy ground.

The clamour of the world—that is the setting of our
crowded lives. You would not thank me to-day for a Church
service devised to be an escape from realism. You would
say, " Don't mock us with illusions : we want facts." God

help the man or the Church that degrades the Christian faith until it is no more than a weak, escapist philosophy ! Our task must be to see the upper room of the first Sacrament against its true background. The light, as in a Rembrandt picture, will shine out all the more vividly because of the deep encircling shadows.

What was the background ? You can divide it into a nearer and a remoter background. The nearer background was the night streets of Jerusalem ; the tense, ominous silence so soon to be broken by that most terrible of sounds, the shouting of an angry crowd ; the conclave in the house of Caiaphas ; the instruction issued to the members of the Sanhedrin to hold themselves ready for an emergency midnight sitting of the court ; the sinister noise of hammering in the prison-yard behind the court-house, where men were working overtime to get three great wooden crosses ready for a triple execution at the dawn ; the very atmosphere vibrant with a strange, uncanny suspense, like those sultry, acrid moments when the earth seems to wait with bated breath for the bursting of the storm. That was the immediate background of this quiet scene in the upper room.

And beyond that lay the remoter background. The looming shadow of Caesar and the dark despotism of Rome, " the boast of heraldry, the pomp of power," the thunder of marching legions, the godless worship of brute force, the domineering menace of materialist politics, the curse of spiritual wickedness in high places—that was the setting of this hushed hour of Sacrament and peace.

The parallel is clear. We gather to the Holy Table now, conscious that the setting of our feast to-day is a world tossed with tempest and darkened with dreadful tragedy, shaken and convulsed by wild, unleashed forces of violence, madness and iniquity. Beyond this quiet place and this sacred hour, that is the background.

Now comes the question, urgent, challenging—Is this thing we are doing here relevant ? Has it any sense in a world

like that ? Is it not frightfully incongruous and inapposite ?
What is the use of an hour like this, with these immense,
insistent worries and perplexities hammering at the door ?
Are we not, to put it crudely, dodging the facts ? Are we not
guilty of a retreat from life ? Is this thing relevant ?

Let us go back for a moment to that upper room. Let us
ask, Was *that* relevant ? In Caesar's arrogant, uproarious
world of vice and force, had *that* any meaning ?

One thing, at any rate, we can say : it has lasted better.
It saw Caesar's sun fall out of the sky. The upper room at
Jerusalem has outlived empires. The message of that holy
hour has braved two thousand years, and been the brightness
of innumerable lives. The quiet words have stood the test
of time better than the deeds of emperors who thought they
were writing history with a pen of iron on the everlasting
rock !

Do you remember Thomas Hardy's vivid picture of the
abiding quality of love ?

> " Yonder a maid and her wight
> Come whispering by :
> War's annals will cloud into night
> Ere their story die."

Who can doubt that the message of the upper room will
go echoing on long after all the colossal, world-bestriding
Caesars have ceased to be even a blot on memory's page ?
It is said that Napoleon's soldiers, entering Milan, desecrated
the House of God and tethered their horses before Leonardo
da Vinci's great picture of the Last Supper. They did not
know that the scene of which the picture spoke would be a
live thing—dynamically alive in the hearts of millions—long
after Napoleon's annals had clouded into night and nothing-
ness. There was a glorious challenge that Theodore Beza
flung out to the King of Navarre. " Sire, it belongs in truth
to the Church of God, in the name of which I speak, to
receive blows and to give them, but it will please your

Majesty to take notice that it is an anvil which has worn out many hammers ! " How many assaults of the enemy has the Holy Table of our Lord worn down and triumphantly outlived ? Something happened in that upper room, something was begun, which is destined to endure to the last syllable of recorded time. " Where is He now ? " cried Ibsen's Emperor Julian, trying desperately to dethrone the Galilean from the world's imagination, yet unable to convince himself that Golgotha had been the end, " Where is He now ? What if He goes on and on, suffers and dies and conquers again and again, from world to world ? " So the scene enacted within the four walls of a Jerusalem guest-chamber had the stuff of eternity in it. Does that not argue its relevance ? I submit that at the very least we can say that anything which has proved itself so enduring must have a strong case for present validity. It would *seem* to be relevant.

Can we go further ? I think we can. I think it can be shown that the upper room, whether against the dark background of the age of the Caesars, or in the tragic setting of this present time, is trebly relevant.

First, it has *the relevance of power*.

Look at the little group of disciples gathered round the table that night. Those men were facing a dangerous, hostile world, a world that dealt in crucifixions, concentration camps, martyrdoms. What was their most urgent need at that moment ? What was the supreme requirement of the cause they represented ? Was it not power ? Power to " withstand in the evil day, and, having done all, to stand " ? Silently, inarticulately, their hearts were crying—" O give us that ! We are weak and helpless and resourceless : for God's sake, give us that ! "

But now, see ! this was the very thing Jesus was doing. For as the dear, familiar voice went on speaking to them that night so intimately, something was happening beneath

the surface. He was putting His very Spirit into them. He
was " strengthening them with might by His Spirit in the
inner man." Every quiet word was adding on to them something more of the resources of God, something that would
grow and multiply until one day it filled the earth. Against
the stormy background of the night and all the rumbling
menace of the dark, the upper room was relevant with the
decisive relevance of power.

And to-day, in this service, we are not playing at ritual
in a crashing, heedless world, nor fiddling while Rome burns ;
nor even, like the psalmist, crying for the wings of a dove
that we may fly away for an hour from the pressure of
tormenting facts, and be at rest. We are here for the power
that is going to help us to face the dark more manfully, the
power which—thanks be to heaven—can assure us that our
spirit shall not break in the hour of testing, but shall encounter every day of dread like a conquering child of God.
Believe me, that is what this historic Sacrament has meant
for generations of men and women, our own forefathers in
the faith. Shall it mean less for us ?

Matthew Arnold, you will remember, described a walk
one sweltering summer day through some of the vilest slums
of East London :

> " 'Twas August, and the fierce sun overhead
> Smote on the squalid streets of Bethnal Green,
> And the pale weaver, through his windows seen
> In Spitalfields, look'd thrice dispirited.
>
> I met a preacher there I knew, and said :
> ' Ill and o'erwork'd, how fare you in this scene ? '
> ' Bravely ! ' said he ; ' for I of late have been
> Much cheer'd with thoughts of Christ, *the living bread.*' "

That man was not lying or romancing, or mouthing pious
phrases. He was living in that hell like a victor, because
he had been with Jesus in the upper room. What a glorious
cry it was that broke, as the old chronicler tells us, from the
lips of Asa, King of Judah, as he faced one of the darkest

and most desperate moments of his life—" O Lord our God, we rest on Thee, and in Thy name we go against this multitude ! " Is that not a marvellous summary of the two sides of this human life of ours—resting back upon God, and then in the strength of that going to do battle with the thousand troubles of the world ? You cannot go, with any verve or attack, against the multitude of problems, difficulties and perplexities that swarm around your path, unless you have also learnt to say—" O God, I rest on Thee ! " That is why, in this bewildering and bewildered world, the upper room will never be an anachronism, nor the Sacrament ever out of date. Its relevance is the relevance of power.

Second, it is *the relevance of judgment.*

It is impossible to visualize with any degree of imagination that scene of long ago, and not have the thought borne in upon you that what you are witnessing is the judgment of the world. In the upper room, I see Jesus kneeling with towel and basin at His followers' feet : and something within me says—there is the world's infernal pride, judged ! I see Him breaking the bread in token of His own immeasurable sacrifice : and I know—there is the world's hectoring, domineering selfishness, revealed and dragged into the light, and judged ! I hear the quiet voice speaking its words of infinite tenderness and pity and compassion : there are all our rancours, bitternesses and hatreds—judged ! I sense that wonderful tranquillity, that heart of peace, that calm ineffable certainty of God : and I realize, there are all our faithless fears, our worries, our crass spiritual blindness— judged ! To outward appearance, on the dark betrayal night, Christ was coming under the judgment of Caesar. In reality, that upper room was the judgment of the world.

Is it not so still ? Here is this Table to which we have come. Do we realize what our presence here means, or ought to mean ? Do we understand what we are committing

14

ourselves to, by our action to-day ? St. Paul put it challeng-
ingly to the members of the Corinthian Church. "As often
as ye eat this bread, and drink this cup, ye do shew the
Lord's death till He come." In other words, every congregation at the Sacrament is engaged in a dramatic act of
witness. You show this thing forth ! You proclaim it before
the eyes of men. Over against the standards of the world,
in the teeth of the whole dominant scale of values, you affirm
Christ's values when He accepted the cross. You line
yourself up with the spirit and attitude of Calvary. You
take your stand with One who believed in love rather than
hate ; in the power of spirit, not the force of matter ; in
character and compassion, not cleverness and contempt ;
in a God-centred quietness and confidence, not a self-centred
aggressiveness and pride. You are showing forth the Lord's
death. You are declaring that the values which that death
enshrined—mercy, pity, peace and love—are on the throne
of the universe, life's ultimate realities. That is why I say
this Table of Christ's passion is the judgment of the world.
How can it be irrelevant, when it is *that* ? Indeed, we are
all judged here. For here there is nothing hid, that shall
not be revealed. Here we are searched and known. "Here,
O my Lord, I see Thee face to face " ; and in the light of
that vision, things in my life long cherished and condoned
seem suddenly shabby and pitiful and mean, and I repent in
dust and ashes. The relevance of the upper room is the
relevance of judgment—a judgment which saves even while
it smites ; and while it searches, heals.

Finally, it is *the relevance of eternity*.

We have tried to paint in the dark background of that
first Sacrament, the sea of paganism surging in its strength
and pride right up to the very doors of the guest-chamber
where Jesus and His friends were gathered. But look well
at that background, and behind the show of bombast and
defiance you will find one fear stalking there, grim and livid,

the fear of death. The world which lay beyond the little circle of light where Jesus sat—all the way from the narrow lanes of Jerusalem to the boulevards of Athens and the battlements of Rome—was a death-haunted world. Alike to Caesar on his throne and to the meanest serf in the gutter, death was the enemy. What could even the imperial sceptre do to stay the onset of this ruthless foe ? What could the wisdom of the philsophers do, or the music of the poets, or the might of the men of war ?

> " To die, to sleep;
> To sleep : perchance to dream— "

perchance to sleep without any hope of waking, to be robbed of love, joy, consciousness, personality, to face that terrible prospect, dust and ashes and annihilation—that was the haunting shadow on the world's soul. That was the misery of man.

But here in the upper room was a miracle ! Here was One facing that last enemy of the race with absolute composure. Why ? Because He—He alone—knew God the Father's love as it really was, a power, a determined passion, far too resolute and mighty ever to be thwarted or robbed by the severity of death. Why should men dread death if God in His love has endowed them with His own eternity ? Jesus, on the night in which He was betrayed, was meeting man's grimmest fear, and cancelling it out for ever.

That upper room not relevant ? I begin to wonder whether anything else is relevant compared with this !

For death still stalks through the world, monstrous, greedy, insatiable, all-devouring. If you are not sure of the eternal hope, how futile all your quest for peace, how precarious all your gladness ! To take just one point, think what life must lose, if human affection is finite and destructible, if death writes " Finis " to the story of a great love. I cannot now dwell on this ; but there are some lines of a

poem that convey the almost intolerable anguish of that
thought.

> " Bend down your head a little ; let me see
> Or think I see your eyes ; yes, I am going.
> For us there waiteth in this world of Earth
> No bridal torch, no clasp of wedded arms,
> No voice of children at the fireside knees ;
> Breaks at my feet the ocean I shall sail
> To that wan world, obscure as destiny,
> Wherein our fathers rest ; and I shall change
> To something other than I am, and lacking
> The memory and love of thee, and between us two
> Perchance no love shall be for evermore.
> So kiss me while my lips are warm."

There speaks the bondage of the fear of death and of its
separating stroke. And deep in the secret heart of multitudes
to-day there lies the thought—" If any certainty of the life
immortal could chase my doubts away, how glorious it would
be ! How supremely relevant to my need ! If there is any
sure word of God to lighten my darkness, let me hear it !
If any one can answer death's grim challenge, let him
speak ! "

The voice has spoken. It has spoken at the Holy Table
long ago. It is speaking in our Sacrament to-day.

> " I heard the voice of Jesus say,
> ' I am this dark world's Light.' "

Will you not trust Christ's certainty, rather than your own
doubt ? " In My Father's house are many mansions. If
it were not so, I would have told you." Strong is the peace,
serene the courage of souls who have reached that sure
conviction. " This," exclaimed James Guthrie, starting
from his sleep as the dawn streamed in at his prison window
on the morning of his execution, " this is the day that the
Lord hath made ! " " This," cried Perpetua, going out into
the Carthaginian arena to be trampled to death by the wild
beasts, " this is my day of coronation ! " And what a

spirit of expectant triumph breathes in Walt Whitman's
lines—

> " Joy, shipmate, joy !
> (Pleased to my soul at death I cry,)
> Our life is closed—our. life begins,
> The long, long anchorage we leave,
> The ship is clear at last, she leaps !
> She swiftly courses from the shore,
> Joy, shipmate, joy ! "

Come unto Me, says Jesus, and I will whisper to you in this
Sacrament the secret of death's defeat, the shining secret of
the communion of saints ! And you shall find rest for your
soul.

XX

VISION AND SACRAMENT

A COMMUNION MEDITATION

" Also they saw God, and did eat and drink."—Ex. xxiv. 11.

THIS story carries us back to a time when Israel's future was in gravest jeopardy. Clouds and darkness shrouded the whole adventure. None of those who had set their faces towards the far land of promise knew whether they would survive the terrible ordeal of the march and reach that goal of their desiring. It might be that the desert would swallow them up, and all the host perish without memorial. Their hopes and dreams, their destiny, their very existence were precarious and problematical. One fact only was fixed and sure and certain : *they saw God*.

But what does that mean ? Does not the Old Testament elsewhere declare that to look upon God is death ? Does not the Gospel itself remind us that " no man hath seen God at any time " ? Do not our own hearts tell us that we shall never see God face to face until the earth-dream here is over, and we awake in the light of the eternal morning ? Do we not sing, perhaps with a touch of wistfulness in our voice—

> " Jesus, these eyes have never seen
> That radiant form of Thine ;
> The veil of sense hangs dark between
> Thy blessèd face and mine " ?

Yes, that is all true enough ; but this, thank God, is also true—that there are times in the life of every one of us when the unseen grows suddenly and coercively real, times when all need of argument to support and prove our faith is at an end, for something which is its own best evidence has spoken

206

to us incontrovertibly, Some one alive and personal has tracked us down. Such moments of direct encounter with the divine authenticate themselves immediately in our experience. The veil of sense seems to have become so thin that it is hardly a veil at all, and behind it there can be seen moving something which is stronger than the iron hills and gentler than a mother's love, Some one keeping watch within the shadows and holding all the keys of destiny in His control —and we know then that we have seen God.

Once when that famous surgeon, the late Lord Moynihan of Leeds, had been invited to operate before a distinguished group of fellow surgeons, some one asked him afterwards how he could possibly work with such a crowd around him. " Well," he said, " it is like this : there are just three people in the theatre when I operate—the patient and myself." " Three ? " said his friend, " but that is only two. Who is the other ? " And the surgeon answered, " God." Do you not think that to reach some such steady awareness of the divine must be by far the best and most important thing that can ever happen to us in this world ? And to miss it, if it is attainable, must be the ultimate tragedy. It is lamentable that a man should go on working, year in and year out, and never see his work with the light of God upon it. It is sad beyond words that two people who fall in love should lose completely the greatest thrill and crowning glory of that experience—which is to see God in the heart of their love.

When Hazlitt was a young lad his mind was listless and inert, and his faculties unawakened. But it happened that one day Coleridge came to visit his father, and that evening young Hazlitt accompanied the poet for several miles on his homeward way. In one of his essays he tells what that walk meant for him—how it gave him a totally new world with far-stretching horizons, and opened up before him magic realms of thought and vision of which until then he had never even dreamed. But on all the high-roads of the spirit

there is no encounter that so surely makes all things new as
an encounter with the living God. That transforms life
utterly and imparts to it a depth and dignity unknown before.
It is far and away the most vital event that can ever happen
to us. And something like that is what had come to those
men of Israel gathered on Mount Sinai's rugged slopes.
" Also," runs the narrative, " they saw God."

It would, indeed, be true to say that all through Scripture,
from the opening prologue of Genesis to the last crashing
chords of the Book of Revelation, that is the dominant
note, the note which really makes the music : " this man,
and the next, saw God." Moses, wandering one day in
troubled mood along a lonely desert track, turned aside to
see a bush on fire—and suddenly, almost before he realized
what he was doing, he was putting off his shoes from his
feet, and bowing his face to the earth, for the ground was
holy : he saw God. Isaiah, standing in the temple, a young
aristocrat and courtier who had lost his king, felt the very
air beginning to tremble ; and looking up, he saw that the
place which had seemed so dim and empty a moment before
was flooded with a supernatural glory now : " in the year
that King Uzziah died, I saw the Lord." Ezekiel, sitting
sad among the songless exiles by the rivers of Babylon,
watched with awe the heavens opening above his head ;
and as his wondering gaze was drawn higher and still higher,
he saw four living creatures, and above them the radiant
firmament, and above the firament a throne, and above the
throne the face of the Lord God Almighty. John, the
apocalyptist, exiled on Patmos for the faith of Christ, was
worshipping in the Spirit on the Lord's Day, when suddenly
like a trumpet shattering the silence a great voice pealed
forth and cried, " I am Alpha and Omega, the first and the
last ! " And turning swiftly round to find whence that
strange voice came, he saw One whose eyes were like a flame
of fire, whose face was as the sun shining in its strength :
" and when I saw Him I fell at His feet as dead." All

through Scripture, from the garden where God walked with man in the cool of the day, to the Celestial City where the ransomed behold His glory, this is the refrain : " Also they saw God."

Is there anything our generation needs more urgently than to recapture that vision ? Panaceas for our modern distresses are offered us in plenty. The solving word for man's predicament, we are told, is education ; or else it is evolution ; or, if not that, then internationalism, or political science, or economic readjustment, or humanism, or rationalization, or psychology. But all these proffered remedies are a mere tinkering with the problem ; and man is beginning to see that unless some power from the beyond takes a grip of the tragic situation, there is no prospect before him but chaos and disaster. It is simple truth to say that the prime necessity of the hour is a new discovery of God. As John Ruskin put it years ago, " It is not the weariness of mortality but the strength of divinity which we have to recognize ; and that is just what we now never recognize, but think that we are to do great things by help of iron bars and perspiration ; alas ! we shall do nothing that way, but lose some pounds of our own weight." Or in the better and more downright words of Holy Writ, " Where there is no vision, the people perish." Where there is no feeling for eternal things, any strutting upstart tyranny can devastate the world. There can be no recall to sanity, or equity, or peace, till there has been a recall to God.

Does that sound too vague, and general, and remote ? Then let us bring it right home to ourselves. Where do we stand in this matter ? Cardinal Newman once defined a religious man as " one who has a ruling sense of God's presence." Is that the background of our common days, of our thinking and our planning, of our work, our friendships, our leisure, our love, our experiences of frustration and fulfilment—a ruling sense of a divine pervading presence ? That, beyond all question, is the most reinforcing factor in life : there is nothing that can so equip a man with courage and calm and indomitable hope as the experience of having looked, in some hour when all the barriers were down, straight into the very heart of things, and of seeing there—as the disciples saw when they gazed into the eyes of Jesus—the all-conquering love of God. That makes a mark on a man for ever. " By these things men live, and in all these things is the life of my spirit." By such encounters with God there come a poise, a dignity, a rhythm, into the otherwise jangled music of life, and men march with steadied nerves and surer steps upon their way. Happy those of whom in this difficult world it can be said : " Also they saw God."

But what is most significant about this text is surely the startling collocation of ideas. " Also they saw God—*and did eat and drink.*" Ought it not to have been something very different ? Should it not, for instance, be this : " Also they saw God—and fled in terror " ? Or, " They saw God—and were paralysed with shame " ? Or, at least, " They saw God—and bowed their heads and worshipped " ? Yet here it stands : " They saw God—and did eat and drink." What can you make of that ? Is it not an extraordinary association of divergent ideas ? And yet, on second thoughts, is not this precisely what we ourselves are intending to do in the Sacrament to-day, to see God—yes, that most certainly, if we can—and then, to eat and drink together ? So it was with the disciples, when the risen Christ came back to them on the shore of the Sea of Tiberias : they saw Him, and knew it was the Lord, and He bade them come and dine.

It seems to me that this eating and drinking by those Israelites who had just seen God implied three things. It meant, first, *something about the character of the God they saw.* It meant that they were beginning to see Him as a friendly God, a God in whose presence the simplest and most homely actions seemed right and fitting. Separated though they were by the waste of centuries from Christ's decisive disclosure of the friendliness of God, some glimmering of that wonderful truth was already dawning upon their minds. " Thou preparest a table before me in the presence of mine enemies " : and to-day God Himself was the host, and they were children in a father's house. They were at home, and could be simple and natural : " They saw God, and did eat and drink."

Now that is a vital part of the meaning of the Sacrament we celebrate here : our very presence at the Table declares our faith that the God of our worship is friendly and a Father. I may know that God is holy, and yet not dare to approach Him. I may know that God is wise, and be filled with terrible misgiving at the prospect of encountering Him. I may know that God is mighty, and feel like dust and ashes when He draws near. But Jesus shows me that God is love —and immediately God's House becomes home, with a table spread for His children : and I sit down to eat and drink in His presence.

" Let a man examine himself," said St. Paul, reminding us that there can be no true participation in this sacred mystery without awe and godly fear and deep searchings of heart. Yet to-day I would fain help you to realize how simple and how friendly is this feast. In that lovely book, the Life of Temple Gairdner, it is told that one morning in the Church at Cairo, before Communion, Gairdner was kneeling at the altar, praying for God's blessing on his people in the Sacrament, when a child stumped up quite close to his praying form, and passed into the vestry where he had left a toy. Some one afterwards made an apology, but Gairdner with a smile replied, " I liked it ! I thought the little fellow seemed so much at home in his Father's House." What Gairdner there felt about the House of God I would we all could feel about the Table to which by a royal summons we are now invited. For to be where Jesus is, is to be in the most homely and friendly place on earth. There is a story of a girl who in a mood of restlessness flung away from home, and was swallowed up in a great city's shadows. Her mother went after her, and found her lonely and miserable and destitute, and brought her back. It was dark when the door of the old home was reached ; and there the girl stopped. "Mother," she said, "I cannot go in. I cannot face father." "But your father is longing to see you," said her mother. "He has been waiting for this day, hungering to have you home." But still she stood there hesitating, afraid to meet her father's gaze. "Mother," she said at last, "will you go in and turn down the lights ? " And so in the darkness the reconciliation was effected. But there is no need of lowered lights and the cover of the dark when a soul from its wanderings turns home to God. We have all so much to make us abashed and contrite and shamefaced and afraid : but God has no grudge against us. He has brought us to His banqueting-house, and His banner over us is love. Here all is friendliness and sunshine and grace and welcome. Let us rejoice in the light of the Lord ! "They saw God, and did eat and drink."

But this wilderness Sacrament meant something more. It meant, in the second place, that those men, having seen God, had realized *a new fellowship with one another*. The communal meal, in ancient times, was a symbol of unity, a sign of fellowship between those who partook. And so doubtless it was here. They ate and drank together in token of the new and vital bond which had been established between them. Their vision of God resulted in a deepened fellowship amongst themselves.

Now, it is not hard to understand why a religious experience should have that effect, or why men who have seen God should suddenly find themselves looking upon one another with a love not known before. The supreme instance, of course, is what happened in the early Church. Those men, gathered in Jerusalem, had seen God in Jesus. The Word had been made flesh, and dwelt among them, and they had beheld His glory. He had lived, and died, and risen before their eyes ; and now at Pentecost, the magnificence of His glory was overwhelmingly revealed. What was the result ? The immediate result was the coming into being of a fellowship of matchless strength and beauty. Having seen God, they loved one another with a love which even yet makes the pages of the old story shine. Here was a fellowship that simply overflowed and obliterated all the age-long barriers of Jew and Gentile, and brought scorned barbarian, cultured Athenian, and elect Israelite to the same Holy Table together, with no shadow of difference among them at all. Here was a fellowship that set them to pray for one another, not only when they came together on the Lord's Day, but also in their own homes, to remember one another by name at the throne of grace ; and there is nothing like that for reconciling differences and leading to a true community of mind and hand and heart. Here was a fellowship which needed but little organization or exposition, because it was born of the Spirit, and its strength was in deeds, not words ; a fellowship not precariously dependent upon a careful balancing of opposing views, nor at the mercy of whims and prejudices, but gloriously free and strong, because in it all divisions of temperament had been transcended and all discords healed. And behind it, as the creating and sustaining force, was one cardinal decisive fact : those men and women had seen God. That was the secret of the fellowship, its inward driving-power and motive : and the weekly " love-feasts " were its outward expression. " They saw God, and did eat and drink."

Right across the centuries, then, this fact stands clearly written—that it is the men who have seen God (and in a true sense, only they) who know the way of fellowship. It is when you have experienced the constraining love of Jesus in the secret place of personal devotion that the love of the

brethren comes mightily into its own. There is a beautiful
thought in one of George Macdonald's poems—

> " Two clear souls
> That see a truth, and, turning, see at once
> Each the other's face glow in that truth's delight,
> Are drawn like lovers."

That is what happened in the early Church. Those men and
women had seen the truth of God at Calvary and the empty
tomb ; and turning, saw one another's faces lit up and
glowing in that truth's delight : and that drew them together,
loving one another fervently in Christ. There is no fellowship
in the world like the fellowship of those who have had a
common experience of Jesus. If the Church of to-day were
shining and throbbing with that kind of fellowship—which
is so utterly different from ordinary cameraderie and socia-
bility, things which you can get apart from religion altogether,
in a club or a drawing-room or almost anywhere ; if the
Church were alive with that far deeper quality of fellowship
of which the world has simply no conception, of which so
many Christians even have hardly come in sight (and therefore do not know what they are missing) ; if the Church were
vitalized in that sense, what an impact it could make on this
generation, and how it would go forth in the greatness of its
strength, mighty to save ! The fact is that if our fellowship
with one another is defective, it is because there is something
lacking in our fellowship with God. If my personal relationships are at the mercy of my likes and dislikes and preferences,
if they are controlled by the apparatus of mental criticism,
it is a sure sign that my relationship to God lacks reality and
steadfastness. But what do all the deep divergences in the
world amount to—Jew or Greek, barbarian, Scythian,
bond or free—when a man has found Christ and can say,
" Mine eyes have seen the King " ? Surely in the fact of
Christ there is far more to unite us than there can be anywhere else to sunder us ! Men and women whose lives centre

in a common experience of God cannot help being one.
Always the vision creates the fellowship, and from the love
of Christ the beloved community springs. " They saw God,
and did eat and drink."

One other aspect of this wilderness Sacrament remains
to be observed. It meant a discernment of the divine
friendliness, and a discovery of human fellowship : but more
than that, it meant *the signing of a covenant*. It meant the
ratification of a pact. In those days it was a recognized
method of proclaiming that a pact had been sealed and was
now operative : the contracting parties would partake of
food and drink together. The meal confirmed the covenant.
Hence our text implies an act of deliberate self-commitment.
It was those desert pilgrims' token of dedication to the high
God of their salvation.

This, too, is in our Sacrament here to-day. Can any of
us see God, as He has come to us in Christ, and not seek to
give ourselves to Him, to fulfil His will for ever ? Can you
see Jesus on the deadly tree, despised, rejected, reviled, yet
reviling not again ; bearing shame and insult unspeakable,
yet never answering except to pardon ; enduring to the
awful end because He was so sure that evil's monstrous
triumph would be its ultimate defeat, and that if His heart
broke, the very breaking of it might be the mending and the
healing of the world—can you look upon that and not want
to give yourself to be mastered and gripped by a grace so
wonderful and mighty ?

There is a very memorable page in that lovely book *Letters
to a Friend* by Winifred Holtby. Winifred Holtby was one
of a brilliant group of Oxford women : she was not indeed
an orthodox Christian—perhaps she would have preferred
to call herself a humanist—but she was a most beautiful
character, and her untimely death at the age of thirty-seven
was a sore loss to English literature. One of the letters tells
how she was present at a dedication service for a Somerville

College girl, a fellow-student of her own, who was going out to China as a missionary. " It must be nice," she wrote, " to decide to dedicate oneself to one particular form of service as she did when she was about twelve, and then train, prepare, and go and do it. And on your going, to have eight hundred people to pray over you and say that you do right. There is a satisfactory definiteness and conviction there about things." And then, more wistfully, she adds this : " The difficulty is to what can one dedicate oneself. I am blown about by a wandering wind of great pity and sorrow and desire, while my weakness and self-indulgence and timidity keep me tied to earth." That sudden confession, with its swift sense of deep, unanswered longing—" The difficulty is to what can one dedicate oneself ? "—surely focuses the feeling of thousands of big-hearted, generous and lovable people to-day. It must be fine to have one fixed goal in life, to have found a settled purpose, to be a dedicated spirit. But dedicated—to what ? Ah, that is the terrible difficulty ! And the years pass, and the sands of time run out, and some would say that they are no nearer to that settled serenity than they were ten years ago, are still being blown about by wandering winds of restlessness and desire, with no fixed definite anchorage.

But if to-day I were to tell you of One who entered history nineteen hundred years ago and has been at work in history ever since ; One who has laid upon the sons of men a spell from which they can never now get free ; One in whom God Himself has spoken and still speaks above the shouting of dictators and the warring noises of this frenzied earth ; One who has given innumerable people just like ourselves something worth living for, yes, and worth dying for—if I were to tell you of such a One, do you not think you might have to consider dedicating yourself anew to Him ? And if I were to go on and tell you that He is still alive, and really here ; that we are not in this Church to listen to a polite discussion about something which happened long ago, but to come to a decision about something which is happening now ; not to participate in a form of historic ritual, but to face the urgent challenge of the incarnate God—if I were to tell you that that is the issue, would you not feel impelled to dedicate, with rekindled passionate devotion, your whole being to His command ? I do tell you now that that is precisely the issue ; and that here in the silence Christ stands and waits for your response.

" They saw God, and did eat and drink." So let us sit down together at the Table now, rejoicing in the friendliness of God, recognizing our fellowship in Christ, and dedicating our lives to be His alone, and His for evermore.

XXI

THE CRY OF THE MARTYRS

" I saw under the altar the souls of them that were slain for the word of God, and for the testimony which they held : and they cried with a loud voice, saying, How long, O Lord, holy and true, dost thou not judge and avenge our blood on them that dwell on the earth ? "—Rev. vi. 9, 10.

HOW long ! That is a cry, a clamorous, impatient demand, which breaks out again and again from the pages of Holy Writ. There was a psalmist, baffled by the inscrutable ways of a God who could sit in heaven watching the vast tragedy of earth, and doing nothing : " Lord," he cried, flinging out a challenge trenchant almost to the point of sarcasm, " how long wilt Thou look on ? " There was another whose vexation was more intimate and personal. " How long," he exclaimed, " wilt Thou forget me, O Lord ? "—and then added, as a kind of stinging afterthought, " For ever ? " Turn over the pages of your prophets. Isaiah receives his commission as a herald of judgment. " Then said I, Lord, how long ? " Habakkuk broods hotly on the apparent dumbness of God in the face of oppression and tyranny. " O Lord, how long shall I cry, and Thou wilt not hear ! even cry out unto Thee of violence, and Thou wilt not save ! " Jeremiah bears on his heart the burden of the strife of nations. " O thou sword of the Lord, how long will it be ere thou be quiet ? Put up thyself into thy scabbard, rest, and be still." Sometimes, it is true, the positions are reversed, and this cry " How long ? " is heard upon the lips of God Himself. " The Lord said unto Moses, How long will this people provoke Me ? How long will it be ere they believe Me, for all the signs which I have shewed among them ? " And the evangelists record an hour when from the soul of Jesus, confronted with the dullness, the impassivity, the sheer obstinate inertia of human unbelief, there broke the cry, " O faithless and perverse generation ! How long shall I be with you ? How long shall I suffer you ? "—and then, referring to the case which they had all said was downright incurable, " Bring him hither to Me ! " But most often when we hear this question, it is not from God's side, but from man's side, that it comes, impeaching the government of the universe. " How long, O Lord, how long ? "

I think you will agree that there are few things more daunting to faith than the slowness of providence and the silence of God. How long, cries the impatient heart, must we go on praying " Thy kingdom come," only to see the powers of evil digging themselves in defiantly, consolidating their position more securely ? How long are our own lives, and the lives of our children and our children's children, to be the pawns and playthings of the bitter gods of war ? How long are the sons of each new generation to be sent forth down the same hard road where their fathers went before them, that Via Dolorosa on which we had fondly hoped that God by this time would have stationed some angel with a flaming sword of peace, to bar the way, and to proclaim to all the human race " Never again " ? " We are so busy," wrote the late Winifred Holtby, " with our patient erections of scientific invention. And we don't seem able to pull our spiritual standard up to the level of our material civilization." There is the real crux of the human predicament—this widening gap between man's command of Nature and his command of himself, this outdistancing of ethics by invention, of the spirit by the flesh. How long are we to look on helplessly ?

There are other questions too. How long is the Church to watch and wait for the fire from heaven to fall ? How long till Ezekiel's vision is renewed, and the dead bones stand up and live, " an exceeding great army " ? How long till the winds of God awake and blow away the winter mists of a

dull and formal religion, and all the gates of a new springtime of the faith lift up their heads to let the King come in ?

And there are our own lives, so disconcertingly difficult
to change, so frequently defeated in the fight of faith, so
easily betrayed out of all Christian equanimity into worry,
and fretting, and personal resentments, and moods and
prejudices and coldness and uncharity—which are just
common sin. We bear ourselves philosophically no doubt :
but honestly, are we satisfied ? We are going to travel this
road but once : are we convinced that we are making enough
of our opportunities ? Do we really believe that the character
we have fashioned for ourselves is passing muster in the sight
of God ? Are there not doubts, regrets, sudden aches of
shame, a haunting sense of unfulfilment like that which speaks
in Jeremiah's unbearably poignant words—" The harvest is
past, the summer is ended, and we are not saved " ? Is there
any conceivable possibility that Jesus should ever be able
to point at us and say—" Now there is what My religion can
do for a man in the realm of character : there is an authentic
illustration of what My disciples are meant to be " ? That
consummation seems vast leagues away. How long, O Lord,
how long ?

Sometimes, indeed, it is different. Sometimes we can
really see God in swift, decisive action. If we had lived in
the days of Wilberforce, when one of the foulest things on
earth, the tree of slavery, was torn up from the roots ; or if
we had been born in the age of the Wesleys, when through
the length and breadth of the land men heard the sound of
the chariots of the Lord ; or if our lot had been cast with the
early Church, when a Saul of Tarsus was " breathing out
threatenings and slaughter " one moment, and broken into
silence before the reproachful face of Christ the next—then
we should have had there before our very eyes the living
evidence of that sublime, dramatic word with which this old
Book so abruptly launches itself out upon our minds and
souls, " God said, Let there be light : and there was light."

As swift as that it happens sometimes. Have you had no instantaneous answers to prayer ? "Before they call, I will answer : and while they are yet speaking, I will hear." "Surely," says the Christ of the Revelation, "I come quickly."

> "At times, with sudden glory,
> He speaks, and all is done ;
> Without one stroke of battle
> The victory is won."

That is what we like. We want desperately to have things happening. We have a passion to see results, "something accomplished, something done," something perhaps never needing to be done again. To spend a lifetime with nothing visibly achieved—how pathetic that, we feel ! A doctor, ah, there, we say, is a type of career worth envying ! For he can save lives, can have the immense satisfaction of knowing that there are people going about their work to-day whom he has literally rescued from the gates of death. A carpenter, a shipbuilder, an artist, a gardener—to all is given the thrill, the delight, of seeing results. Nor need a minister be ashamed to confess the huge difference it makes to him to know, sometimes by a letter from a total stranger, sometimes by the simple word of a friend, that the divine grace has been secretly at work, comforting one soul here in sore perplexity, challenging another there in doubt or apathy ; and that his labour has not been in vain in the Lord.

But so often it is not like that. So often the eager passion for results seems thwarted. Resolutely we strive to build a better world, and demonic forces mock our endeavour. We protest to our own souls that we " will not cease from mental fight " until we have wrought out and actualized the dreams for which our brethren died ; and still man's inhumanity to man desolates the earth. Nothing seems to move. The world's malady is endemic and persistent. Man's heart remains unchanged. If only God would co-operate more visibly ! If only providence were less lethargic, would take a grip instead of leaving things to drag and drift! "That Thou doest, do quickly!" At such times, faith has to fight for its life, perhaps breaks beneath the strain; and from all quarters, grim disquieting questions come thronging in around us. Did they die utterly in vain? Are peace and goodwill illusions? Is the dream of the kingdom of heaven a sham? Will God's will ever be done upon the earth? Are our personal strivings leading anywhere? Or must we write as an epitaph on the graves of a thousand shattered hopes—

> "the struggle nought availeth,
> The labour and the wounds are vain,
> The enemy faints not, nor faileth,
> And as things have been they remain"?

Is that the final word?

"I saw under the altar the souls of them that were slain for the word of God, and for the testimony which they held: and they cried with a loud voice, saying, How long, O Lord, holy and true, dost Thou not judge and avenge our blood?" Behind that lay the story of two frightful persecutions. Here was the young Church of God, which had weathered the storm and hurricane of the reign of Nero, had come out of that great tribulation battered and reeling but with the flag of the cross still flying—only to find looming ahead of it in the next generation a still fiercer and more menacing danger. For the decree of Domitian established Caesarism throughout the world, making the State an object of worship, and the Emperor himself an incarnation of God. Rank idolatry and blasphemy, the Church called it, and refused to bow its head or burn incense at that hateful shrine: whereupon with a violence which knew no bounds the fury of the persecutor was let loose. The darkness deepened into midnight, and God gave no sign. The terror raged, the hail of death descended, and God gave no sign. The Church of which Jesus had said that it was founded upon rock, and that the gates of hell would never prevail against it, seemed doomed to

perish utterly ; and still God gave no sign. It was then that
this man John, meditating and brooding in his own soul upon
the mystery, seemed suddenly to hear a shout, a challenge
from beneath the high altar of God in heaven, where the souls
of the martyrs lay : " How long, O Lord, holy and true, dost
Thou not judge and avenge ? "

That does not mean, of course, that this man conceived
of the noble army of martyrs as having died with vengeance
in their hearts. Not so had they learned Christ. Their spirit
was that of Stephen when he prayed, while the stones were
flying round him, " Lord, lay not this sin to their charge " ;
of Jesus Himself, crying from the cross, " Father, forgive
them, for they know not what they do." It was with no
thoughts of revenge or retribution, but only with psalms of
praise upon their lips, that these men went down into the
dark valley of death.

No, what John's vision means is this, that all the cruel
sufferings of noble souls, all the sacrifice and torture, all the
lives laid down for freedom, truth, and justice, all the tears
shed by mothers and by lovers for the memory of the un-
returning—these are facts which, to those who see them and
meditate upon them, challenge the government of the
universe. The very occurrence of such facts is bound to
constitute, if no explanation is forthcoming, a solemn im-
peachment of God. It is not that the sufferers claim revenge
—they don't : they have won their immortality, and there
is nothing in their hearts but love. But it is this—that the
tragic element in life, as represented by their sufferings,
cries out insistently to be interpreted, lays on God Himself
the terrible onus of vindicating and justifying the way in
which His world is run.

Very often it seems that providence has nothing to answer,
and no defence to make at the bar of man's outraged soul.
" If I were God," the human spirit begins to think, " I would
set about rectifying a thousand glaring wrongs this moment !
I would refuse to tolerate injustice and oppression on My

earth another day. I would overthrow governments. I
would stop wars. I would restrain tyrants. I would deal
once and for all with the powers of evil. I would break them
with a rod of iron, and dash them in pieces like a potter's
vessel." And all the answer that comes through from the
beyond is this—" My thoughts are not your thoughts, neither
are your ways My ways." Whereupon we fling back, " No,
that's obvious! That is just what we are saying. If God
thought as we do, it would be a better and juster world. But
as it is — if He does not intervene now, this very day,
to-morrow all hope may be gone ! "

> " Too late for love, too late for joy,
>   Too late, too late !
> You loiter'd on the road too long,
>   You trifled at the gate :
> The enchanted princess in her tower
>   Slept, died, behind the grate ;
> Her heart was starving all this while—
>   You made it wait."

So here in John's vision. The Church was the enchanted
princess, the bride of Christ. But how the Bridegroom tarried!
" How long, O Lord, will You loiter on the road ? Through
all the night of persecution, the heart of the Church has been
starving for Your coming, to bring release and the songs of
the morning. You have made it wait ! " It is the age-long
question—" Does God know ? Can He realize, from our
side of it, what the agony of waiting means ? Does He have
any inkling of the anguish of going out into the dark, with
one's dearest dreams unfulfilled ? Does God know what it
means to die in faith, not having received the promises ?
Of course He doesn't ! He can't ! "

But this is precisely where the Gospel comes in. " God
does know," it says—and suddenly points us to a cross. Say
not that the burden of the mystery, the bitterness of defeat,
the anguish of the dark, are unknown to Him. God has been
there—and He knows. Have you suffered ? His feet climbed

Calvary. Have you lost hope ? He saw the last star go out.
Have you wondered why life should be so hard ? He cried
" Why ? Why ? " to the blackening heavens. Have you
been disappointed ? He died with all He had ever lived for
apparently in ruin. He knows ! For He, too, more even than
the martyr souls beneath the altar, has met the full impact
of the withering blast of evil. He, too, has " died in faith, not
having received the promises." And in that very act He has
verified the promises for ever, and opened the kingdom of
heaven to all believers.

Here, then, there emerges, from the very heart of the
Gospel, the divine answer to the human cry " How long ? "
It is an answer in three words—the patience of Christ, the
victory of God, the communion of saints.

Do you remember Paul's prayer for the Thessalonian
Church ? " May the Lord direct your hearts into *the patience
of Christ*." If only these fretful hearts of ours could learn the
mind of Jesus, His brave tenacity of hope ! See how marvellously it shines out from the narrative of the evangelists.
Here was Jesus, His heart ablaze with a passion to save the
whole suffering human race, dreaming that magnificent,
audacious dream of a new creation in which all the kingdoms
of the world and the glory of them would be a tribute at the
feet of God : and providence kept Him thirty years in the
narrow lanes of Nazareth and at a carpenter's bench. And
when at last His hour came and He went forth on His mission,
when He drew great crowds around Him by His preaching,
it was only to see them, as the days went by, dwindling
steadily away—many who had hailed Him at the first with
boundless enthusiasm growing suddenly cold and distant
and disaffected, as though the magic of His personality had
somehow lost its grip, His own family misunderstanding
Him and scheming to put Him under restraint, His best
friends abandoning Him to His fate ; and then the shadow
of death at last, with all the gallant hopes frustrated (or so

it seemed) and all the dream-castles crumbled into dust and ruin. And yet He laid His life down undaunted and serene, because He was quite sure that some day, in God's good time, it would all come gloriously true.

Can we not make that spirit ours ? Cannot we, as Paul would say, " put on the Lord Jesus Christ " ? People complain, " There is so little to show after nineteen hundred years of Christianity ! " Nineteen hundred years ? But what if, as God sees things, a thousand years are but as yesterday when it is past, and as a watch in the night ? Get a truer perspective ! What are nineteen hundred years to the rolling aeons that lie behind us, or to the untold ages that may still be to come ? We are only standing in the dawn of the Gospel day as yet. May the Lord direct our hearts into the patience of Christ !

The second solving word is *the victory of God.* On this the New Testament is absolutely categorical and emphatic : God's will, though it may be hindered for a time and obstructed by human blindness and folly and sin, cannot finally be defeated. When Christians make that assertion, they are not being merely rhetorical, nor allowing the wish to be father to the thought, nor inventing a fool's paradise as a refuge from disconcerting realities. They are building on the solid rock of history. If God must conquer in the end, it is because in point of fact He has conquered already. Look at the cross. Was there ever, to outward seeming, such a crushing defeat of all the spiritual values ? Was ever evil more conspicuously triumphant ? But look again. Let a deeper insight reveal the truth. Get closer to Calvary. Who was conqueror there ? Has that cross not been, ever since it happened, God's supreme instrument of blessing and salvation ? Is it not precisely out of that hour and power of deepest darkness that there has come for multitudes " the light that shone when hope was born " ? In other words, evil, at the very point of its supreme achievement, has been met and mastered and defeated. In crucifying Christ, it shot its bolt ; and now that cross, with the Resurrection to seal it, remains for ever as the guarantee of the ultimate triumph of the divine will. No wonder St. Paul, even when confronted with the terrible might and majesty of Roman paganism, was able to stand his ground and cry, " I am not ashamed of the Gospel of Christ ! I am proud of it ! "

" Certainly I must confess," wrote Sir Philip Sidney, " I never heard the old song of Percy and Douglas, that I found not my heart moved more than with a trumpet." And we Christians have something so infinitely more moving and heart-stirring and trumpet-toned. Give thanks for the cross ! For it is the pledge of the future, the assurance of the final victory of God.

One other solving word remains—*the communion of saints*. See how vividly that is brought out here in Revelation. The cry of the noble army of martyrs was not left unanswered. " It was said unto them, that they should rest for a little season, until their fellow-servants also and their brethren " —that is to say, the generation of Christians then upon the earth—had fought the good fight through to the end. Is that not a glorious reminder of the solidarity of the Church visible and militant with the Church invisible and triumphant, the unity of God's people in this world with God's saints in heaven ?

What a thrilling thing ordinary Churchgoing might become, did we but keep that constantly in mind ! How it would save us from the defeatist spirit in religion ! So often our attitude seems to say—" We Christians are a pitiful minority. Here is a congregation gathered in the House of God in the name of Jesus ; but for every one of us here, are there not hundreds of men and women for whom our Christ means nothing ? Is not our religion just an insignificant ripple on the surface of life's throbbing sea ? " When that mood gets hold of us, we would do well to pause and remember the mighty invisible host with whom we hold high fellowship every time we gather here, the " great multitude which no man can number, of all nations, and kindreds, and people, and tongues, standing before the throne, and before the Lamb, clothed with white robes, and palms in their hands," and the perfect praise of heaven upon their lips.   When we are inclined to attach but small importance to our Church and congregation and to our own place in the Christian community, let us think ourselves anew into the full width and sweep and magnificence of the heritage which is ours in worship : " Therefore with angels and archangels, and with all the company of heaven, we laud and magnify Thy glorious name."   That is what it means to have a place within the Church, which is the Body of Christ : we belong to it on earth, they belong to it in heaven, they (if you care to put it so) being Christ's right hand, we His left—and yet all one, because all members of the same body, " one army of the living God ! "   Where is the man with soul so dead that he can think of that and not feel thrilled and challenged and compelled to a new nobility of life ?

> " O blest communion, fellowship divine !
> We feebly struggle, they in glory shine ;
> Yet all are one in Thee, for all are Thine.
> Hallelujah ! "

I believe in the communion of saints.   I believe in the death-defying unity of the family of God.   I believe in the fellowship of all servants of the King in heaven and earth, above, beneath.   I believe in the life everlasting !   And to Him who has brought that life to light be glory for ever and ever.

XXII

SIGNPOSTS TO IMMORTALITY

" Death is swallowed up in victory."—1 Cor. xv. 54.
" That mortality might be swallowed up of life."—2 Cor. v. 4.

THERE are many people to-day who regard the Christian faith in immortality, not indeed as untrue, but as irrelevant. They are not prepared actively to support or to combat the idea of a future life. It does not concern them one way or the other. They are simply not interested.

Let us be quite fair to this attitude. It would be very foolish to brand it off-hand as irreligious. In point of fact, it is conjoined in many cases with real nobility of character ; and some at least of those who adopt it are devoted and highly-principled souls whose sincerity it would be absurd to question.

If they were to put their feelings on this matter into words, they might say to us something like this : " We believe God has put us into this world to do our duty here, quite independently of what may or may not be coming hereafter. We believe that every wrong which exists in the world to-day, every injustice in the social order, every sordid and tragic fact throughout the whole human scene, is calling on us to be up and doing now, instead of waiting for the millennium and dreaming pleasant dreams of a blissful future that will redress the balance of man's sufferings upon the earth. We feel that what is needed most is a religion that will stab the spirit broad awake and sting it into energy and activity here and now, not a religion that will dope it into quietism and acquiescence with the anaesthetic of a sentimental other-worldliness. We must work while it is day : the night cometh when no man can work."

There is much that is noble in that attitude, much that is essentially Christian. But the mind of man cannot permanently rest satisfied there. There are instinctive questions which cannot so easily be silenced. Man may toil and struggle and sweat for a better order of things upon the earth ; but deep in his heart he wants to know—Is all this effort of mine rational ? Is it leading anywhere ? Is it backed up and sanctioned by anything ultimate and eternal in the order of the universe ? And there is the question-mark raised by death. We may talk glibly and unthinkingly enough about " the transience of life " ; but inevitably there comes a day when we begin to realize that life's transience is now a desperately real fact for ourselves. The boundless time which once seemed at our disposal is reduced to a narrow span ; and there is so much still to do, and so many things which we once hoped to achieve will never now be done ; and is it all over when the darkness falls ? Even if you crush down that question as it concerns yourself, can you crush it down as it concerns some other whom you love, some one whose love has been the crowning blessing of your life ? Surely then the question leaps to meet you irresistibly. When death raids your dearest affections, will you dream of saying that immortality is irrelevant ? Will the question as to whether death is ruthlessly final and catastrophic, or only the gateway to a larger and lovelier life, find you indifferent and unconcerned ?

> " A shadow flits before me,
> Not thou, but like to thee :
> Ah, Christ ! that it were possible
> For one short hour to see
> The souls we loved, that they might tell us
> What and where they be ! "

Belief in the hereafter is no abstract article of faith. It is not like believing in the existence of the planet Jupiter or in the historicity of Julius Caesar. These are things which do not actively concern us, one way or the other. But this matters personally and vitally and overwhelmingly. " I believe in the life everlasting."

Granted, however, that this belief is relevant, is it true ? It may comfort the heart, but can it also satisfy the intellect ? Is it not possible that the critics of religion are right when they say that this is just another instance of the working of a perfectly familiar and recognizable psychological process, an illustration of the human mind's unconscious but inveterate tendency to believe what it wants to believe, and to assign objective validity to what is nothing more nor less than its own subjective desire ?   When Robert Browning wrote, " God took her to Himself, as you would lift a sleeping child from a dark uneasy bed into your arms and the light," was that just a poet's fancy trying to ease the smart and pain of an intolerable grief, and to cover up grim facts with the protective camouflage of illusion—or was it really true ? In short, is life everlasting a creation, for their own comfort, of broken hearts in the bitterness of bereavement, or is it actual fact ?   Is it man's invention, or is it God's reality ?

Now obviously it is not possible to give a coercive demonstration of the life beyond the grave as you might demonstrate a proposition in Euclid.   But this we can do : we can notice how many signposts there are, in thought and life and experience, pointing in the direction of immortality and making the Christian belief far more credible than any alternative.   Let us look at some of these now.

The first signpost to immortality is *the fact of the reality of the unseen.*   It is the existence of a spiritual order here and now, every whit as real as the material order in which our lives are set.   If we start there, going right back to this prior question, and clarifying in our own minds the implications of an invisible environment pressing in upon us at this very moment, we shall find that half the difficulties in the way of a belief in immortality are eliminated and disappear.

But can we start there ?   Have we any right to talk about

the reality of the unseen ? Is that an intellectually respectable proposition ?

Here we touch the very nerve of the whole issue between religion and materialism. This question of the reality of the unseen is the crux. We find it desperately hard, do we not, to break with our mental habit of judging by appearances ? This is precisely the trouble about belief in life after death. All the appearances are against it. Death looks so final. The collapse of the bodily powers in death is so radical and complete. And because the outward appearances are against survival, men say it is not true.

Now the point to notice is that such subservience to the appearance of things is not only irreligious : it is actually unscientific. If there is one dogma which modern science is proclaiming, it is this—that things are not what they seem, and that if you judge by appearances you are almost certain to be wrong. This Church building looks solid and substantial enough ; but science tells us that every stone in the walls, every beam in the roof, solid and substantial as it appears, is in reality a mass of whirling electrons. In other words, if we persist in judging by appearance, the very stones will cry out against us. In fact, science is almost beginning to hint that matter itself is spiritual. You can see, then, the anomaly of the situation : you have people calling themselves scientific realists, on the ground that they trust their five senses implicitly and will not admit the reality of anything they cannot touch and handle and see. The truth is, the very science they profess disowns them now. " We are no longer tempted," declares Eddington in *Science and the Unseen World*, " to condemn the spiritual aspects of our nature as illusory because of their lack of concreteness. We have travelled far from the standpoint which identifies the real with the concrete." Some of our latter-day realists would do well to ponder that.

It is a great and most liberating discovery that we need no longer allow the visible and the tangible and the appearance of things to monopolize and tyrannize us : for it is precisely the things we cannot see that are the most basic things in the universe. Love is invisible ; yet love drives the wheels of life. Truth is invisible ; but it haunts man like a passion. Personality is invisible ; but what a dynamic force personality is ! Conscience is invisible ; yet where conscience reigns, there are certain things men would die rather than do. Wordsworth was meditating of something invisible when he wrote the moving lines—

" I have felt
A presence that disturbs me with the joy
Of elevated thoughts ; a sense sublime
Of something far more deeply interfused,
Whose dwelling is the light of setting suns,
And the round ocean and the living air,
And the blue sky, and in the mind of man."

Yet to multitudes of men and women the still small voice of that invisible disturbing presence has meant more than all the raucous clamour of the world. " Reality as actually experienced," writes Aldous Huxley in a passage of impressive personal testimony, " contains love, beauty, mystical ecstasy, intimations of Godhead. Science did not and still does not possess intellectual instruments with which to deal with these aspects of reality." That is a deeply significant confession. It is surely clear beyond doubt or cavil that the unseen spiritual forces are the bedrock reality out of which the whole complex structure of life and history and experience is hewn. In Robert Louis Stevenson's phrase, they are " the nails and axles of the universe."

May we not therefore say that the really marvellous thing is this—not that we should pass into an unseen world when this life on earth is over, but that we have an unseen world all round us now ; not that death should usher us into eternity, but that we are eternal already ? The fact of the reality of the unseen, to those who have grasped it, removes out of the way half the difficulties to belief in the life beyond, and makes the Christian doctrine suddenly credible and convincing. It is the first signpost pointing decisively towards immortality.

Following the path of our inquiry further, we come upon a second signpost pointing in the same direction. It is *the rationality of the universe.*

I propose that for a moment we should try the experiment of looking at life with the doctrine of immortality left out. Suppose we decide to abandon the Christian conviction and to drop belief in the hereafter. Do you see the position to which we are now driven ? We have now to believe that life has brought this marvellous thing called personality into being, with all its splendid powers of love and heroism and nobility, only to annihilate it in the end. We have to believe that the universe, having toiled and travailed and agonized to produce its crowning creation, proceeds then to throw it out on the scrap-heap of death. We have to believe that the spirit which was in Beethoven when he was working at white-heat on the Ninth Symphony, or in Leonardo as he painted the " Last Supper," or in Martin Luther crying " Here stand I ; I can no other ; so help me God," or in Father Damien living the Christ life among the lepers—is of no more significance or ultimate value than the leaves which go flying down the street before the autumn winds, " cast as rubbish to the void." We have to believe that souls which have shone with the radiance of faith and hope and love and honour and valour and self-sacrifice can be finished irrevocably and for ever by a microbe, or a piece of shrapnel, or a careless driver's twist of the wheel of a car.

Such is the position to which we are logically forced by the denial of the Christian doctrine of immortality. Look it fairly and squarely in the face, and you will see that it is not the Christian believer who is irrational, but his sceptical opponent. The latter is working with a philosophy of life which reduces every trace of purpose in the universe to myth and moonshine and delusion. No doubt the Christian faith is difficult : but what of the alternative ? Will you find that easier ? Which gives the more satisfying interpretation of all the facts ? Belief may have to meet the challenge and assault of many a dark perplexing mystery ; but try to maintain a secure, consistent unbelief, and you will find that the difficulties confronting you are now a hundredfold more serious and insurmountable. It is by the vista of its eternal hope that Christianity makes sense of the universe : reject that vista, and immediately you are entangled in a host of problems far more embarrassing and intractable than those you are seeking to escape. It would indeed be no exaggeration to say that the alternative to the Christian position involves a surrender of intellect which it is an outrage to demand. There, then, is our second signpost pointing towards immortality— the rationality of the universe.

Let us pursue our quest a stage further. The third sign-post is *the character of God.*

It is vitally important to get this clear. Have you realized that what is at stake in all discussion about the life beyond is nothing less than the character of God Himself ?

Why do I say that ? Here is man, with all those strong, quenchless longings which God has put into his heart. Here is this strange, restless creature, never quite at home in this seen and temporal world, dissatisfied with his own frustrations and imperfections, conscious of powers within himself requiring a different climate and a wider horizon for their full development and fruition. Here is man for ever clutching the inviolable hope that the heart of the universe is friendly, that the power which made him loves him, and that the end will be, not a sheer precipice and a fall to the abyss of nothing-ness, but a leaning back upon everlasting arms. The question is, Has God put that faith into man's·heart just to mock him ? Do you suppose that a good God would allow man to cherish such longings, and then shatter them as a callous jest ? Is the great Creator having a fiendish game with his human creatures ? Are we to write over the whole story of man such words as Thomas Hardy's, " The President of the Immortals had finished his sport with Tess " ? You see, what is at stake in this question of immortality is far more than the nature of man : it is the character of God.

Now if you believe Jesus, if God cares for the individual as Jesus said He did, if the very hairs of your head are all numbered and the paths of your feet all guided, if round your life there is the besetting pressure of the everlasting mercy, do you think a love so infinite and sublime is going to be defeated at the last by an incident like death ? If the great Father has loved His children enough to go into the far country after them, to climb the terrible slopes of Calvary for them, to send the urgency and passion of His Holy Spirit to revive and rescue them, to cause all the bells of heaven to ring for the salvation of one of them coming home at last out of darkness into light ; if God *so* loved the world—do you imagine that He will consent to have His love baulked and thwarted and robbed by death at the end of the day ? " Thou wilt not leave my soul in Hades." God's love cannot finally be frustrated. If it means breaking the bands of death to satisfy that love, then break those bands He will. For when God loves once, He loves for ever. It is impossible to overemphasize the importance of this argument for the life eternal : for it is Christ's argument. The third sure signpost pointing to immortality is the character of God.

A further decisive signpost now appears. It is *the Christian experience of regeneration*. From the days when the Word was made flesh and walked in Galilee down to the present hour, men have always declared that fellowship with Christ has brought them the final confirmation of their dreams of a blessed hereafter. Why is this ? It is not only that Jesus, who knew more about life and death than any one else, was utterly sure of the life eternal. It is not only that He said quite plainly, "If it were not so, I would have told you." It is not only that, speaking in the name of God, He promised men the gift of immortality—a fact which confronts us with the solemn alternative that either the belief in the hereafter is true, or else Jesus deliberately misled us. It is not only that. Far more than that, it is this—that all down the Christian centuries countless men and women, entering into fellowship with Christ, have found eternal life *as a present possession*. "We have passed from death unto life," cried one of them. We are not waiting for the great transition to come to us at the journey's end. It has happened already, through our fellowship with Jesus. We have passed over into a new realm. The bitterness of death is behind us. The eternal order has projected itself out of the future into the present ; we have felt the power of an endless life go thrilling through our experience. We possess it now !

"Some morning you will read in the papers," said Moody the evangelist once to a group of friends, "that D. L. Moody is dead. Don't believe a word of it ! At that moment I shall be more alive than I am now. I was born of the flesh in 1837—I was born of the Spirit in 1856. That which is born of the flesh may die : that which is born of the Spirit shall live for ever." He was right. Death cannot touch this glorious thing which is ours in fellowship with Jesus. "He that believeth on the Son *hath* everlasting life " : and death lies dead for ever.

Finally, there is the signpost of *the Resurrection of Christ Himself*. Think how it thrilled the first disciples to know that from the mortal conflict in which He had faced the full weight of the onslaught of the powers of darkness their Master had emerged triumphant, and that the measure of His victory was that death itself, the last enemy of man, had had to submit ! The glory of that victory chased away the dread of the unknown, and carried them through martyrdom with songs upon their lips. The valley of the shadow had lost its terrors, and the grave its gloom, for Christ had conquered there. Death, they said, had met its match on the day when Jesus had looked into its grim visage. It had been vanquished all along the line. Mortality had been swallowed up of life.

We who are sons of the Resurrection have been liberated for ever from the bondage of the ultimate fear.

> " Death is a fearful thing :
> To die, and go we know not where."

So cried Shakespeare's Claudio. But we who believe in a risen Redeemer have passed beyond the reach of that harrowing dismay. We have received a kingdom which cannot be shaken. The darkest mystery has been lit up by a gleam of glory from another world, and from behind the clouds of our mortality there has broken forth the light of heaven.

Let us, then, who are children of the light, walk in it with gladness, singing the songs of that City of God towards which we travel, and rejoicing in the magnificent, impregnable conviction that Christ's victory is the earnest of the victory of His brethren. And when the last mile comes, we shall find that it is no unshepherded way, and that

> " Christ leads me through no darker rooms
> Than He went through before."

For the power which raised Him from the dead and gave Him glory shall resurrect us also, when the last darkness falls, to the daybreak of an eternal morning.

XXIII

GOD'S GLORY IN THE MORNING

"And in the morning, then ye shall see the glory of the Lord."—
Ex. xvi. 7.

LET us take these lovely words of hope and promise out
of their historic framework in the record of Israel's
deliverance from Egypt, and let us seek to read their message
for ourselves. Do they not bring suggestively before our
minds some of the daybreak experiences which in the mercy
of God come to us men and women from time to time on our
way through life, some of the different kinds of dawn and
morning which lighten our human darkness and reveal the
splendours of the eternal ?

"In the morning, then ye shall see the glory of the Lord."
Let us take it, first, quite literally : for *every new day that
comes to us*, every morning that awakens us from sleeping,
is a fresh divine revelation. There is a deep sense in which
it is true to say that each returning dawn, with the scattering
of the night shadows before the sun, is not only a physical
fact in the realm of inanimate Nature, but a moral fact in
the realm of the soul.

Consider the matter like this. You lay down to sleep some
night feeling dreadfully depressed in spirit. Your work had
been going badly, and circumstances and people had been
tiresome and difficult, and you were beginning to wonder
where you would ever find strength or heart to carry on at all.
Life was becoming too much for you, and you could scarce
stand up to it any longer. And then next morning came,
and somehow everything was different : in Shakespeare's
vivid phrase, sleep had " knit up the ravell'd sleave of care,"
and the difficulties which had seemed absolutely overwhelm-

239

ing the night before had shrunk to truer proportions now, and the joyous strength of a confident serenity was in your heart. That is what I mean by saying that a new day is not only a physical fact of Nature, but a moral fact for the soul.

But there is something more than that. There is this, that when a new day dawns there speaks a voice, for those who have ears to hear, the heartening, rallying voice of God, proclaiming " Here is a fresh, unspoilt opportunity ! Here is a clean page of the book ; and even though some of the earlier pages have been full of blots and blunders, though the record has been marred by smudges and mistakes which shame you bitterly to think of them, here is this page, untouched and spotless, waiting for the narrative you will write on it to-day. All the past is finished and forgiven. This is your hour of opportunity. Behold, I make all things new."

That miracle of renovation can happen every morning. And all that you require, in order to know the joy and thrill of it yourself, is the resolve to begin each day by surrendering your life to God, as definitely as if you had never done it before. I am growing more and more convinced that a great part of the secret of achieving steadfastness and serenity in face of the battle of life is this—not only to commit your way to God in some high decisive moment of conversion, but to do that very thing every morning, to go down upon your knees and say, " Dear God, I do not ask to see the distant scene ; but here, for the next twenty-four hours, is my life—I give it back to Thee, to guard, and bless, and control ! " That is why the morning seasons of prayer are so immensely and vitally important. A period of recollection and communion with God before the business of the crowded hours begins—that will give the daily divine miracle its chance to work out in your experience, and will make all things as new and fresh and fair as when the morning stars sang together when the world was young. And what the heart of the poet sang, as he thought of his beloved, your heart will want to echo, thinking of your God—

> " Awake, my heart, to be loved, awake, awake !
> The darkness silvers away, the morn doth break,
> It leaps in the sky : unrisen lustres slake
> The o'ertaken moon. Awake, O heart, awake ! "

For it is a great thing to be beloved by God. And so " in the morning "—any morning, every morning—" then ye shall see the glory of the Lord."

Let us pass on to consider, in the next place, how true these words are of *the Lord's Day* in particular. When the Romans built their great wall across the north of England, they placed, at intervals of a mile apart, towers rising above the ordinary level of the wall ; and there the sentinels were set to stand and watch. And when God built the battlements of our human life He placed at every seventh day a tower, a day thrust up above life's common levels, for the safeguarding of our souls. Hence we can take this text and make it read : In the morning of God's own day, in the morning when the Church bells are summoning to worship, then shall ye see the glory of the Lord !

What underlies the Churchgoing habit, if not the wistful hope that this promise may indeed come true ? It is not mere custom, or sentiment, or gregariousness, or routine that turns the steps of men and women week by week towards the House of God. It is the deep, unspoken longing that somewhere in the services of the day a vital contact with God may be achieved ; and that somehow, incredible as it may often seem, Christ will be able to use these services— with all their glaring, lamentable deficiencies, their human bungling and inadequacy—for the fulfilment of His promise, " Where two or three are gathered together in My name, there am I in the midst of them." As a rule, people do not say in so many words what the Greeks said to Philip long ago, " Sir,

we would see Jesus : " but whether they say it or not, it is
that they mean. Some turn in to the sanctuary, scarce
knowing what has drawn them there ; some have never done
much self-analysis in these matters at all ; some leave their
motives quite inarticulate. Yet if their deep, inmost hearts
could speak the truth aloud, this is what we should hear
them say : " I have come hoping, longing, desperately
needing to meet God. This is what has brought me—nothing
formal or superficial or trite or sentimental, but only this,
that ' as the heart panteth after the water-brooks, so panteth
my soul after Thee, O God ! ' " For man cannot live by bread
alone. He needs God. He needs the resources of the Spirit.
He needs the width and sweep of the eternal. And when the
morning of the Lord's Day brings him to the place of worship,
he is longing that every barrier should go down, and every
well-meaning, blundering intermediary should stand out of
the way, that Christ and his own soul may meet. " Sir, I
would see Jesus ! " The thrill and romance of it is that,
because Christ is as good as His word—because, even as He
promised, He is here—this vital contact with the divine can
and does most surely happen. For still He comes to meet
His own, as long ago and far away He came to Mary, keeping
vigil in the dusk of Easter dawn. " In the morning "—the
morning of His own day—" then shall ye see the glory of
the Lord."

Passing on again, we notice in the third place how true
these words are of *the morning of life*. Wordsworth was not
simply romancing when he cried, " Heaven lies about us in
our infancy ! " How near the angels are to childhood, and
what clouds of glory it comes trailing from God who is its
home ! With what eyes of wonder the child gazes out upon
the fascinating surprises of the world ! With what zest he
reconnoitres his own small corner of the universe ! There is
" nothing common or unclean," when the heart is young.
The child is born to love, and marvel, and traffic with a world

unseen ; and of such, said Jesus, is the kingdom of heaven.
" In the morning "—life's unspoilt childhood morning—
" then ye shall see the glory of the Lord."

But does it last ? Shades of the prison-house come
closing in ; and to keep the child-heart of unwearied wonder
in this dull and disillusioning world is desperately difficult.
The magic and the glamour of the morning are banished by
the light of common day. There is a modern version of
" Twinkle, twinkle, little star," a laconic lament for the loss
of mystery—

> " Twinkle, twinkle, giant star,
> I know exactly what you are,
> An incandescent ball of gas,
> Condensing to a solid mass.
>
> Twinkle, twinkle, giant star,
> I need not wonder what you are,
> For seen by spectroscopic ken,
> You're helium and hydrogen."

But it is not only advancing knowledge which threatens to
despoil with its sophisticating touch the magic of the
morning : far more than that, it is the sheer pressure of life
that does the damage, dulling our sensibility, blunting the
fine point of conscience, and blurring our souls with sin—
until from the afternoon of life we look back ruefully to what
we once were in the morning—

> " Sing me a song of a lad that is gone,
> Say, could that lad be I ?
> .   .   .   .   .
> Billow and breeze, islands and seas,
> Mountains of rain and sun,
> All that was good, all that was fair,
> All that was me is gone."

But if you believe Christ, that tragedy need never
happen : or if it has been beginning, then it can be arrested
and annulled. " Here in My gospel," declares Jesus, " I
offer you the secret of the child-heart that inherits the kingdom of God. I offer the perpetual power of inward daily

renewal to keep your spirit fresh and young and full of wonder. Learn of Me, make Me your travelling Companion along the road, permit Me to cleanse your vision and to quicken your receptivity and to bestow upon you the authentic insight of the pure in heart—and dullness and languor will fly away ; even the hardest miles will find your spirit undismayed and your courage unabated and your peace of mind unbroken. Go through the world with Me, and it will always be morning with you, full of zest and loveliness and hope ; and in the morning, then ye shall see the glory of the Lord."

Viewing these words of promise again from a different angle, I find a message here about the coming of *seasons of religious quickening and revival*. Think of the world as it was nineteen hundred years ago before the angels sang at Bethlehem, that proud imperial world which was beginning to go rotten at the core, festering with sin, with all its gods dead, and all its wisdom bankrupt, and all its morals in chaos. Desperate voices were crying then out of the darkness, " Watchman, what of the night ? " and weary eyes were straining vainly through the gloom. There is a marvellous passage at the opening of the *Agamemnon* of Aeschylus. A solitary watchman crouches on the palace-roof at midnight. Every night, for weary months, he has been stationed there—

> " Conning the nightly concourse of the stars
> That shine majestical in yon clear heaven,"

and waiting for the gleam of the bonfire that shall announce the fall of Troy and the ending of the Trojan war. Suddenly, clear through the darkness, the flame of the beacon leaps up the sky ; and the watchman on the battlements, his long vigil over and the tension snapped, springs to his feet and cries aloud—

> " All hail ! thou light in darkness, harbinger of day ! "

So it was when " the fullness of the time was come, and God

sent forth His Son." Through the thick darkness of a pagan
world's confusion and corruption and despair, the divine
beacon of hope appeared.

> " Far from Thee our footsteps wandered,
>   On dark paths of sin and shame ;
> But our midnight turned to morning,
>   When the Lord of glory came."

It was just as if that lost and hopeless world stirred in its
sleep, and murmured the name " Immanuel "—God with us
—and looked up, and saw far down the eastern horizon the
flush of dawn. And men knew that the dark age was over,
and that ancient night was vanquished : and in the morning
they saw the glory of the Lord.

Has it not been so at every great revival of religion ?
I think of the darkness which enveloped medieval Europe
when the Franciscan movement was born. Very memorable
and moving are the words in which G. K. Chesterton has
described that new invasion of the living God into history :
" While it was yet twilight a figure appeared silently and
suddenly on a little hill above the city, dark against the
fading darkness. For it was the end of a long and stern night,
a night of vigil, not unvisited by stars. He stood with his
hands lifted, as in so many statues and pictures, and about
him was a burst of birds singing ; and behind him was the
break of day." That was St. Francis, bringing back the
morning : and in the morning men saw the glory of the Lord.

I think, too, of Scotland in the sixteenth century, and of
the darkness and bondage of those grim and bitter years ;
when suddenly, at Stirling, the voice of a preacher rang forth
in challenge to the highest in the land. " My Lords, greater
than armies is goodness, greater than swords is freedom.
Scotland ! Scotland ! lift up thy banner and be free."
That was John Knox, another herald of the dawn ; and in
the morning men saw the glory of the Lord.

And so our thoughts travel down the centuries to this
present age in which our lot is cast, when hatred and bitter-

ness, broken hopes and rampant, militant paganism have again brought a great darkness over the earth—a darkness which is so deep that many voices are beginning now to ask, " Why does God allow it ? Has He abdicated the throne ? Is Christ's day done ? Are Christian ethics finally discredited ? Is this the closing act that marks the exit of the Christian faith from the scene of human history ? " But the man who has once looked into the face of his Redeemer will meet the thrust and challenge of such questions dauntless and un-afraid. He will answer, in the words of one who had witnessed faith fighting for its life in days even grimmer than our own, " I am not ashamed of the Gospel of Christ—I am proud of it—for it is the power of God ! " Having seen that power in action at the cross, and victorious at the tomb, he will add his own confession : " I believe in the righteous purpose which, though it may be temporarily thwarted and set at naught, cannot ultimately be defeated. I believe in Christ as against anti-Christ, in faith and hope and love as against godlessness and denial and cynicism and tyranny. I believe in the dawn as against the darkness ! " Is it not Hilaire Belloc who tells how once a friend and himself were climbing by night in the Pyrenean Mountains ? Suddenly a terrific storm and hurricane burst upon them. " This," exclaimed his friend in awe, " feels like the end of the world ! " " Not so," replied Belloc, who had been there before, " this is how dawn comes in the Pyrenees." Do not let us say when days of darkness visit us, and faith is strained, and vain is the help of man—" This is the end of Christianity as a living force upon the earth." May not the truth rather be that this is how dawn comes in God's world ? So it was when God awakened an astonished England from the uneasy, nightmare slumbers of its deep degeneracy, to hear His word by the voice of His servant John Wesley. Again and again the very extremity of the human situation has been the opportunity of the Spirit of the Lord. And so, with courage in our hearts, we still may pray—

"Rise, happy morn, rise, holy morn,
Draw forth the cheerful day from night :
O Father, touch the east, and light
The light that shone when Hope was born."

"Though the vision tarry," said an old prophet, "wait for it ; because it will surely come." And in the morning, then ye shall see the glory of the Lord.

This leads to a fifth suggestion. Our text tells of *the restoring of the soul* by the grace of God after those periods of dryness and darkness and deadness which every Christian knows. Is it not one of the great mysteries of the spiritual life—recognized frankly even in the experience of the saints —that sometimes, for days or months on end, the lights burn low, and ardour fails, and a desolate sense of forsakenness besets and flogs the soul ? In every congregation you are sure to find some from whom God seems for the time to have withdrawn the clear shining of His face. Doubt lays its chilling hand upon the spirit, and the precious things of religion—prayer, the Word and the Sacraments, the fellow-ship of the Church and the summons to the Christian crusade —lose their savour. In such times of spiritual dryness and barrenness, even the contemplation of the cross and the message of the Easter victory may leave the heart impassive and unmoved. Where once all was eagerness and radiance and assurance, now weariness and listlessness and gloom prevail ; and out of the encompassing shadows there arises, like some dire spectre of the dark, the grim question, " Have I been mistaken utterly ? What if the practice of the presence of God is the product of an obdurate credulity, and religion a vast delusion ? " " O Lord," cried Jeremiah in such an hour, " Thou hast deceived me, and I was deceived ! "

This is the dark night of the soul, and most of God's people have to face it somewhere on the road. We cannot enter now into a discussion of the causes of this most perplexing and desolating experience : sometimes doubtless it is occasioned by our own failure, whether conscious or unconscious, to " keep ourselves in the love of God," but sometimes it seems to be sent deliberately by an inscrutable providence to train and discipline the soul, and to initiate it into the deeper secrets of true blessedness. Be that as it may, let those who are passing through this difficult experience of darkness and eclipse take courage. Have you not read of eleven men who had seen all the lights of life go out, and had barricaded themselves behind impenetrable walls of uttermost despair ? " When the doors were shut, came Jesus and stood in the midst, and said ' Peace be unto you.' " All the saints who have ever lived can tell you of the misery of barren hours and days of dereliction, for they have passed that way themselves, and yours is no unfamiliar road : but they will also tell you, with the ringing and triumphant certainty of irrefutable experience—" His going forth is sure as the morning ! " Hold on, then, through the weary hours of darkness. Remember that this world which has the tears of Calvary in it has also the songs of Easter ; and " he that goeth forth and weepeth, bearing precious seed, shall doubtless come again with rejoicing, bringing his sheaves with him." To-day there may be nothing for you but sheer naked faith, fighting doggedly against terrific odds of doubt : but God does not mock His children with a night which has no ending, and to every man who stands faithful through these midnight experiences of the soul there come at length the blessed daybreak hours, and the dawn music of an inviolable hope, and the vision of the sun of righteousness arising with healing in his wings. Your spirit will be stronger for having had to agonize and wrestle in the dark ; and in the morning, then ye shall see the glory of the Lord.

Last of all, I want to take these words and hold them above the darkness of the grave. Is there not a great message here about *death and the dawning of eternity* ? Here in this present human life we are permitted to know something of beauty, truth, and goodness, to read something of the ultimate plan and meaning of the universe, to see something of the splendour of the majesty of God. Yet the very best that we can see and know on earth is but a poor fraction of what must be waiting yonder to be revealed.

We can find a parable of this in modern science. There are whole ranges of colour, the scientist tells us, which our physical eyes cannot perceive. True, we can see all the colours of the rainbow, ranging from red at the one end of the spectrum to violet at the other. But now we are assured that this is only a comparatively small fraction of the colours which really exist ; that beyond the red rays at one end of the spectrum there are the infra-red, beyond the violet at the other the ultra-violet, and out beyond these again whole unimaginable reaches of colour which we never see at all, because our eyes as at present constituted cannot get hold of them. In short, what we do see is only a tiny segment of the whole. If this is true of our physical eyes, is it not likely to be true of the inner eye of our soul ? Here on earth we do apprehend something of the eternal spiritual realities ; we do see, even if through a glass darkly, something of the marvel of the kingdom and the beauty of the King. But our present mortal spectrum—how poor a fraction of the whole ! And beyond the best insights we can ever hope to have in this dark, shadowed existence of time and sin and limitation, what reaches of glory must be waiting for us yonder in the morning ! We are going to find the answers to all questions unanswered here. We are to see the dearest faces we have loved and lost. We are to gaze upon that one Face which has haunted the dreams of humanity since the day when God walked with men in Galilee, the Head that once was crowned with thorns and is crowned with glory now.

There was a December day in Edinburgh in 1666 when Hugh Mackail, youngest and bravest of the Covenanting preachers, was brought before his judges and condemned to

17

the scaffold. They gave him four days to live : then back to the Tolbooth the soldiers led him. Many in the watching crowd were weeping as he went—so young he seemed, so terrible his coming fate. But in his own eyes no tears were seen, no trace of self-pity or regret on the radiant, eager face of this young Galahad of the cross. " Trust in God ! " he cried, and his eyes were shining—" Trust in God ! " Then, suddenly catching a glimpse of a friend among the crowd, " Good news," he cried, " good news ! I am within four days' journey of enjoying the sight of Jesus Christ ! "

Death ? What is death, if that is beyond it ? In the morning, then shall ye see the glory of the Lord.

XXIV

THE STRONG NAME OF THE TRINITY

"The grace of the Lord Jesus Christ, and the love of God, and the communion of the Holy Ghost, be with you all."—2 COR. xiii. 14.

TO-DAY is Trinity Sunday ; and of all Christian doctrines, the doctrine of the Trinity is at once the most controversial and the most unassailable. It is the most controversial, as you will see if you cast a glance back along the line of theological debate through nineteen hundred years ; nevertheless, it is the most unassailable, as you will soon discover if you try the experiment of running a Christian life with one or more of the three Persons of the Trinity left out.

There is one point which, right at the outset, ought to be made emphatically clear. It is this, that in its origins the doctrine of the Trinity came, not from the dialectic of philosophers nor out of the lecture-room of any neo-platonic Academy, but straight out of the experience of ordinary men and women. It did not spring from the dexterous manipulation of abstract ideas : it sprang from the presence of concrete facts and realities. Now that is important ; for it means that this doctrine impinges upon, and strikes home to, the experience of ordinary people like ourselves to-day.

It all began in the New Testament. It began in the experience of the post-Pentecost Church. It began quite simply and intuitively and untheologically. It began when men made this discovery—that they could not say all they meant by the word " God " until they had said Father, Son, Spirit.

Now I submit that the best way to vivify to our own minds

the meaning of Trinity Sunday is to get right back to that. Why should not we, in this matter, be as simple and direct as the New Testament, as factual and experimental as the Christians of the early Church ? You cannot say all that the mysterious word " God " means for you, you cannot convey or describe what that transcendent name connotes, until you have said Father, Son, Spirit. That is true Trinitarianism—as decisively simple, and as simply decisive as that.

I am not saying, of course, that this line of approach removes the baffling and incomprehensible element of mystery in this doctrine. Listen to the Creed which bears the name of Athanasius, struggling with language in the effort to expound the mystery—" The Catholic Faith is this : that we worship one God in Trinity, and Trinity in Unity ; neither confounding the Persons, nor dividing the Substance. For there is one Person of the Father, another of the Son, and another of the Holy Ghost. But the Godhead of the Father, and of the Son, and of the Holy Ghost, is all one : the Glory equal, the Majesty co-eternal. . . . And in this Trinity none is afore, or after other : none is greater, or less than another ; but the whole three Persons are co-eternal together and co-equal." So through the ages, men have struggled with words in the desperate endeavour to elucidate the nature of the God they worshipped, words often misleading, always inadequate. I do not think we ought to despise their efforts. I am sure it is a wrong thing to engage in the modern popular abuse of creeds (so often indulged in by those who ought to know better), to set aside with a wave of the hand those wrestlings of the human soul with the ineffable mystery of God. To do that is essentially cheap and vulgar. No one could do it who had any sense of history.

At the same time, it has to be admitted frankly that, even after all the massive thinking of the centuries, there is mystery in the doctrine of the Trinity still. And some would say that that fact alone is sufficient to discredit and disprove this article of our belief. "You Christians," we are told, "when you sing your hymns about ' Three in One, and One in Three,' are simply romancing, mythologizing ! You are dwelling in some crude, fantastic region of hyperbole and make-believe. You are the pathetic victims of your own credulity and muddled thinking. You are not dealing with anything solid and substantial and real ! " Let us not be perturbed by the criticism. The little intellectualist, wanting everything brought within the compass of his logic, sus- picious of any doctrine which "breaks through language and escapes," may have an air of being omniscient, but he is quite ludicrously wrong. To say that, mark you, is not to oppose his intellectualism. For indeed we want not less, but more, hard thinking in religion. And the fact of Christ, on which for us Christians all our religion is based, is (to put it no higher) the most rational fact in all the world. I am not denying the value or the validity of the intellectual approach. But I do say that what some of those are needing who are endlessly discussing religion, and rejecting what cannot be squared with the standards which their logic sets, nor measured with the intellectual foot-rule of finite minds—what they are needing most is to stop discussing and get down on their knees. That is the only attitude in which the ultimate truths of religion are ever discerned. "The natural man," declares St. Paul, "receiveth not the things of the Spirit of God." For all his pride of intellect, for all his patronizing attitude to the eternal and ineffable mystery, he simply does not know these things, "because," says Paul, "they are spiritually discerned." "I thank Thee, O Father," cried Christ, "because Thou hast hid these things from the wise and prudent, and hast revealed them unto babes ! "

So with this doctrine of the Trinity—paradoxical and problematical to the mind, as the history of the Christian centuries bears witness, yet clear and unassailable to faith, as your own experience decisively declares. And I beg you, on this Trinity Sunday, to get right back to what is simple

and direct and your very own. Is it not true that you cannot
say all that is contained for you in the word " God," until
you have said Father, Son, Spirit ? That is to believe in the
Trinity.

I ask you to notice that it was along this line of personal
experience, and none other, that Paul—like all the Christians
of that early age—arrived at his conception of the Triune
God. It was not speculative theorizing, it was the plain
facts of his own soul's history, that made him say " The
grace of the Lord Jesus Christ, and the love of God, and the
communion of the Holy Ghost, be with you all."

Here, then, the whole meaning of Trinity Sunday is
concentrated ; this is what we celebrate to-day ; this
threefold personal activity of the divine is the true message
of this festival. It is therefore fitting that we should take
the familiar words, these three short crucial phrases, and try
for a few moments to let their meaning sink right in.

" *The grace of the Lord Jesus Christ* "—how significant
that Paul starts there ! He starts with God the Redeemer,
God revealed in Christ the Son, the Saviour. Why did he
not start with God the Creator, God the sovereign Ruler,
God the all-embracing Providence of this vast, tremendous
universe, God away off in His heaven paternally regarding
the work of His hands, and rejoicing that it was good :
" all's right with the world " ? Why did he not lead off
with that ? Why did he begin with God the Son, the
Redeemer ?

Surely the reason is this, that as soon as the human mind
begins reflecting at all on life and experience, it is brought
relentlessly face to face with the grim and frightening fact
that in this world as we know it, in our own inmost nature
as we know it, something is radically wrong. Man looks
outward upon a world where foul iniquities and callous
cruelties and monstrous tyrannies walk open and unashamed ;
he looks inward to his own frustrated, shame-scarred,

disappointed soul ; and his cry is not only " O world, so broken and corrupt, who can deliver you and set you right ? " —it is this, " O wretched man that I am ! who shall deliver me ? " Paul started where he did, because man's first and basic need is deliverance.

No humanism can help him here. No pacts or politics can meet this need. Ethical systems, text-books of morality, codes of doing one's duty and playing the game—they have no answer for man's deepest questioning, no, nor has the philosopher's conception of God the impersonal Absolute, nor the mystic's idea of a vague, aesthetic pantheism. One answer alone will suffice—the answer of the supernatural breaking through into history, the eternal getting a footing in time, the divine intersecting the human from above and from outside, God going forth in redemptive action, a second Adam to the fight and to the rescue, a Man upon a cross, love dragged through the fearful pit and the miry clay, a Conqueror defeating death and hell, a victorious Lord inaugurating a new creation. But that answer—the one and only answer which could ever meet the tragic human situation —has in point of fact arrived upon the scene. That this has happened, as a matter of history, is the crucial declaration of Christianity. And it is all summed up in the words, " The grace of the Lord Jesus Christ."

Hence Paul, basing his Trinitarian benediction on personal experience, basing indeed on what had happened years before when proud Saul of Tarsus was unhorsed outside the Damascus gate, puts the grace of Jesus first. And what I seem to hear him saying to us on Trinity Sunday is this : " Remember that when this redeeming personality of Jesus of Nazareth confronts you in judgment and in mercy, you are being confronted by God. This that happened at Bethlehem and Capernaum and Calvary is the divine in action for your salvation. This is the heart of the eternal brought near, made bare, for you. Receive this Jesus, and you receive into your own being the life of the spiritual world. Adore

Him, and it is the everlasting Godhead you are adoring."
And so we bow, and make our prayer—

> "Almighty Son, Incarnate Word,
> Our Prophet, Priest, Redeemer, Lord,
> Before Thy throne we sinners bend;
> To us Thy saving grace extend."

" The grace of the Lord Jesus Christ."

" *And the love of God,*" he proceeds. Do you grasp the
sequence of his thought ? It is through his experience of
the grace of Christ the Son that Paul reaches his conviction
of the love of God the Father. What he has seen for himself
in the eyes of the Jesus of the Damascus road—that same
mercy and compassion he now traces back into the very
pattern of the universe, finds in them the inmost realities of
life and the clue to the dark enigma of creation, sees them
upon the throne at the right hand of power. It is by standing
on the vantage-point of redemption ground, by standing
alone with Jesus at the viewpoint of the hill of Calvary, that
he sees, afar off, range after range of towering peaks—the
righteousness and sovereignty and wisdom and justice and
everlasting mercy of God.

It is fundamentally important to get the sequence of the
apostle's thought quite clear—first the experience of the
grace of Jesus, and then through that, and only through that,
the certainty of the loving Fatherhood of God.

So many people talk to-day about the Fatherhood of God
as though it were an easy discovery, in fact quite commonplace and axiomatic and self-evident. Easy ? It can be
the costliest of all discoveries. Always it is bought with a
price. It is not a " walk-over " for faith—this item in the
creed—it is a hard victory. Axiomatic ? Turn to Nature.
Is the Fatherhood of God so palpable and obvious there ?
If it is, then why were not Lucretius and Swinburne, with
their marvellously sensitive insight into Nature, amongst
the greatest believers and heralds of faith whom literature

has ever produced, instead of being—as in point of fact they were—the great protagonists and preachers of the spirit of denial ? We are wrong if we cheaply assume that " love divine, all loves excelling " is categorical and unmistakable in nature. " In sober truth," said John Stuart Mill, " nearly all the things which men are hanged or imprisoned for doing to one another are Nature's everyday performances." Is it, then, self-evident in history ? Ask Europe in the twentieth century about that ! Ask the homeless and the destitute, the dispossessed and the broken and the refugee. Ask the great multitudes who are wondering in their hearts why God, if He is righteous and powerful and loving, does not intervene, and make all persecutors bite the dust. Or is it self-evident in the individual life ? Are there not things—disease and trial and bereavement, broken dreams and disillusionment and hours of black depression, and through it all the uncertain tenure on which we hold our lease of life—things which seem to cry out against the Fatherhood of God and the love of heaven ? No, whatever it is, it is not self-evident.

But is it true ? That is the crucial question. That is what the human heart craves to know. If you could pierce through all the problems and perplexities to the inmost core and centre of creation, to the very seat of government of the universe, what would you find there ? Would it be blind Fate, or a personal Friend ? Would it be a dead machine, grinding on irresistibly in accordance with ruthless laws, or would it be a loving Father of us all ? Is the heart of the eternal most wonderfully kind, or was Faber just making a pretty piece of poetry when he said that ? Is righteousness omnipotent ? Is love sovereign ? Is God upon the throne ? We Christians stand up in grim and difficult days like the present, and sing—

> " The beam that shines from Zion hill
>   Shall lighten every land ;
>   The King who reigns in Salem's towers
>   Shall all the world command."

Is that real, or is it just the silly pretence of the defeated ?

I want you to realize that the only way to answer that question decisively is the way by which Paul reached his answer. You can never be absolutely sure that righteous love is on the throne of the universe, until you have met redeeming grace in the secret place of your own soul. Or rather, let me turn that round now, and say—you cannot experience the grace of Jesus, and ever doubt the love of God again. If once at the cross you have seen Christ facing the full force of life's tragic mystery, all the concentrated might of suffering, sin, and death, and conquering in His love, then you know that here is a power which has come forth from the very heart of reality, from the bosom of the Father, and shall yet subdue all things unto itself. " The grace of the Lord Jesus Christ, and "—through that—"the love of God."

" *And the communion of the Holy Ghost* "—that is the final word. None of us has said all we mean by " God " until we have included that. You may believe in the Father —God immortal, invisible, eternal and transcendent, beyond the bounds of time and history. You may believe in the Son—God manifest in the flesh, dramatically breaking through into the temporal and the historic. But what you need to bring all this home to yourself, to make it valid and effective and personal in daily living, is not only God in the eternities, or God in history—it is God in you, making your heart His dwelling-place. That is the Spirit. That is " the communion of the Holy Ghost."

It is this that in every age has made, and still makes, the saints—not necessarily a deeper learning, not always a higher culture, certainly not a self-confident dogmatism that truculently condemns all who disagree or a pugnacious assertiveness that narrows the gates of the kingdom ; but something purely supernatural within, something strong and masterful yet winsome and kindly, as in St. Francis, as in George Herbert, as in humble men and women you have known—the indwelling of the eternal world, the fellowship of the unseen, the communion of the Holy Ghost.

Without this, even the Gospel must remain a closed book to us for ever. Without the work of the Spirit in our hearts, even Jesus is a great unknown. " He shall receive of Mine," said Jesus, " and shall shew it unto you "—He shall convince you of My truth, He shall authenticate to you My power and My divinity, He shall make My living presence the most intimate and unchallengeable reality of your life.

Some years ago a little company of Russian peasants met for worship, knowing full well that their gathering was illegal, and that if they were discovered they would be haled before the dread tribunal and would be liable to incur the ruthless penalty of the law. While their worship was proceeding, suddenly the door was flung open, and there entered an agent of the secret police, followed by a body of his men. " Take these people's names," he commanded ; and the names were written down, thirty of them. They were warned to wait their summons, and then the agent turned to go. But one old man in the little group stopped him at the door and said, " There is one name you have not got." The officer looked at him in surprise. " I assure you that you are mistaken," he retorted, " I have them all ! " " Believe me," said the old peasant, " there is one name you have not got." " Well, we'll prove it," exclaimed the agent impatiently, " we'll count again ! " And they did—verified every name they had taken, and recounted the number. There were thirty. " You see ? " cried the official of police, " I have them all, every one. I told you I had ! " But still the peasant persisted. " There is one name you have not got." " Who is it, then ? " demanded the other. " Speak out—who is it ? " " The Lord Jesus Christ," was the answer. " He is here ! " " Ah," sneered the officer, " that is a different matter." These pestilential Christians, wasting his precious time with their trumped-up story, a senseless, maudlin sham! But that old peasant was right. Jesus, in point of fact, *was* there. " Where two or three are gathered together in My name, there am I in the midst." And it is the Holy Ghost alone who does that. " He will make Me real to you," said Jesus. " He will validate Me to your experience. He will take this Gospel of Mine out of history, out of the eternities, and plant it deeply in your hearts and ratify it redeemingly to your souls." It is the Holy Ghost who makes us certain of Christ's presence with us now, and of the love of God the Father brooding over all.

One thing more remains to be said, and it is this. Remember that the great apostolic word on which we have been dwelling is not a credal statement, it is not a theological summary—it is a benediction. It is an invocation : " *be with you all.*" " O God the Father," Paul is praying, " in Thy righteous love, O God the Son in Thy redeeming grace, O God the Holy Ghost in Thy most intimate communion, look upon these children of Thine, this Church which Thou hast founded, these dear men and women Thou hast sent me here to serve—remember them, great Triune God, and be with them all ! " And down the ages, wherever God's people have assembled for worship, that cry to heaven has been renewed. I beg you here and now to claim your rightful place within the blessing. Yours can be the grace of Christ, yours the love of God, yours the communion of the Spirit. Go forth into the world in the joy and serenity of that high faith ; and say, with that brave soldier of the cross St. Patrick—

> " I bind unto myself to-day
> The strong Name of the Trinity ! "

THE END